SMALL

IS THE NEW

BIG

ALSO BY SETH GODIN

BOOKS

The Big Moo (editor)
Permission Marketing
Unleashing the Ideavirus
The Big Red Fez
Survival Is Not Enough
Purple Cow
Free Prize Inside!
All Marketers Are Liars

e-books

Really Bad Powerpoint
What Should Google Do?
Knock Knock*
Who's There*
Everyone's an Expert
Flipping the Funnel*

BLOG

www.sethgodin.com (click on my head)*

WEB SITES

Changethis.com (founder)
Squidoo.com (original squid)

*included or excerpted in this book

SMALL

IS THE NEW

BIG

AND 183 OTHER RIFFS, RANTS,
AND REMARKABLE BUSINESS IDEAS

Seth Godin

PORTFOLIO

PORTFOLIO

Published by the Penguin Group
Penguin Group (USA) Inc., 375 Hudson Street, New York, New York 10014, U.S.A.
Penguin Group (Canada), 90 Eglinton Avenue East, Suite 700, Toronto, Ontario,
Canada, M4P 2Y3 (a division of Pearson Penguin Canada Inc.)
Penguin Books Ltd, 80 Strand, London WC2R 0RL, England
Penguin Ireland, 25 St. Stephen's Green, Dublin 2, Ireland (a division of Penguin Books Ltd)
Penguin Books Australia Ltd, 250 Camberwell Road, Camberwell, Victoria 3124,
Australia (a division of Pearson Australia Group Pty Ltd)
Penguin Books India Pvt Ltd, 11 Community Centre, Panchsheel Park,
New Delhi – 110 017, India
Penguin Group (NZ), Cnr Airborne and Rosedale Roads, Albany, Auckland 1310,
New Zealand (a division of Pearson New Zealand Ltd)
Penguin Books (South Africa) (Pty) Ltd, 24 Sturdee Avenue, Rosebank,
Johannesburg 2196, South Africa

Penguin Books Ltd, Registered Offices: 80 Strand, London WC2R 0RL, England

First published in 2006 by Portfolio, a member of Penguin Group (USA) Inc.

10 9 8 7 6 5 4 3 2 1

Portions of this book first appeared in *Fast Company* magazine.

Photograph on page 284 used by permission of Ibex Outdoor Clothing LLC.

Publisher's Note
This publication is designed to provide accurate and authoritative information in regard to
the subject matter covered. It is sold with the understanding that the publisher is not
engaged in rendering legal, accounting or other professional services. If you require legal
advice or other expert assistance, you should seek the services of a competent professional.

LIBRARY OF CONGRESS CATALOGING IN PUBLICATION DATA

Godin, Seth.
    Small is the new big and 183 other riffs, rants, and remarkable business ideas /
Seth Godin.
    p. cm.
    ISBN 1-59184-126-7
1. Success in business. 2. Simplicity. 3. Common sense. 4. Interpersonal relations. I. Title.
HF5386.G553 2006
658.4'09—dc22   2006041626

Printed in the United States of America
Set in Janson Text with Avenir
Designed by Daniel Lagin

Don't read this book all at once.

It took eight years to write, and if you read it in one sitting, it'll give you a headache.

Diffusion of Innovations (fifth edition) by Everett M. Rogers is more than 450 pages long. I'm reading it right now, and it's good. It, like most business books, is designed for someone seeking mastery of a particular bit of knowledge. It starts at the beginning and goes to the end. It lays out an argument and supports it with enough research and details to prove, beyond any doubt, that the author is correct.

Small Is the New Big is not that kind of book.

If you want a narrative and lots of research, you're in the wrong place. Quick, put this book down and buy something else.

But I'm betting you don't need another dense book. You don't need more proof, either. What you need is a small prod, or perhaps an aggressive whack. If you're like most of the people who read my blog or come to the talks I give, you're looking for a spark, something to ignite your energy and get you started doing what you already realize is going to work.

Derek Sivers read one of my books and wrote, "This book is

inspiring, as in 'causing immediate action' not just 'made me feel warm.'" If you want warm, take a bath. I'm trying to get you to do something. Today.

Here's the deal: read a few pages. Find what you need. Make copies for your co-workers. Repeat every few days. Then give this book to your kids, who aren't as stuck as we are and can really run with it.

If you're here for a little idea that could change everything, I think you'll find it. Have fun.

Seth Godin
seth@sethgodin.com

NEW RULES, NEW WINNERS

Small is the new big. Recent changes in the way that things are made and talked about mean that *big is no longer an advantage*. In fact, it's the opposite. If you want to be big, act small.

Consumers have more power than ever before.
Treating them like they don't matter doesn't work.

Multiple channels of information mean that
it's almost impossible to live a lie.
Authentic stories spread and last.

The ability to change fast
is the single best asset
in a world that's changing fast.

Blogs matter. If you want to grow, you'll need to
touch the information-hungry, idea-sharing people
who read (and write) them.

There are *no side effects*. Just effects.

Indulge *short* attention spans.

Aretha was right. *Respect is the secret to success in dealing with people.*

> Do something that matters.

HOW DARE YOU?

How can you squander even one more day not taking advantage of the greatest shifts of our generation? How dare you settle for less when the world has made it so easy for you to be remarkable?

I DARE YOU

I dare you to read any ten of these essays and still be comfortable settling for what you've got. You don't have to settle for the status quo, for being good enough, for getting by, for working all night.

CONTENTS

If you want to know . . .

INTRODUCTION: YOU'RE SMARTER THAN THEY THINK

You're smarter than your boss or your friends or your organization believes. And you are way smarter than the marketers selling to you every day give you credit for, that's for sure.

I've been betting on the intelligence of my readers for almost a decade, and that bet keeps paying off.

They just don't get it. Not you, *you* get it. It's the other guys who don't. The people who deceive or cut corners or refuse to change in the face of overwhelming opportunity and evidence.

Sometimes it's hard for me to figure out exactly what I do for a living. Looking through some of my PowerPoint slides, I saw an image that clarified my thinking. It helped me understand what it is I do all day.

The picture is of a propane filling station in Canada, with a landmark twenty-foot-tall propane tank out front. This gas station also happens to sell fireworks.

That's what I do. I sell fireworks.

The people who buy my books or read my blog or hire me to speak to their organization *already know* what to do next. They're smart, even brilliant, when it comes to growing an organization, building a business, or spreading an idea. They already know how to design a great Web site or compose a successful blog posting. But they're stuck.

They're stuck because society, or their bosses, or their spouses, or their co-workers won't let them do what they already know they should do. It's like their briefcases are filled with compressed propane, but they can't get anything to happen.

So that's where I come in. I bring fireworks with me. Not particularly loud or powerful ones, but fireworks capable of attracting attention—and, more important, igniting the propane you've already got.

And what I've discovered is that different people respond differently to various messages.

Some of my e-mail tells me that people's lives have been changed and organizations supercharged as the direct result of a six-hour seminar I did—a seminar that left me exhausted for days. Others seem to get a spark from a two-line blog post, while still others need the comforting reassurance of a hardcover book to set their inner genius free.

After I posted my one-thousandth blog post, I realized that many of these fireworks I was busy igniting weren't reaching the audience that wanted (and maybe needed) to read them. My blog readers were having a blast (no pun intended) but others, those who wanted stimulation in a different format, were missing all the fun.

So here they are, in a handy, portable, nearly waterproof format, 100 percent recyclable, of course. The most explosive, viral, intuitive, obvious, spreadable, and quotable ideas from almost a decade of my writing books, then a column, and now a blog. I guarantee you'll find some that don't work for you. But I'm certain that you're smart enough to recognize the stuff you've always wanted to do buried deep inside one of these riffs. And I'm betting that once you're inspired you'll actually make something happen.

SMALL

IS THE NEW

BIG

AAA AUTO PARTS

AAA Auto Parts is not, contrary to what you might believe, named after Alfred A. Archos. Nope, the owner had precisely the same strategy in naming his business that Jeff Bezos did when he named Amazon. *To be first in the phone book.*

Be first and be the biggest. Who can argue with a strategy like that?

Who, exactly, invented alphabetical order? Why does *M* come before *P*?

Not sure it matters, but I'm not sure that alphabetical order matters so much anymore either. Web searches, and digitally augmented word of mouth, low barriers to entry, and quick speed to market are all conspiring to make "first and biggest" a pretty old-fashioned strategy.

Most of this book is about *not* being the biggest and not being disconnected from your customers and your employees and your environment. This first chapter, though, is about not worrying so much about being first. First in the phonebook, or first to market. If your idea is great, people will find you.

In honor of Alfred A. Archos, the chapters that follow are an alphabetical collection of fireworks that might help release that great idea you've been meaning to unleash all along. They're alphabetical for no particularly good reason, which, as it turns out, is the way the world works, too.

ACCOUNTABILITY

Big companies and the Web are draining the civility out of business. Are you ready to embrace accountability and sacrifice anonymity?

I was almost killed on my way to work today. People who know me realize that my brushes with death are fairly common, but this one was instructive. As I was driving down the road, a Verizon repair truck burst out of a driveway, narrowly missed my bumper, and tore across two lanes of traffic. The driver sped off, but not too fast for me to get her license plate number.

Cell phone in hand, I was ready to call her supervisor. This wasn't just a matter of Verizon's annoying suburban commuters—it was truly reckless driving. A matter of life and death! Alas, I couldn't call: There was no DON'T LIKE MY DRIVING? bumper sticker. No phone number to call.

Have you ever noticed that people you know are far less likely to cut you off in traffic, curse at you, or steal your parking space than total strangers seem to be? There's a reason: Anonymity is the enemy of civility.

I wonder if the Verizon driver would have behaved differently if that bumper sticker had been on the truck.

In a town of two hundred people, you can't get away with bad behavior. Sooner or later, even bullies need the help of those around them—and even bullies know that their bad behavior will keep them from getting help. Neighbors are an effective behavior modification tool—once people know who you are, you act differently.

Given total privacy and a cloak of invisibility, many people become coarse. They do selfish things—things that they would never do if a friend (or a video camera) were watching. Pornographic on-line chat rooms would be empty if users had to type in their real names to register. Polluting the Hudson River would be a lot harder to do if you had to meet with neighbors and explain that it was *your* decision to dump those PCBs.

Here's the problem: George Orwell–obsessed critics complain that we're entering the era of Big Brother, where there are no secrets, where marketers know everything there is to know about us. I say that we're entering an era of anonymity. An era where it's easy to hide.

Big companies are one culprit. A big company can do things that a neighbor would never dream of doing—because big companies can hide behind voice mail and "policy." When we get truly angry at a company for bad service (think about United's canceling its flights as a labor-negotiating tactic) or for repeated promise breaking (think about getting your DSL installed), it's largely because anonymous strangers have made our lives miserable. People can deal with disappointment, but they deserve the satisfaction of looking the perpetrator in the eye.

The other force working against personal responsibility is the Internet. I don't know who was responsible for making the Internet an anonymous place, but it was a truly dumb idea. Who suffers from the dark alleys and the lack off accountability that come with online anonymity? Let's take a look:

■ Online auction services such as eBay work poorly in an anonymous environment, and, as we've seen, despite their best efforts, anonymity can lead to theft and fraudulent bidding.

■ E-mail is falling apart, largely as a result of spam. The torrent of anonymous messages that clog our in-boxes would disappear in less than twenty-four hours if all e-mail could be traced to the individuals who send it—with a bill then sent to those people for the costs incurred.

■ Information exchange is increasingly compromised as a result of anonymous rumors. Everything from online stock tips to national news to the decision to go to war becomes suspect when we're unable to figure out who said what.

■ Newsgroups are being rendered useless because individuals are able to show up, rant, rave, and otherwise disrupt a useful conversation— and there's not a thing we can do about it, because we don't know who anyone is and can't lock people out if they are able to change their user names and then come back.

Stop for a minute and consider how well the real-world analogs for these services work, and how much better they'd work in an online environment with no anonymity.

Could you imagine a workplace where everyone came in wearing a mask? People would sit wherever they wanted to, take anything that interested them, say whatever they felt like saying—and then they'd disappear, possibly forever. Nothing would get done.

Here's a humble suggestion: Let's build a parallel Internet, a Net where no one is welcome unless they have a verifiable identity. Let's require everyone to take responsibility for their actions if they want to participate in our new online society.

Which Internet would you want to visit, the anonymous one or the one where everyone is secure in who they are dealing with?

But won't privacy go out the window in a world with no anonymity?

Anonymity and privacy are not the same. Years ago, we had far less anonymity and far more privacy. While the Internet and the shields built around large corporations have increased anonymity, it doesn't seem as if privacy has increased. And by the way, is privacy necessarily such a good thing?

What if there were no privacy? What if everyone knew how much money you made, what you paid in taxes, what you gave to charity, and how many dogs you had? And let's add just two more assumptions to the mix. One: The government doesn't get over-thrown and replaced with blue-helmeted thought-controlling soldiers enforcing a new world order. Two: We're all equally exposed. You have no anonymity and no privacy—but no one else gets any either.

What would happen? I'm not proposing that I want a world like that—but I do think that the idea is worth discussing. Somewhere along the way, we seem to have come to the conclusion that rampant anonymous chaos, aided and abetted by tiny circles of privacy, is the best way to ensure our future as a civil society. I think that if I had a choice, I'd live in the village where everyone knew my name.

At least we'd all drive better.

ACORNS, INFECTED

**CHANGE IN ACORN WEEVIL
INFESTATION RATE OVER TIME**

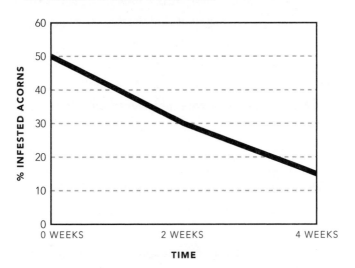

The percentage of the work you get paid to do goes down *as you get paid more.*

A talented doctor spends no more than ten or fifteen minutes a day performing the service that she's actually renowned for.

An insightful Web designer spends just a few minutes a day doing insightful Web design.

A great lawyer might be pushed to the edge of his talents once or twice a week.

The same goes for salespeople, farmers, novelists, and hockey players. The baseline level of talent in most professions is pretty high, and the really exceptional people shine only rarely.

There's too much overhead. A doctor needs to fill out forms, meet salespeople, answer phone calls, travel from hospital to hospital, manage her staff, and, every once in a while, see a patient. And most of those patients are run-of-the-mill cases that a medical student could handle.

I'm talking about knowledge workers, obviously. Factory workers get paid for showing up, for moving things from pile A to pile B. The irony, of course, is that low-paid jobs are structured so that you can be productive all day long. Knowledge workers, on the other hand, get paid extra when they show insight and creativity or do what others can't. But packaging that knowledge is expensive, time-consuming, and not particularly enjoyable for most people. As you get better at what you do, it seems as though you spend more and more time on the packaging and less on the doing.

(Yes, I know the chart above is about infected acorns, but it had the right slope.)

The exception?

The intense conversations you can have with your customers and prospects, especially via a blog. Once you get the system and the structure set up, five minutes of effort can give you four minutes of high-leverage idea time in front of the people you're trying to influence.

This is pure, unadulterated leverage. The stuff you actually get paid for, with no overhead.

When the net is broken (spam, pop-ups, CC lists, most instant messaging) it just adds more "time overhead" to what you do. But when it's working, it allows ideas to be stripped down to their essence and lets you really push them. Push the ideas, push your organization, push yourself.

The temptation we face, now that the overhead of time and hassle is diminishing, is to invent *new* overhead so that we can stall. Stalling feels safe, stalling gives us insulation, stalling makes it easier to avoid the important stuff we're actually rewarded for.

So don't stall. Start now. Expose your ideas. Interact.

ARTISTS CARE ABOUT THE ART

Fifteen years ago, on the streets of SoHo (the artsy district of Manhattan) my wife and I were window-shopping for art we couldn't afford. Outside of one of the galleries, literally on the street, we saw an artist selling out of the back of his car. We bought a painting for about $100 and congratulated ourselves on "buying art in SoHo" at a discount. The artist was friendly and we wished him luck.

Knut Masco, the artist, specialized in painting on the backs of old windows. He decorated the wooden frames and painted on the glass. He was a committed street artist and made a name for himself when he joined in with some other artists and sued Rudolph Giuliani for banning the sale of their work (a surprisingly large number of people don't remember the original, bullying version of Mayor Giuliani). They won and that was the last we heard of Knut.

Two months ago, the Masco in our house fell off the wall and shattered into a billion pieces. We were heartbroken. "This is a job for Google!" I cried, and off I went to find Knut. Nothing doing. He had vanished. Hours of searching turned up nothing but the lawsuit. No one had seen or heard from Knut in a decade.

I hopped over to the amazing Google Answers (answers .Google.com), posted a query, said it was worth $75 to find him, and within a day, the researcher found Knut . . . living in Israel . . . under another name . . . no longer making art!

I sent Knut an e-mail, discovered that his new name was Boaz, and described our need for a new painting. He quickly agreed—even though he couldn't find any old windows and would have to build a new old window from scratch, even though he hadn't painted in a while, and even though he didn't know who we were. I offered to pay in advance, but he wouldn't hear of it.

Two months later, I get an e-mail saying that the painting is ready and has been shipped. I send him a check, made out to his new name, on faith. A day later, a painting arrives by Federal Express, from Israel, with a handwritten invoice.

The painting is terrific—even better than the original. But more important to us is the story. Not sure what you can do with it, but I thought you'd want to hear it.

ATKINS

Today at the supermarket, a woman asked me to reach up to a high shelf to grab her a one-ounce bag of Atkins-brand crunchy chips. Probably $2 a bag, which works out to $32 a pound.

She looked at the bag, saw the label on the front that read, "Only five carbs," and then asked me to put it back.

She apologized, and told me that her limit was four.

Wow.

Here's a person who didn't even know what a carbohydrate was six months ago and has been so swayed by the Atkins idea that she's now too puritanical to even eat the Atkins-branded products.

This didn't happen because of advertising. It happened because of the power of the idea.

BENCHMARKS = MEDIOCRITY

I can benchmark everything now.

I can benchmark my morning workout. The rowing machine tells me if today's workout was a personal best. Even better, I can go online and compare my workout to the efforts of thousands of other people.

On my way to work, I can track my car's mileage (my record is 89 mpg). Once there, I can watch the status of my books on Amazon, comparing their sales to those of every other book published in the English language, and then go check out JungleScan.com, where I can track the book's performance over the last ninety days.

The problem with benchmarking is that nothing but continuous improvement (except maybe spectacular results) satisfies very much. Who wants to know that they will never again be able to beat their personal best rowing time? What entrepreneur wants to embrace the fact that the wait time at her new restaurant franchise is 20 percent behind the leader's and there's no obvious way to improve it?

Our interconnected, five-hundred-channel world lets us be picky. We can want a husband who is as tall as that guy, as rich as this guy, and as loyal as my brother-in-law. We can ask for an apartment that is in just the right location, with just the right view and just the right rent, and then reject it because the carpeting in the hallway isn't as nice as the carpeting in the building next door. Monster.com lets us see five thousand resumes for every job opening and imagine that we can find someone with this guy's education and that woman's professional experience who works as cheap as this person and is as local as that one.

In the old days, data was a lot harder to come by. You didn't know everything about everyone. All the options weren't right there, laid out in Froogle and compared by Epinions.com. We didn't have reality

TV shows where each and every component of a singer's presentation or a bridal prospect's shtick were painstakingly compared.

Yes, benchmarking is terrific. Benchmarking is the reason that cars got so much better over the last twenty years. Benchmarking has the ability to make the mediocre better than average, and it pushes us to always outperform ourselves and others.

But it stresses us out. A benchmarked service business or product (or even a benchmarked relationship) is always under pressure. It's hard to be number one, and even harder when the universe we choose to measure ourselves against is so vast.

Of course, the baby boomers have this problem even worse. (And we're all boomers, aren't we? Even if you're not, we boomers don't care, because it's all about us.) Boomers are getting older. We can benchmark our eyesight, our rowing speed, our memory, or even our ability to come up with great ideas at a moment's notice. As a result, we benchmark ourselves into a funk. We get stressed because we have to acknowledge that nothing is as good as it was before.

In addition to the stress it creates, benchmarking against the universe actually encourages us to be mediocre, to be average, to just do what everyone else is doing. The folks who invented the Mini (or the Hummer, for that matter) didn't benchmark their way to the cutting edge. Comparisons to other cars would never have brought about these fashionable exceptions. What really works is not having every little thing be up to the usual standards—what works is everything being good enough, and one or two elements of a product or service being *amazing*.

So, I'm officially letting go. I'm going to stop comparing everything to my all-time best, to your all-time best, to everyone's all-time best. I've stopped checking Amazon. Instead of benchmarking everything, perhaps we win when we accept that the best we can do is the best we can do and then try to find the guts to do one thing that's remarkable.

BILLBOARDS THAT CHANGE

I've gotten about a dozen e-mails about Google's clever way of indicating that they keep adding storage to Gmail.

Every time you visit your Gmail account, you notice that the amount of storage you've been given has gone up.

The same thing is true for the billboard on the bank near the house in Buffalo, New York, where I grew up. It didn't matter how many times we had looked at it before, we always looked at it again when we drove by. Why?

Because the time and temperature were always changing!

Why bother reading something if you already know what it says?

The best stories change over time. They change in ways that fascinate the consumer, and, more important, they change in ways that are fun or interesting to talk about.

BLUEGRASS AND THE CELLO PLAYER

Jeff Reed writes:

> I am the music director of an orchestra that is entering its sixth season, located in a town of fifty thousand people. Our budget was about $15,000 the first season and it will be nearly $500,000 this season. We have always had balanced budgets and will finish this season (ends July 1) with about a $20,000 surplus. This is happening at a time when many orchestras have ended in bankruptcy or are finishing with large deficits. I owe much of our success to you.
>
> Having read several studies on why orchestras are failing, I

have learned (which came as no surprise) that people these days don't want to hear one type of music (which is what orchestras usually offer—only classical) and that audiences get bored without a visual element in a concert (merely watching the musicians isn't enough).

To respond to these studies, we created what we think is a Purple Cow: an orchestra that programs Beethoven and the Beatles on the same concert (usually, orchestras perform only "serious" music on one concert and have a pop orchestra to do the "light" stuff—they usually use two different orchestra names, even though the same musicians do both concerts!). All of our concerts are centered around themes which tie the various musical styles together, often with an added visual element on a screen above the orchestra. For example, we did "That '20s Show," which featured "serious" music from the 1920s by Shostakovich; a commissioned film score to accompany a silent film (the orchestra played the score while the audience watched the film on a screen above the orchestra); and popular songs by George and Ira Gershwin. We did a bluegrass concert that featured Copland's "Appalachian Spring," standards performed by a bluegrass band, and a new composition for bluegrass band and orchestra.

I don't know how remarkable all of this is nationally or internationally, but it is certainly working in Bowling Green, Kentucky. Our audiences have grown from one hundred the first season to an average of eight hundred this past season (some concerts sell as many as two thousand tickets).

I just finished reading *All Marketers Are Liars*. My question is: What story are we telling or should we be telling? It seems like we are telling quite a few, for example: (1) orchestras don't have to be boring (which deals with a common perception); (2) We think outside the Bachs (sorry for the pun), which seems to make people feel good about the fact that they want to hear several different types of music and that they aren't stupid if they get bored listening to some classical music. All of our season themes are along those lines: Anything Goes, Thinking Outside the Bachs, Bluegrass to Baroque, etc.

I thought it would be fun to answer Jeff's questions here. The fact is, he's already 99 percent of the way there.

Most orchestras are run by people who are focused on the "truth" of what they do. They are performing the canon, doing it with skill and passion. They offer their community the best of what they are able to produce, and hope that those who are intelligent and genteel enough will appreciate what they have to offer. If people don't come, it's some sort of commentary on the declining state of our culture, not, in their view, a reflection of the story they're telling.

Every once in a while, a traditional orchestra decides to go slumming to raise money. They program a pop concert or bring in PDQ Bach. The problem with this is that they're still talking to the same people they always talk to, so it's not enough. For that reason, and because organizing the pop concert is seen as an extra, lesser task, few orchestras really get very good at this sort of programming.

Jeff, on the other hand, has figured out a totally different way to look at the situation. His new vision starts by understanding worldview. There is certainly a tiny population in Bowling Green that walks around with the worldview, "I love traditional classical music and will pay to see it live." These people would be an easy sale, but there are very few of them.

There's a much larger group that has a worldview that says, "I'm interested in live music and enjoy an evening out. I want to do something fun and something that doesn't make me feel bored or stupid." These are the same people who read movie reviews and movie ads not because they have to, but because they *want* to. These are the people who don't skip over the entertainment section of their local paper.

In walks Jeff's group with a simple story, well told. "We're not slumming, we don't look down on you, and we're here to have fun, too." By taking advantage of clever programming, slide shows, and other nontraditional techniques, Jeff is busy putting on a show—a show that people want to experience.

I don't think Jeff needs help telling his story. The challenge now is to make it easy for other people to tell that story to their friends. I'd obsess about getting permission to contact my fans (via e-mail, or a traditional newsletter) so that I can regularly deliver news to them that's easy to spread. I'd offer "bring a friend" evenings and discounts, and start programming in venues outside of the traditional theater.

The thing to remember here is: *If your target audience isn't listening, it's not their fault, it's yours.* If one story isn't working, change what you do, not how loudly you yell (or whine). Nice work, Jeff.

BON JOVI AND THE PIRATES

Bon Jovi, the fabled rock band, is trying to fight piracy. At first glance, it's straight out of *Permission Marketing.* The band is offering listeners who buy a copy of their new CD a chance to enter their serial number online and get concert tickets, fan info, etc.

The good news is that the music business is starting to see that the relationship between artists and fans is worth far more than the profit on a single CD. Last year, for the first time in more than five years, no record in the United States sold more than five million copies. This shows that reliably reaching a small audience who *wants* to hear from you is a far better strategy than attempting to sell to everyone in the world.

The bad news is that Bon Jovi, in the words of the *Wall Street Journal,* is "battling the pirates," which makes it seem that they view fans (the only people who are busy trying to get free copies of their music) as the enemy. Why should I go to the site and register my e-mail address and a lot of personal information? What's in it for me? Is the access to tickets just bait, or is it really a reward for my long-term attention and investment?

Here's the challenge—we need to remember who we're working for. Whether you're selling music or steel, the rules are the same. We're working for the people who pay us (with attention). Bon Jovi is making a really brave first step, but they have to take their time. They should not be greedy, or start spamming those fans who take a step and enroll.

BRANDING IS DEAD; LONG LIVE BRANDING

Here's my take:

1. The data is irrefutable. The number of massive megabrands and their value (in terms of the premium consumers are willing to pay) is shrinking, and fast. You can't charge as much for a Sony DVD player or a Marlboro cigarette as you used to.

2. The number of new microbrands is exploding. Blogger Hugh MacLeod, founder of gapingvoid.com, is a brand now. If we define the word "brand" as shorthand for a set of commercial attributes, emotions, stories, whatever, then any blogger with a following has a brand. And the same goes for the thousands of microbrews, perfumes, and hot-sauce products. All are brands, all cluttering the shelves of our minds.

3. There's a difference between brands and *branding*. Brands exist whether you want them to or not. Brands aren't going to go away anytime soon. Brands are a useful shorthand for a complicated asset within an organization. Branding, on the other hand, is a thing you do. And as an activity, branding is problematic. Branding is ill defined, usually vacuous, often expensive, and totally

unpredictable. You shouldn't aim to be someone who does branding.

Markets engage in conversations, but marketing often doesn't. The reality is that most brands are actually monologues, not dialogues. A conversation might create a better, more robust, more useful brand but, alas, most organizations can't handle that truth. So they do their best to do it the old way.

Big brands are dying. Little brands are doing great. Branding is a weird gig.

There. Let's hope that riff helps my brand a bit.

BRAND MY CAR, BRAND ME

I saw a bumper sticker that I really liked. It said, IS IT TRANSPORTATION OR A LIFESTYLE? Of course, you never see a bumper sticker like that on a Mercedes. It was on a beater of a Subaru, naturally.

Then I noticed that the *Wall Street Journal* has started running a regular feature on which celebrities and industry luminaries are buying which car in which city.

It's a little odd, if you think about it. Here's one of the biggest purchases the average person makes, and we're interested in which famous people are endorsing our choices.

But then the real question hit me. The car dominates our culture. It has a huge impact on our cities, on our balance of trade, on the environment, and on world politics. If everyone gave up SUVs and drove hybrids, we'd essentially be independent of foreign oil and a major threat to the atmosphere would virtually disappear (as would asthma, smog, etc.). But almost no one suggests this as a potential solution to some of our country's problems.

Why? Because somehow we've marketed this formula to ourselves: car = self-esteem.

I mean, I love my Miata. I drive it with a smile on my face, and I like to believe that I really drive it the way it was designed to be driven. Of course, SUV users like to justify their purchase in exactly the same way I do. Why do we care so much about what we drive? I certainly don't give the same thought to my shoes or the kind of pen I use. What would happen if there were no car choices (except maybe the paint job)?

Imagine for a second that all the time and money and competitive drive we put into buying, cleaning, improving, tuning, and tweaking our cars needed to be spent in other ways.

What if there were only two choices? You could either get a big car (a slow, ugly van) or a little car (a slightly less slow sedan) and that was it? In our postindustrial age, would this radical change grind capitalism to a halt?

In the name of national security, world peace, and environmental longevity, it's an interesting thought exercise, isn't it?

From a marketing point of view, the discussion is even more interesting. When you take away an expensive option for expressing one's self-esteem (cars, for example), human beings quickly find substitutes. It might be Timberland boots downtown, or Prada bags uptown. Both are ridiculously overpriced for the utility they deliver, but it's the story we tell ourselves that matters, the label, the image, the peace of mind.

How do some marketers create this aura of self-esteem while others fail?

I think when traditional marketers talk about "brand," self-esteem value is what they mean. A true brand is something where the self-esteem value far exceeds the utility. It might be Heinz ketchup or a Rolex watch or a Marlboro cigarette, but in each case there's a truly emotional connection between the brand and the user.

Alas, almost all marketers fail in creating a brand. Fortunately, the allure of a powerful brand (like Disney) appears to keep the nonwinners (like Six Flags) trying.

I'm way off the topic of cars here, but I'm really not. What I'm worried about now are side effects—the unintended consequences of excellent branding. I'm not in favor of the government's getting in the middle of this, but I sure wish I could figure out how to market our way out of this problem. It's one of the great tragedies of our profession, imho.

A BRIEF HISTORY OF HARD WORK, ADJUSTED FOR RISK

Your great-grandfather knew what it meant to work hard. He hauled hay all day long, making sure that the cows got fed. In *Fast Food Nation* (Houghton Mifflin, 2001), Eric Schlosser writes about a worker who ruptured his vertebrae, wrecked his hands, burned his lungs, and was eventually hit by a train as part of his fifteen-year career at a slaughterhouse. Now *that's* hard work.

The meaning of hard work in a manual-labor economy was clear. Without the leverage of machines and organizations, working hard meant producing more. Producing more, of course, was the best way to feed your family.

Those days are long gone. Most of us don't use our bodies as though they are machines—unless we're paying for the privilege and getting a workout at the gym. These days, 35 percent of the American workforce sits at a desk. Yes, we sit there a lot of hours, but the only heavy lifting that we're likely to do involves putting a new water bottle on the cooler. So do you still think that you work hard?

You could argue, "Hey, I work weekends and pull all-nighters. I start early and stay late. I'm always on, always connected with a BlackBerry. The FedEx guy knows which hotel to visit when I'm on vacation." Sorry. Even if you're a workaholic, you're not working very hard at all.

Sure, you're working *long*, but today "long" and "hard" mean two different things. In the old days, we could measure how much grain someone harvested or how many pieces of steel he made. Hard work meant *more* work. But the past doesn't necessarily lead to the future. Our future in the workplace is not about time at all. The future is about work that's really and truly hard, not just time-consuming. It's about the kind of work that requires us to push ourselves, not just punch the clock. Hard work is where our future job security, our financial profit, and our future joy lie.

It's hard work to make difficult emotional decisions, such as quitting a job and setting out on your own. It's hard work to invent a new system, service, or process that's remarkable. It's hard work to tell your boss that he's being intellectually and emotionally lazy. It's hard work to tell senior management to abandon something that it has been doing for a long time in favor of a new and apparently risky alternative. It's hard work to make good decisions with less than all of the data. It's much easier to stand by and watch the company fade into oblivion.

Today, working hard is about taking apparent risk. Not a crazy risk like betting the entire company on an untested product. No, an apparent risk: something that the competition (and your co-workers) believe is unsafe but that you realize is in fact far more conservative than sticking with the status quo.

Richard Branson doesn't work more hours than you do. Neither does Steve Ballmer or Carly Fiorina. Robyn Waters, the woman who revolutionized what Target sells—and helped the company trounce Kmart—probably worked fewer hours than you do in an average week.

None of the people who are racking up amazing success stories and creating cool stuff are doing it just by working more hours than you are. And I hate to say it, but they're not smarter than you either. They're succeeding by doing hard work.

As the economy plods along, many of us are choosing to take the easy way out. We're going to work for the Man, letting him do all the hard work while we put in the long hours. We're going back to the future, to a definition of work that embraces the grindstone.

Some people (a precious few, so far) are realizing that this temporary recession is the best opportunity that they've ever had. They're working harder than ever—mentally—and taking all sorts of emotional and personal risks that are bound to pay off.

Hard work is about risk. It begins when you deal with the things that you'd rather not deal with: fear of failure, fear of standing out, fear of rejection. Hard work is about training yourself to leap over this barrier, tunnel under that barrier, drive through the other barrier and, after you've done that, to do it again the next day.

The big insight: The riskier your (smart) co-worker's hard work appears to be, the safer it really is. It's the people having difficult conversations, inventing remarkable products, and pushing the envelope (and, perhaps, still going home at 5:00 P.M.) who are building a recession-proof future for themselves.

So tomorrow, when you go to work, really sweat. Your time is worth the effort.

BURGERVILLE

As I travel around spreading the word of the Purple Cow, a lot of people appear confused about just what "remarkable" means. "Remarkable" does not mean elitist. It doesn't mean weird, either. It doesn't mean cheap or expensive or big or small. "Remarkable" is any or all of these things. It's just something worth talking about.

This month's *Gourmet* magazine talks about a chain of burger places in the Northwest called Burgerville. It's not that expensive, and it's *amazing*. We're talking chocolate hazelnut shakes. (Fresh, local, and wild) salmon salad with Tillamook cheese. Onion rings that (ready for this?) are only available when onions are in season.

I didn't know onions *had* a season.

Worth a detour. Worth talking about. That's remarkable.

CAMP, MICKEY ROONEY, AND YOUR MARKETING PROBLEM

My friend Tim wrote me a note asking if I had any tips as to where he might go to improve his public speaking. I was flattered that he asked, and then took a minute to think about where I learned how to speak in public.

Answer? Camp Arowhon.

Wait, there's more. I also learned marketing there.

My summer camp was a marketplace (a loud one). Everyone had to do something, but what you did was up to you. So the canoeing instructor (that was me) was always competing with the sailing instructor (that was Mike) and the others to get people to come to our dock. If no one came, you were a failure and you didn't get asked back.

I discovered that:

1. No one cared about me. They didn't care about how hard I'd trained, how little I'd slept, or how much effort I was putting into my job.

2. People were rarely willing to try something new. If they'd never done it, they didn't want to start anytime soon.

3. Word of mouth was electric.

4. You didn't get many chances to screw up.

5. If you didn't risk screwing up, you would certainly fail.

The biggest and best discovery, though, was how willing people (even sullen teenagers—and if you think selling to cranky purchasing agents is hard . . .) are to suspend their disbelief. One week, I persuaded three hundred people that Paul McCartney was coming to visit the camp, checking the place out for his daughter. It was only at the last minute, when a friend of mine, impersonating Sir Paul, fell out of the approaching motorboat and was (allegedly) mangled by the spinning rotor, that people figured out that it wasn't really him.

My point, and I do have one, is that marketing is a show, a Judy Garland/Mickey Rooney-esque form of entertainment designed to satisfy wants, not needs. We need to take it a lot less seriously (no matter if we're marketing social security fixes or a world religion) even as we take more risks. If you're not growing now, playing it safe isn't going to help you grow tomorrow.

My advice to Tim is the same advice I've got for you, whether you're speaking in public or running ads. Be fearless, but wear a life jacket.

CARLY NEVER HAD A CHANCE

The reason Carly Fiorina had so much trouble at Hewlett-Packard is that HP was competing too hard with Dell. If you're going to be the standard, you need to be boring. If you're boring, you've got to be cheap. Cheap and standard is what Dell does best, and I don't see how you can beat them at that game.

As the choices available to businesses and consumers become increasingly clear and easily comparable, you've got to either be different . . . or cheaper. You will fail if you try to do both—or neither.

CEO BLOGS

Apparently, blogs written by CEOs are the newest thing. I just got off the phone with one CEO who's itching to start, and read an e-mail from another who just started.

Here's the problem. Blogs work when they are based on:

Candor
Urgency
Timeliness
Pithiness
Controversy
(Utility, maybe, if you want six)

Does this sound like a CEO to you?

If you can't be at least four of the six things listed above, please don't bother. People have a choice (4.5 million choices, in fact) and nobody is going to read your blog, link to your blog, or quote your blog unless there's something in it for them.

Save the fluff for the annual report.

CHANGE JUNKIES

Hi. My name is Seth, and I have a problem: I'm a change junkie. If the world around me isn't changing, I get bored and become inefficient.

On second thought, that's not really my problem. My problem is that while I'm busy advocating change, insisting on change, and teaching change, deep down inside *I hate change*. Change is inconvenient, painful, and frightening.

I should know: In the past year, I've moved twice, I've sold two businesses, and I've gladly gone from having thirty employees to having more than seventy—before going all the way down to zero employees. It's been one hell of a ride, but frankly there were times when all of that changing gave me a real headache. I guess you need to be careful about what you wish for—because you just might get it.

Quite a paradox, no? I love change! I hate change! So how do people like me manage to rationalize those extremes? On the one hand, it's obvious that if you don't move quickly, you're dead. On the other hand, it's obvious that changing to keep up with the new realities of the workplace is painful and exhausting. Question one: Are we doomed to lives marked by ever increasing pain, as the ever faster business world damns us to becoming digital nomads?

A few decades ago, I found myself eating lunch at an outdoor café in Vienna, Virginia. It was 1994—just about the time when America Online was beginning to show up on people's radar—and I was having lunch with Steve Case and the three other top people at AOL. I went home feeling enthusiastic about AOL's prospects, but I stuck to a rule that I have against taking money out of my IRA to buy stock. I think AOL was trading at about $7 per share at the time. It has since gone as high as $125. Needless to say, my IRA hasn't had nearly the return that AOL's stock has had since 1994. Question two: Why was I unwilling to make that investment?

Five years later, I was lucky enough to work with David Filo and Jerry Yang, the two visionaries who created Yahoo! At about the same time that they were launching Yahoo!, I was thinking about precisely the same opportunity. But instead of starting a company that would eventually be worth more than $30 billion, I wrote a book called *The Smiley Dictionary: Cool Things to Do with Your Keyboard*. Total royalty earnings to date: $9,000.

Question three: Why a book and not a Web site? Here's one answer: I was running a book business, and every opportunity that I saw looked like a book opportunity. David and Jerry, on the other hand, had no preexisting framework, no installed base. So, when they saw that opportunity, they viewed it for what it could be rather than tailoring it to what they already were.

Which raises question four: Why is it that the big opportunities, the really obvious chances that we get to improve our businesses and our careers, almost always pass us by? Go back to what I said about change: Big opportunities bring change, and change is painful. As long as "opportunity" means change, and as long as "change" means pain, we will continue to miss our chances.

So I have a very simple proposition for all of us change-addicted and change-conflicted new-economy warriors: Instead of embracing and celebrating change—or lying about it and pretending to embrace it—I think we ought to stop talking about change altogether. Let's ignore it, avoid it, and sidestep it. Instead of spending time thinking about change, let's all sign up for zooming lessons.

"Zooming" is about stretching your limits without threatening your foundation. It's about handling new ideas, new opportunities, and new challenges without triggering the change avoidance reflex. You already zoom every day: Whenever you buy a new CD or read a new issue of the newspaper, you don't have to contend with all of the emotions that we associate with "change." You're zooming—doing the same thing as usual, only different.

Eating at a different Thai restaurant, trying a new airline—for most of us, none of these things represent change. This is the stuff of exploration; it's the kind of thing that we're eager to do. That's why the guidebook business is booming, and why adventure travel is a growth industry. These products and services offer safe adventure— the chance to do the same thing as usual, only different.

There are all kinds of zoomers, and all kinds of categories in which you can learn to zoom. The late John Hammond was a world-class zoomer. Hammond was the guy at Columbia Records who discovered Billie Holiday, Count Basie, Aretha Franklin, Bob Dylan, and Bruce Springsteen. What made him a zoomer? He defined "the same thing as usual, only different" pretty broadly. He didn't spend his days trying to find folk singers, jazz singers, or AOR-crossover funky white singers. No, Hammond just looked for singers.

By choosing to zoom across such a large area, he was able to listen to anyone, anytime, without getting stressed out. He didn't plague himself with rigid rules and standards; he just wanted to find something great. Hammond had broad "zoomwidth." I'm betting that if you had asked him whether finding all of those different kinds of singers meant that he had to "change" every day, he would have said no. He viewed each day not as a high-stress, change-filled event but as part of his zooming continuum.

Compare Hammond's zoomwidth to your own. Or compare it with your company's zoomwidth. Martha Stewart, for example, had no trouble turning her book-writing business into a billion-dollar media empire—without compromising what she stands for (okay, maybe a little). But the folks at *Rolling Stone* were too entrenched in the magazine paradigm to see that they could have been what MTV has become—without having to change their foundation. The people at Omaha Steaks realized that however they sold their steaks—by phone, by mail, or on the Net—it was all the same thing, only different. By contrast, it took Lands' End years to sell products online.

I grew up during the glory days of franchised restaurants— McDonald's, Baskin-Robbins, Carvel, Pizza Hut. None of them had any zoomwidth at all. The structure of these organizations made any sort of adjustment seem like a major threat rather than an opportunity. Today, as the population changes and as people's needs change, many of these chains are facing a major crisis. Kentucky Fried Chicken had to change its name to KFC—so that it could start selling nonfried foods!

Compare this mentality with that of the Limited, a company that gladly zooms its merchandise at every single store at least once a month, whether it needs to or not. At Limited stores, introducing new clothing style is easy: Managers don't have to go very far up in the organization to get approval. They just zoom—and it happens.

Question five: Why is there so much pain in the business world? One reason is that most companies are now stretched beyond their zoomwidth. Everything is seen as a threat; nothing new is perceived as an opportunity. Instead of changing, companies need to zoom. By increasing its zoomwidth—by hiring people who love to zoom—a company can grow, adapt, and maybe even transform itself.

Here is my handy, five-step zoom starter checklist—five simple things that you can do right away to practice zooming.

1. For dinner tonight, try a food that you've never tasted. Then try another one tomorrow night.

2. On your way to work tomorrow, listen to a CD from a musical genre that you hate or that's new to you.

3. Every week, read a magazine that you've never read before.

4. Once a week, meet with someone from outside your area of expertise. Go to a trade show on a topic in which you have no interest whatsoever.

5. Change the layout of your office.

Sounds silly, doesn't it? Like a bad self-improvement book. But if you can master these five steps, you'll find it much easier to sign Bob Dylan when you think you're looking for Count Basie. In other words, you'll discover that the art of zooming makes it easier for you to view everything as an opportunity.

Question six: Isn't all of this just a lot of semantic maneuvering? Why waste time on a word or two? The zoomer's answer: Words are important. They give you a lens through which you can see why you (and your company) are finding it so hard to move as quickly as you'd like.

The next time your company is looking at a big, life-threatening change, stop! Ignore the scary, life-or-death, change-or-die issue. Ask yourself question seven: How much room do you have to zoom? After all, a company with an appetite for zooming will always be quicker, more nimble, and more fun than one that's doomed never to zoom.

CHECK THIS BOX

Newspapers are in trouble. eBay has sucked the life out of classifieds. People have stopped reading papers. Today more folks read the *New York Times* online than the print version.

Is the future of newspapers to trick people into receiving spam?

My wife e-mailed me a link to an article in the *Los Angeles Times*. In order to read it, I had to register. Here's the last part of the online registration process:

> From time to time, we may send you e-mail announcements on new features, products and services from latimes.com and selected advertisers and affiliates. Sending you occasional advertising and announcements is necessary for us to continue providing our rich news content. We will try to limit the amount of advertising you receive. Information is used as described in our Privacy Policy. Some advertisers may prefer to contact you directly. Please check this box if you prefer not to be e-mailed directly by advertisers unaffiliated with latimes.com. Note you may continue to receive certain other e-mail from latimes.com and our Affiliates as described in our Privacy Policy.
>
> IMPORTANT: After you complete registration, you will immediately be sent a confirmation e-mail. Please click on the link in that e-mail as soon as possible to fully activate your account for site access.
>
> Your browser MUST accept cookies in order to successfully register and log in. You may also need to adjust your firewall or browser security to register.
>
> By registering, you agree to our Terms of Service

Notice that the box *isn't* checked. That's the universal symbol for, "We're honest and we want genuine permission from you before we send you stuff by e-mail. So if you want it, please check here." A quick reader sees the unchecked box, smiles, and moves on.

I was glad to see that. But then I read the text. It says that the *un*checked box means that they *will* send you spam unless you affirmatively *check* it to say that you *don't* want to receive unsolicited e-mail. (Even without the italics I'm adding, it's still confusing.)

So, let's be clear here: In order to ensure its future in a world where everyone is online, one of the great newspapers on the planet is relying on second-order trickery (because ordinary opt-out isn't nefarious enough). Do you really think they're building much of an asset here? Can you imagine that three years from now the publisher is going to say, "I'm sure glad we tricked a million people into having no leg to stand on when we busily spam them!" Hardly.

CHINA (ALL THAT TEA!)

Imagine, for a second, that you're China.

Over the next few years, you're going to buy half a billion or so cars, pave most of the country, buy billions of barrels of oil—all part of modernization.

The thing about China is that the government isn't shy about being authoritarian.

So what if the Chinese government decided to decree what it means for something to be legally sold as a car?

What if a Chinese car:

- got 40 mpg or more?
- had low emissions?
- was small enough to fit into a standard, x-by-y-size parking space (which is smaller than, say, a Buick)?
- had a built-in transponder to track stolen cars?
- had built-in cell phone capability?
- had a transmitter that alerted the local authorities whenever you drove faster than the legal speed limit?
- had built-in baby seat anchors?
- had brights that automatically dimmed whenever another car approached?

- was recyclable?

- had digital key systems that made it easy to share cars?

- had insurance paid for with a gas tax?

- allowed local roads to "talk" to the car about potential hazards?

- had a body that was ugly but easy to repair after an accident?

- had a transponder that broadcast when it was stuck in traffic and received input on how to avoid existing jams?

- had a "follow me" feature that allowed each car to be set to follow the car ahead (at low speeds) to increase the efficiency of traffic flow?

- had ten other features I can't think of but you can?

How would that change the future of China? The definition of a car?

And what on Earth does this have to do with you and your life and your career?

I think there are entire classes of products and services (from charities to political parties to cars) that are about to be completely reimagined and upgraded. The accumulating weight of new technology, new networking abilities, and ecological and economic demands means that incremental Band-Aid improvements cease to pay off and wholesale replacement occurs instead.

Think about the iPod. The iPod is not a better CD player. It's part of a totally new system.

China has the luxury of starting from scratch (though it appears, based on the sales of Maybachs and Land Rovers, that they're blowing it the same way others have), but either way, it's going to happen to just about every industry.

Imagine the positive effects that will result from your industry's being networked and rebuilt and reinvented. Who's going to go first? Maybe you?

CHRISTMAS CARD SPAM

Call me Scrooge if you want to, but I can't help but notice a new trend. Call it Christmas card spam.

Christmas cards used to be handwritten and thoughtful. They took a lot of time and were thus sent just to people who actually wanted to receive them.

Then professional printers stepped in and Christmas cards became a bulk item. Businesses get them by the hundreds. Almost anyone can count on dozens of cards every year. You might not have wanted to get a Christmas card from your Xerox-machine-service guy, but hey, it only took a second to chuck it in the mailbox so he sent out three hundred cards.

You didn't get too much of this junk, though, because the cost of the card and the stamp made it prohibitively expensive for the Xerox guy to send one thousand or four thousand cards.

Today, thanks to the zero-cost nature of e-mail, the equation has been completely reversed. The cost to the sender of a card is essentially zero. The cost to the recipient, however, is significant. This stupid snowman card (who, exactly, is Telemak and why are they writing to me?) took about twenty seconds to receive via my DSL connection. Watching my e-mail take five or six minutes to arrive is enough to induce Dickensian feelings, for sure. Telemak must have sent ten thousand cards . . . costing the recipients about fifty hours of download time.

So, one more treasured tradition trashed by new media.

Happy Holidays!

CLEAN FIRE TRUCKS

I live in a neighborhood where all the firehouses are run by volunteers. I don't know how my family, my neighbors, and I would get by without them—like firefighters everywhere, they do brave work with little credit.

One thing you'll notice is how clean the trucks are. "Why are the trucks so clean?" a friend asked. After all, a clean fire truck isn't a lot better at putting out fires than a smudged one.

The answer: Because when there isn't a fire, the firemen wait for the siren to ring. And while they're waiting, they clean the truck.

Sounds a lot like where you work. Most organizations are staffed with people waiting for the alarm to ring. Instead of going out to the community and working to prevent new fires, the mind-set is that firemen are working to put out the fires that have started. Hotel desk clerks don't write letters or make calls to generate new business— they stand at the desk waiting for business to arrive. Software engineers are often overwhelmed with an endless list of programming fires—and rarely get a chance to think about what they ought to build next.

The structure of most organizations (and every single school I've ever encountered!) supports this. It's about cleaning your plate, finishing your assignments and following instructions. Initiative is hard to measure and direct and reward. Task completion, on the other hand, is a factory orientation that is predictable and feels safe.

In fast-changing markets, clean fire trucks show attention to detail but rarely lead to growth and success.

What a great way to describe a stuck but busy organization. "They sure have clean fire trucks."

CLIFF CLIMBING (PLEASE DON'T FALL OFF)

I got business plans from two different friends today.

Both of these guys are big thinkers, entrepreneurs through and through and destined for greatness. And both of their plans had precisely the same problem. It's a problem that's becoming very common—for products, for services, online and off. The problem is caused by our networked world, the quest for the Purple Cow, and the goal of reaching a Tipping Point.

In the old days, there was pretty much only one way to grow a business. Start small, make some money, get a little bigger, repeat. Over time, you could fund your way to bigness. Venture capitalists can help you jump-start, sure, but raising $100 million or $400 million to skip all the steps on the way to bigness is rare indeed.

Procter & Gamble started small. They sold Ivory soap, then Crisco, and slowly, bit by bit, they grew the company.

Your business has to work when it's small in order to survive to the point where it gets big.

A magazine, for example, can't have a business plan that says it will accept no ads until it's bigger than *Time* or *Newsweek*. A new technology won't take off if the business plan says it won't be profitable until it becomes the industry standard.

Dolby Digital is the exception, the one everyone likes to remember. It works because it is adopted by the entire audio industry (projectors, processors, etc.). But it had to get there.

I call a business that depends on the win at the end of the cycle for its success a "cliff business." This is a business that doesn't slope upward, but one that runs flat until, miraculously, it hits critical mass and suddenly dominates the world.

In our networked world, cliff businesses are a site to behold. eBay or Microsoft, for example, are cliff businesses, natural monopolies that work when everyone uses them. That's one of eBay's best assets—everyone wants to use the system that everyone is using.

The problem is that it's almost impossible to bootstrap a cliff business. The Bluetooth standard, for example, is a great thing—once every cell phone and laptop uses it. But it took more than five years of high-overhead standards setting and meetings and commissions and committees before it even began to take off. Had Bluetooth been a business, it would have disappeared long ago.

The best businesses online started with little fanfare (Blogger, or ICQ, for example). They didn't spend a fortune trying to intentionally jump up the cliff. Doing it on purpose is difficult indeed. That's one reason you don't want your kids to grow up to be songwriters trying to write Top 40 hits. It's a great gig if you can get it, but you can't count on getting it.

So, if your product or your service or your business is going to be nothing but trouble until it hits big, I think it's better to pick something else to launch. Something remarkable and cheap and likely to make customers and investors happy long before you get to the cliff.

CLIFFSNOTES

Nine percent of all *USA Today* bestsellers are diet books. Yet today the *New England Journal of Medicine* reports that two years after going on a diet, on average, people weigh *more* than when they started.

Also worth noting: The CliffsNotes of *The Scarlet Letter* outsells the real book more than three to one.

CLINGING TO YOUR JOB TITLE?

Something really scary happened to me. I flew to England to give a speech. And on the way there, while on the plane, I had a panic attack.

It's not that I'm afraid of flying. No, I had the attack because I'm afraid of going through customs. Now, I've never tried to smuggle anything in my life, and my passport is in fine order. But I've always had this phobia about being unjustly incarcerated by an uncaring bureaucrat in a foreign country. That's the main reason why I've never torn one of those tags off of a mattress or pillow. But this time, my fear was the result of something slightly more rational: a form. This was no ordinary form; it was an official government document.

The form wasn't that big—maybe about four inches by six inches. It asked for a bunch of rudimentary information, such as my name and address. But on the reverse side of the form, in tiny writing, near the bottom of the page, was a question that struck absolute terror in my heart: Customs asked for my occupation.

Suddenly, I was beset by doubts and fears, uncertainties and unanswerables! I felt a new-economy identity crisis looming. What am I? The government of the United Kingdom wanted to know. It insisted on knowing. And if I supplied the wrong answer, if I lied on the form, who knew what would happen? I could spend years rotting in the basement of some prison, eating porridge for breakfast and bangers and mash for dinner.

Am I a writer? An entrepreneur? A typesetter? A traveling salesman? A public speaker? An accountant (though an admittedly poor one)? A marketer? I could go on and on. On any given day, I probably have fifteen or twenty "occupations."

That's when it hit me: The world is changing. The days of "milkman," "mailman," and "soldier" are pretty much gone. Most of the people I know and work with would have had just as much trouble as I had with the occupation question (although I don't think that any of them would have had a panic attack).

What are you?

Does clinging to an occupation make you better at it? Does it make it easier for you to identify the folks you'd like to work with, the people who can help you do your job—or does it just obfuscate things and drag you into meetings that you shouldn't be in? Does it supply an employment security blanket, a comfortable totem from the old economy that you can carry with you to give you a sense—genuine or false—of stability? Or, even worse, do you use your title as a shield, so that when people ask you for help, you can say, "Sorry, that's not my job"?

While we're at it, what is your job description? Is it a hopeful, optimistic, powerful document that gives you permission to explore new opportunities and to get something done? Or is it a defensive shield that makes it easy for you to identify what's not your responsibility? Companies that don't have any employees who have the phrase "increase our international presence" in their job description rarely take the time and risks necessary to develop an international presence. Organizations that provide their employees with carefully worded job descriptions are giving them permission to ignore excellent business opportunities, and, in doing so, are losing out every day.

While we're on the subject of failed bureaucracies, inert organizations, and brain-dead "corpocracies," why don't big companies publish their org charts and phone directories? Put 'em online, I say. A vice president at IBM once spent a full hour drawing an org chart for me, in an attempt to make her company more accessible, because she realized that a fortress mentality wasn't good for IBM. Of course, as soon as she'd finished drawing the two-page chart, IBM announced a reorg. So much for making it easy to do business with IBM.

The other day, out of boredom, I engaged in one of my favorite hobbies: I called Microsoft at (425) 882-8080. "Hello," I said. "Could you please tell me the name and extension of the person who's in charge of marketing Windows 2000?" (Note: That person's name is not much of a secret. A quick Web search will get you what you need.)

"I'm sorry, sir. I can't divulge that sort of information," a courteous but officious receptionist responded, as if I were the first person ever to have the audacity to ask for such private information. It was as if I'd asked her for the Windows source code, rather than for a marketer's name and extension.

Here's the New Economy Customs Form Question of the Month: What sorts of bad things would happen if every vendor, every analyst, every customer, and, yes, even every headhunter knew exactly who did what, why, and how—at Microsoft or at your company? What would be the big deal if your true occupation were trumpeted far and wide?

How can a company be fast if everyone on the team doesn't know who's in charge of what? How can a company be permeable to the outside world if the outside world doesn't know whom to talk to? Is it really possible to create a system of rapid, informal communication that keeps all parts of an organization in sync? When an invoice comes in, you route it to the guy in accounts payable, because that's his occupation. But whose job is it to decide whether using MP3 technology to improve customer satisfaction is a good idea?

Which leads us right back to where we started. It is unlikely that you have just one occupation. And rather than pretend that we all have just one occupation—as the British government seems so intent on doing—maybe we ought to embrace the "multipational" nature of our jobs. ("Multipational" is a new word that I've invented. It means "having more than one occupation at a time"; it's the workplace equivalent of "multinational.") We could each pick a new, all-purpose title that lets others know what we're really focused on— titles such as "customer joy specialist," or "change agent," or perhaps even "gal who will take a meeting and then work the organization."

It's not silly. It's about communicating—to your peers, to the outside world, and to yourself—what you really do all day.

CLOWN, ARE YOU A?

When it comes to the health of your organization, it's time to stop clowning around.

Being called a clown is rarely a compliment. Unless you want to join the circus, it's not much of a career goal, either. In addition to the obvious—bad makeup and ill-fitting shoes—all clowns have a surprising amount in common. This is because of a simple truth: Clowns are based on real people. They embody what's wrong with human nature, just magnified a bit.

Are you a clown? Do you work with clowns? I break clownhood down into four common traits.

1. Clowns Ignore Science Whether it's the magic of fitting sixteen full-sized clowns into a Volkswagen Beetle or the constant struggle between clowns and gravity, the fruitless conflict between what's real and what a clown desires is a fixture in a clown's act.

Organizations (and politicians) tend to believe that science is optional. It's not. If you run ads and they don't work, it doesn't matter how you spin it; they didn't work. If your industry is changing because of a technological breakthrough, it doesn't matter whether you believe in the breakthrough; it's still there. We may have all sorts of business and theological reasons to challenge a piece of science, but denying reality never leads to a positive outcome.

Kodak, for example, spent years denying, ignoring, or evading the reality of digital photography and its inevitable impact on the film business. And when it recently announced plans to lay off one-fifth of its already decimated workforce, you couldn't help but holler, "You clowns! Did it just now dawn on you that digital cameras were going to catch on?" I felt terrible for the innocent folks who lost their jobs because senior management was busy trying on the big red nose.

Clowns refuse to measure their results, because measurement implies that they accept the reality of the outside world. Wishful thinking is not a replacement for the real world. Only clowns can get away with that.

2. Clowns Don't Plan Ahead Clowns get big laughs from slamming into a brick wall or running to catch up with a car that left without them.

Of course, squirrels and sea monkeys don't plan ahead, either. Humans are the only species that regularly demonstrates foresight, but we manage to do this only on occasion. People are happy to spend themselves into credit card debt to enjoy today (instead of tomorrow and the next thirty years), and they work hard to maintain the illusion that everything is just fine—until it's not. Just look at the folks now bringing you record federal deficits.

3. Clowns Overreact to Bad (and Good) News We all have memories of a clown bursting into tears when he stubs his toe or drops an ice-cream cone. Those same manic clowns are overcome with glee and laughter when something goes right for them.

We sometimes behave like clowns in this regard, too. Witness the dramatic fall in the polls of Howard Dean after one ill-timed scream, the near demise of the Audi after a *60 Minutes* report that questioned its safety, or the irrational mood swings of the stock market.

4. Clowns Aren't Very Nice to One Another From the Three Stooges to the colorful characters at the Ringling Bros. circus, clowns are most famous for willfully inflicting harm upon their fellow clowns. The easiest way to get a big laugh is with a pair of pliers, it appears. If you can't find pliers, a bottle of seltzer will also do nicely.

Why is it so unusual to find a company where the boss cares for his employees? Why is it even more unusual still to find a workforce where teamwork naturally overcomes selfishness? Why do we focus on takeover battles, high-profile firings, and attack-dog politics instead of the gradual, inexorable progress that happens when people with a shared goal work together to accomplish it?

If clownhood is our natural state (and I think it must be), then the alternative must be the anticlown. Success lies in rejecting your inner clown and adopting a long-range view of the world (even if it's just five minutes longer than your peers' view).

We ought to issue little red foam rubber noses to everyone who reads this book. They compress easily, so you can keep one in your wallet. Whenever you're in a meeting and someone starts acting like a real clown, silently whip out the nose and put it on. Imagine the impact of five or ten VPs confronting the CEO with rubber red noses firmly in place. Imagine twenty congressmen as they fight against short-term pork all wearing theirs.

What would Krusty do? Or Chuckles? Bozo? Figure out the behavior of a real clown—and do the opposite.

CLUELESS, WE ARE ALL

We're all clueless. That's the best word I can use to describe the state of the art of marketing.

Three examples:

At the supermarket yesterday, I ran into my friend John, not someone I often see at the Food Emporium. John has a standard grocery list ("Here honey, please go out and get this . . ."). But John wants to show me something on the list. It says,

1 WOMAN'S RAZOR THAT MATCHES OUR BATHROOM.

Wow. Gillette has been making razors for almost a hundred years, and you have to wonder how many hours and how much money they've spent trying to answer that desire—probably .0001 percent of what they spend on blade technology.

Then this morning, I headed to the bank. Some poor guy was arguing with the "customer service manager." The problem? He had $4 in his checking account as he was waiting to close it. The bank charged him a monthly $5 service fee. The fee bounced. Then they charged him $30 for bouncing the fee on an inactive account.

The manager was trying to explain the policy, but the bottom line is that all the bank's real estate, all the ads, all the marble, all the computers—all were wasted, because they were enraging the guy. Over $4.

And finally, leaving the bank, I saw the most amazing interaction (yes, this is true). A woman is first in line. She's withdrawing $1,000 from her account. The teller pushes away from the desk and goes and gets her signature card from the filing cabinet (this is a neighborhood bank—no computers here) to match it against the woman's signature on the withdrawal slip.

The customer turns to me and tells me that:

1. The teller has been working there for twenty years.

2. She (the customer) comes in at least once a week.

3. They always check her signature.

And, ready for this . . .

4. She's been a customer at this bank for seventy years. I am not making this up. She is very proud that she's nearly (nearly!) their longest-serving customer. The account is more than seventy years old. And they check her signature.

Marketing is now officially about wants, not needs. That's what your entire day should be about. Your church, your company, your restaurant, your blog, it doesn't matter. Give me what I want or I'm out of here.

CMO, THE PLIGHT OF THE

I feel sorry for Judy Verses. She's the chief marketing officer of Verizon, a brand that is justifiably reviled by millions of people.

Is Verizon disdained, mistrusted, and avoided because Judy's not doing a good job? Of course not. She's doing a great job.

The reason we hate Verizon is that they act like a monopoly, have ridiculous policies, a lousy call center, a bad attitude, plenty of outbound phone spam, and crazy pricing.

We hate Verizon because of all the things Judy doesn't get to influence or control.

The myth of the CMO is the C part. They don't get to be the chief of the stuff that is really what marketing is all about today. CAO, maybe (chief advertising officer) but not CMO.

If I were the CMO of Verizon, I'd fix the call centers. I'd fire people with a lousy attitude who aren't hesitant about sharing it with a customer. I'd reward the great ones (like the installer who came to my new office last week) and figure out how to get every employee to understand that *they* are the marketing department. And I'd shut down the outbound phone spam center immediately.

Until that happens, the CEO is the CMO, no matter what the title says.

COGS

Since you were five, schools and society have been teaching you to be a cog in the machine of our economy. To do what you're told, to sit in straight lines, and to get the work done.

We have been trained to be cogs in a vast system, workers in a finely tuned factory.

In the early factory era, there was great demand for trained cogs. The cogs even had unions, and cog work was steady, consistent, and respected. There were far worse things than coghood.

Here's how being a cog has changed in the last few years:

1. Cog labor is a lowest-common-denominator activity.

2. If cog labor gets expensive, companies now automate it.

3. If a company can't afford to automate, they move the work somewhere where it's cheaper.

4. If the competition moves, companies figure out how to measure and semiautomate their cog labor to make it cheaper still.

The end result is that it's essentially impossible to become successful or well-off doing a job that is described and measured by someone else.

Worth reading the italics twice, I think.

The only way our country (or your country, depending on where you live), your economy, and, most of all, your family has to get ahead is this: Make up new rules.

People who make up new rules continue to be in very short supply.

COMMISSIONS (HOW TO INVEST THEM)

Over the last decade or two, many neighborhoods have seen the price of homes increase by 1000 percent. Because real-estate agents charge a commission based on selling price, this means that many agents make ten times as much as they used to for selling a house.

Obviously, they're not doing ten times as much work.

Sooner or later, in any business that works on percentages, things change and the commissions come under pressure. You can be defensive about this or you can see it as an opportunity.

One broker in Massachusetts now works by the hour. If I were a broker, I'd take the increased cash flow from higher commissions and spend it as fast as I could. I'd fundamentally change what I offer and include a wide range of free services—from a free paint job to help sell the house to a new big-screen TV for the buyer or the seller. I'd hire assistants and build a permission-based computer system. I'd realize that no industry is static, especially one where the rates change so quickly in just a short time.

Obviously, this is about more than just real estate. If you work by the hour, what would happen if you charged a commission instead? (PR folks? Lawyers?) What happens to the sales process when you flip from success-based to time-based pricing? Or the other way around?

It turns out that real estate, like many other endeavors, is a zero-profit condition. It's so easy to become a broker that once the price of houses rises, the number of brokers rises right along with it. One study found that there are five times as many brokers in San Francisco as there are in one part of Ohio—which, not coincidentally, has housing prices one-fifth as high.

The lesson is that you can avoid the zero-profit condition by creating a huge barrier to entry. And you do that with the assets, the extras, and the skills your competition can't get quickly.

COMPETENCE

Horror stories used to start with "It was a dark and stormy night." No longer. Now they start with "My wife and I decided to add a couple of rooms onto our house."

My wife and I recently decided to enter the house of horrors. But we were determined to avoid disaster. So we took our time and found a competent architect. That was our first mistake.

Then we searched until we found a competent contractor. Great references, solid reputation. That was our second mistake.

Our criteria for the project were, in order, "fast," "good," and "cheap." We were clear about our goals. We set specific dates, and we delivered our objectives in writing.

Unfortunately, our contractor and our architect had both built their reputations, the center of their competency, around "good." "Fast" was not a concept that they really understood. Try as we might, argue as we did, nothing would change their focus. Order windows before the building permit comes through? Too radical. Have two teams working on the project at the same time—one upstairs, the other in the basement? "Well, I guess some might do it that way, but you hired us for our reputation. So you've got to trust that our way is the best way."

Hey, if these guys were building a skyscraper, it would take them forty years to complete it.

Every situation has a silver lining, and mine was that I got a big insight into what competence is. Competent people have a predictable, reliable process for solving a particular set of problems. They solve a problem the same way, every time. That's what makes them reliable. That's what makes them competent.

Competent people are quite proud of the status and success that they get out of being competent. They like being competent. They guard their competence, and they work hard to maintain it.

Bob Dylan, on the other hand, is an incompetent musician. From year to year, from concert to concert, there's just no way to be sure that he'll deliver exactly what you're expecting. Sometimes, he blows the world away with his insight, his energy, and his performance. Other times, he's just so-so. And unlike a truly competent musician, Dylan never delivers a song the same way twice. Remember Dylan's Grammy-winning *Time Out of Mind* album? About the only thing you can be sure of is that when he plays a song from that album in concert, it won't sound anything like the studio version. No, Dylan isn't competent. But he is brilliant.

Over the past twenty to thirty years, we've witnessed an amazing shift in American businesses. Not so long ago, companies were filled with workers who couldn't do their jobs. If you bought a Pacer from American Motors, it wasn't all that surprising to find a tool hidden in a door panel of your new car. Or, when you were trying to put together that shiny red bicycle late on Christmas Eve, it wasn't out of the ordinary to discover that not all of the parts were inside the box. Back then, it wasn't uncommon for shipped products to be dead on arrival. Everyone from lawyers to senior executives to receptionists was dropping the ball on a regular basis.

Then we got sideswiped by global competition, discovered a whole new approach to working, and found religion. We bought into not one but a whole series of revolutions. We reengineered. We bought computers. We adopted Six Sigma quality-management systems that ensured that every process would be robust enough to turn whoever was involved in it into a competent automaton.

Now the receptionist can't lose your messages, because they go straight into voice mail. The assembly line worker can't drop a tool, because it's attached to a machine. The telemarketer who interrupts your dinner is unlikely to overpromise, because the pitch is carefully scripted on paper.

Today, it's much harder to make a bad car, because robots measure everything. It's much harder to be a lousy directory assistance operator, because computers are handling so much of the work.

Oh, there's one other thing: As we've turned human beings into competent components of the giant network known as American business, we've also erected huge barriers to change.

In fact, competence is the enemy of change!

Competent people resist change. Why? Because change threatens to make them less competent. And competent people like being competent. That's who they are, and sometimes that's all they've got. No wonder they're not in a hurry to rock the boat.

Just think of the risks that come with embracing anything other than competence. What would that mean to my contractor? A fresh approach to project management—one that could save me from having snow blow in through that hole in the wall where the window should be—would expose his team to all sorts of risks. It would mean that his reputation as a competent builder would be threatened. Of course, it might also mean a fresh perspective on building, a chance to invent a new, time-sensitive approach to construction, even the possibility of revolutionizing an industry with a reputation for making customers unhappy. But the risks of jeopardizing that *Good Housekeeping* label of competence are just too high.

Do you work for a competent company? A company in which people are hired because they've done a certain job before, in which the upward path is slow and the sideways path is nonexistent? Such companies are especially frustrating to the internal (or the external) change agent. Sadly, Wall Street has traditionally rewarded companies for being competent.

Charlie Trotter's, in Chicago—one of my favorite restaurants—has an incompetent chef. Every night, he offers a different menu of innovative dishes. And sometimes those dishes fail: The beet-kumquat-chocolate soufflé is not worth the calories, and the blood oranges really don't add anything to the poblano mousse—you get the idea. But I'd much rather let this gifted, incompetent chef cook for me than go back to the restaurant that I ate at yesterday in Boston. Staff members at this restaurant will happily make you a banana-orange juice, and they'll gladly offer you a carrot-spinach juice. But they'll refuse, with total amazement at the request, to make you a banana-carrot juice. For just one moment yesterday, I had a flashback to that scene in *Five Easy Pieces* when Jack Nicholson tries to get the maddeningly competent waitress at the frustratingly competent restaurant to bring him some wheat toast.

In the face of change, the competent are helpless. Change means a temporary or permanent threat to their competence. But among the competent, the smart ones realize that change is inevitable—and that they are doomed. Hence the tremendous discomfort among our happily competent population.

In the face of change, some of us are becoming competent at zooming: Our skill set includes the ability to move from opportunity to opportunity doing the same thing, only differently. It's this new breed of competents, of people who in another age might be labeled incompetent, who are going to lead us through the changes that we encounter. Whom should we hire to become zoomers? Which people, and which companies, can take on new challenges, new opportunities?

Here's the weird thing: I think that the incompetent among us are stars in the making. Not the folks who are incompetent because they can't do any better. No, I mean the folks who have the option to become competent but choose to try something new.

The next time you review résumés, try ignoring all of the perfectly qualified applicants. In fact, disqualify everyone who is clearly competent to do the job at hand. Do what Southwest Airlines does: Don't hire people with experience at another airline unless you're sure that they can unlearn what they've learned there. "Competence" is too often another word for "bad attitude." Instead, find the serial incompetents—the folks who are quick enough to master a task and restless enough to try something new. The zoomers.

It's not very surprising that so many new companies that are creating wealth today are run and staffed by very young people. Because they have very little work history, these people haven't fallen prey to becoming competent. They don't have to unlearn bad habits. They're not interested in maintaining their competencies—because, frankly, they don't have any.

But this reliance on the young is dangerous. Why? Because as these new companies get locked into a successful business model, they create a layer of very successful, very young, and in some cases very arrogant managers. And these managers are the most dangerous competents of all: the ones who will do everything in their power to fight the next round of necessary changes, because they're in love with their newfound competence.

Some of the companies that have radically redefined their industries are already seeing rough times. Netscape lost its way and blew its huge lead, not because of Microsoft but because Netscape's own rapid success caused the company to stop innovating. Netscape did a totally competent job of working to leverage its lead—but competence was exactly what brought the company down.

The newly competent in Silicon Valley and elsewhere are guilty of another common mistake: They confuse speed with velocity. The culture of these revolutionary companies is to sprint as fast as possible—all the time. Cars fill the parking lots at these companies on weekends. Want to reach someone in an office cubicle? Call at 10:00 P.M. One woman I met last week lists seven different ways to contact her on her business card!

But this embrace of hard work and moving fast for fast's sake misses the point. It doesn't take a lot of time to change your business plan radically, to reinvent your marketing proposition totally, or to redesign the way you deal with consumers completely. No, it doesn't take time; it takes will. The will to change. The will to take a risk. The will to become incompetent—at least for a while.

Velocity is a company's ability to zig and zag and zoom—to make significant changes when significant changes are necessary. And you can have velocity without speed: Driving around in circles may make your speedometer look impressive, but it won't get you across the country very fast.

Give me five serially incompetent nine-to-five executives with a focus on velocity, and I can change the world—over and over again. I may even get this addition on my house finished.

COOKIES AND THE TECHNICAL IGNORANCE OF JOE SURFER

Jupiter published a report that says that 10 percent of U.S. Net users delete the cookies on their web browser every day and 40 percent do it (in aggregate) every month.

Let's do a reality check here. This is the same population that can't get rid of pop-ups, repeatedly falls for phishing of their PayPal and eBay accounts, still uses Internet Explorer, buys stuff from spammers, doesn't know what RSS is and sends me notes every day that say, "What's a blog?"

Forgive my skepticism, but it's inconceivable to me that 40 percent of Internet users even know how to use their browser to erase their cookies.

The echo chamber effect on the Net is stronger than it is anywhere in the world. Yes, professional women in New York think that lots of women keep their maiden name when they get married (it's actually less than 5 percent). Yes, people who work out all the time figure that most people do, too (they don't). People who run wineries figure that lots of people care about wine (they don't). But on the Net this phenomenon is at its worst. The heavy users figure that everyone else understands what they understand (they don't).

People aren't stupid. They just are too busy or too distracted to care as much as you do about the stuff you care about.

COOKIES (THE OTHER KIND OF COOKIE)

I almost bought some expensive Back to Nature–brand cookies.

Everything about the packaging is perfect. The matte finish. The old-fashioned rolltop on the bag, just like we grew up with. The colors and more.

The only problem is that these cookies are no healthier than most of the others on the shelf. The reason to buy them is that they make it easy to lie to yourself when you feed 'em to your kids.

Is it only my supermarket that is now filled with stuff like this?

COVER, JUDGING A BOOK BY ITS

It's a horrible habit, I admit it. But do I have any other choice? With 95,000 books published every year in the United States alone, how on Earth are you supposed to spend time reading books with bad covers?

Of course, it's not just books. We judge magazines, restaurants, and even people by their covers. (And especially Web sites!) And as a result, we end up skipping great meals, not getting to know terrific people, and missing other terrific opportunities.

So, here's what I do about it:

1. I try to find things with lousy covers and go out of my way to check them out. If the herd is drawn to the obvious, flashy cover, then I'm not going to find insightful, rare information where everyone else is. The unique stuff is hiding.

2. I try to make covers that don't sabotage the work. It's astonishing to me how many packages, jackets, labels, signs, and outfits are chosen because they're safe, boring, and invisible instead of for the only reason that matters—to sell people on finding out what's inside.

CRITICISM

So, why haven't you and your team launched as many Purple Cows as you'd like?

Fear.

Not just the fear of failure. Fear of failure is actually overrated as an excuse. Why? Because if you work for someone, then more often than not the actual cost of the failure is absorbed by the organization, not you. If your product launch fails, they're not going to fire you. The company will make a bit less money and will move on.

What people are afraid of isn't failure. It's blame. Criticism.

We don't *choose* to be remarkable because we're worried about criticism. We hesitate to create innovative movies, launch new human-resource initiatives, design a menu that makes diners take notice, or give an audacious sermon because we're worried, deep down, that someone will hate it and call us on it.

"That's the stupidest thing I've ever heard! What a waste of money. Who's responsible for this?"

Sometimes, the criticism doesn't even have to be that obvious. The fear of hearing, "I'm surprised you launched this without doing more research" is enough to get many people to overresearch, to study something to death. Hey, at least you didn't get criticized.

Fear of criticism is a powerful deterrent because the criticism doesn't actually have to occur for the fear to set in. Watch a few people get criticized for being innovative and it's pretty easy to persuade yourself that the very same thing will happen to you if you're not careful.

Constructive criticism, of course, is a terrific tool. If a critic tells you, "I don't like it," or, "This is disappointing," he's done you no good at all. In fact, quite the opposite is true.

He's used his power to injure without giving you any information to help you to do better next time. Worse, he hasn't given those listening to him any data to make a thoughtful decision on their own. And by refusing to reveal the basis for his criticism, he's being a coward, because there's no way to challenge his opinion.

I admit it. When I get a bad review, my feelings are hurt. After all, it would be nice if a critic said that a title of mine was a breakthrough, an inspirational, thoughtful book that explains how everything, from politics to wine, is marketed through stories.

The lesson here is this: If I had written a boring book, there'd be no criticism. No conversations. *The products and services that get talked about are the ones that are worth talking about.*

So the challenge, as you contemplate your next opportunity to be boring or remarkable, is to answer these questions:

■ If I am criticized for this, will I suffer any measurable losses? Will I lose my job, get hit upside the head with a softball bat, or lose important friendships? If the only side effect of the criticism is that you will feel bad about the criticism, then you have to compare that bad feeling with the benefits you'll get from actually doing something worth doing. Being remarkable is exciting, fun, profitable, and great for your career. Feeling bad wears off.

And then, once you've sold yourself on taking the remarkable path, answer this one:

■ How can I create something that critics will criticize?

CRITICISM (MORE)

According to the New York City Parks Department, there are more than 1,800 statues in the Big Apple. Statues of famous American generals. Brilliant international poets. There's even a statue of Gandhi. But extensive research has shown that there isn't one single statue honoring the memory of a critic.

Is it just me or has criticism gotten a little out of hand?

Here are five ways to be an unfair critic:

Speak in absolutes. That film you saw last night is, of course, "the worst movie I've ever seen in my life." Heap as much negativily into one sentence as possible.

Criticize not just the item in question but also the background of the person or company responsible for it. If you can point out how much you disliked something else from the same source, by all means do so. Inclusion only compounds derision.

Criticize the motivation of the creator. Maybe he's doing it just for the money. Maybe he has some sort of secret political agenda. Better yet, the person behind the creation is certainly some kind of "wannabe"—a Robert Redford wannabe or perhaps a Tom Peters wannabe. In any event, "wannabe" is a great general put-down.

Criticize the taste and judgment of anyone who disagrees with your criticism. An enemy of your criticism is *your* enemy—and also needs to be criticized. Feel free to turn your enemy's criticism back on him—and score extra points if you use his own words against him.

Make threats in your criticism. Possibilities include threats to "tell everyone" or to destroy the reputation or property of whomever you are criticizing. Alternatively, you can claim that *you* were threatened—and that your criticism is only one measure of your unwillingness to bow to threats.

Now, don't get the wrong idea: I'm not hoping that you'll feel sorry for me and for the thousand of other authors and product creators who regularly see their work criticized by uneducated, anonymous teenagers with a personality problem (not that it bothers me, of course; I'm not thin skinned). But the new culture of criticism is hurting you and your company.

Why is it that as soon as a company becomes successful, it ceases to innovate? How is it that the founders of a company seemingly forget, just a few years after they've launched their breakthrough venture, that it was innovation that got them there? They didn't achieve success by worrying about doing the same old thing out of fear of criticism; they achieved it by being willing to take a risk and break the rules.

So here they are: the three curses of criticism that make companies put the brakes on innovation (and worse, put their best employees—the innovators—on the defensive):

■ Successful companies fear external criticism.

■ Successful innovators are more subject to harsh criticism.

■ Less innovative employees have carte blanche to criticize the innovators unfairly.

Did you ever notice that critics are more likely to be harsh about movies and books that come with high expectations? Ask for a list of the worst movies ever made, and people will mention *Waterworld*, *Ishtar*, or some other big-budget spectacular. Surely these movies aren't as bad as some $100,000 exploitation flick made in Tallahassee, Florida, over a long weekend. Yet we're quick to assault the big flops because we're so certain that the folks who squandered all of that money deserve our harsh assessment.

Years ago, Stephen King launched his second online e-book, and it was downloaded by only about 150,000 people. Rather than laud his bravery and insight, or comment on a writer of his stature demonstrating a willingness to take a risk, people wanted to know why the e-book didn't receive a million downloads. The *Wall Street Journal* ran a snide paragraph or two suggesting that Mr. King might be better off waiting for a big corporation to back him next time. After all, this is Stephen King, and thus the critics expect instant success.

This external criticism doesn't just affect individuals, of course. When 3M launches a sequel to the Post-it, or Microsoft unveils a new service, our expectations are set very high indeed. This is partially due to all of the hype: Hype attracts criticism the way that politicians attract lobbyists. When the product inevitably doesn't meet our expectations, we're ready to slaughter it.

It's this sort of mind-set that allows someone to get off an on-time flight from New York to San Francisco, having just flown first-class (using frequent-flier miles), and bitterly complain that the nuts weren't warm enough. Success makes the critics lose perspective. Success means that nothing is good enough.

At your company, this probably means that even though there are countless ways to take your early successes and leverage them into new successes, senior management is afraid to do so. They're afraid to take the risk of being criticized by customers, competitors, or Wall Street: "We can't do that. We might fail!"

Why did all of the retail giants fall to Wal-Mart? Why is Kraft so far behind in organic, nonengineered foods? Why did CBS wait years to launch much of anything on cable or the Internet? Because market leaders are afraid.

The second criticism effect is the fear that top management (often the original innovators) has of being *personally* criticized. This is a fear that successful authors and actors have to deal with all the time. When people become associated with an idea or a company (especially an idea or a company that the public loves and respects), the personal stakes get higher. Not only will those people be open to even greater criticism, but they also risk losing an asset that they've established and now treasure: the respect and devotion of the public.

Do you think that Larry Ellison or Steve Jobs or Tom Clancy or Julia Roberts want to make a product that might flop? Not likely. It's about more than the money for these folks. It's about the aura of wisdom and insight that they've created. Approach one of these people with a daring new idea and you're going to face quite a challenge in getting them to accept it.

But it's the last sort of criticism that makes it so difficult for successful companies to innovate. Whether you work for Ben & Jerry's or JCPenney or Toyota or Wal-Mart, your company is going to be staffed with people who are unfair—and harsh—critics of your new idea. And by the way, that's any new idea, almost anytime.

Why?

Because as companies mature and grow, they are far more likely to hire people to perform tasks, as opposed to hiring people who figure out how to change their jobs for the better. These new people are there because they embrace the status quo. They like their jobs. That's why they took them.

As a result, whatever you want to change at your company has to be unfairly compared with whatever is happening there now. And the comparison goes like this: *The worst possible outcome of what you're proposing must be better than the best possible outcome of what we're doing now.*

I've sat through some meetings that were absolutely surreal. Someone proposes an e-mail campaign that could dramatically increase a company's profitability and market share at the same time that it would decrease customer service costs. Then the vice president of customer service says, "But what about the people who want to call us and end up getting this e-mail instead? What about them?" Now, simple math would show that she's talking about a tiny fraction of customers. Worse, a quick audit would show that virtually everyone who calls in is upset about being put on hold for so long. So, while your proposal might offend a few customers, the critic ignores the thousands of customers who would end up much happier.

I'm not proposing that you run off and try whatever crazy idea pops into your head, ignoring constructive criticism that can make it better. I am asking, though, that you follow these three rules when attending a meeting:

Criticize an idea based on how well it meets its objectives. If you don't like the objectives, criticize those separately.

Fairly compare the idea to the status quo, warts and all. Ignoring your current problems just because you already have them is not fair.

If you don't like an idea, it's your job to come up with something better by Friday. No solution is not a solution.

CUFF LINKS

If cuff links didn't exist and you invented them, would they succeed?

I've got one shirt in my closet with French cuffs. As I looked at it one day, hanging there quite lonely, I got to thinking about cuff links.

Cuff links are arguably a nice way for men to wear jewelry, and they were no doubt functional back in the day. But it's difficult to argue much of a utilitarian use today.

Yet they persist.

They persist because stamping them out completely is essentially impossible. They are an anachronism, part of a system that may never go away. We can't get rid of them until all the shirts are gone, but as long as there are shirts with French cuffs, there will be cuff links, which will only encourage people to buy more French cuffs! Stores can sell plenty of reversible nautical cuff links ("What! You got me cuff links that aren't reversible!?") because the shirt makers support them by selling shirts with holes. If there were no holes, there would be no cuff links. As long as there are holes, there will be a demand for them.

So if you're trying to invent a product or service that requires the rest of the industry to put a hole out there for you to fill, good luck. Starting a new industry standard is really difficult. Leveraging one that already exists is easy.

If you can figure out a way to profit from an existing "hole," you've got yourself a huge advantage.

Audible.com, for example, needed the world to make an MP3 player in order for them to succeed. What a crazy gamble! Fortunately, just in time, it happened. But now that the MP3 player is here, I bet some smart folks are going to figure out something else to put on an audio player. . . . What about city walking tours, with local ads?

CURSIVE VERSUS TYPING

I heard on the radio yesterday that "scientists" are predicting the next big computer breakthrough will be voice recognition. Chips are becoming fast enough that computers will soon be able to understand what we say. Which will make airports very noisy places, but that's a different story.

The other day, I took a four-hour flight sitting next to a very aggressive hunt-and-peck typist. He must have written three thousand words on the flight, nailing each key as hard and as fast as he could.

Then I got home to discover that they're teaching my third grader how to write in cursive.

Something's wrong here.

Cursive is a fundamentally useless skill in this century, and if we were inventing the curriculum from scratch, it wouldn't even show up in the top one thousand things children need to learn. Typing, on the other hand, is way up there, at least until the "scientists" perfect voice recognition. Educators must realize this, but because they don't actually test the efficacy of what they teach, because they don't have an obvious way to figure out what's worth the time and what's not, they still teach cursive.

All organizations are slow to change. Organizations that don't measure their results are even slower.

CUSTOMER SERVICE, A MODEST PROPOSAL FOR

The trend is pretty clear: Move your customer support operations offshore to cut costs. After all, providing customer service is a cost, not a profit center, and if you can cut that cost, you win. Cost savings go straight to the bottom line, they say.

I can do that one better.

I just spent the last few days on the phone (as a customer) with three big companies, engaged in infuriating conversations with over-stressed people. Not just annoying conversations, but time-consuming, too. In two cases, I "won" the discussion, but of course both of us lost. In the other case, they "won," I gave up, and don't expect to talk to them again anytime soon.

Here's the plan:

Someone starts a service that is designed to cut customer service costs close to zero. You pay $.02 on the dollar compared to what you're paying now. The way it works: It's a computerized, totally turnkey operation, located on some desolate island with no people, just computers. Any firm with a customer service "cost problem" can hire them—this company can handle dozens of clients at once. The extremely polite computer voices answer with the name of the firm and use a database to keep track of all the information they receive. They keep people on hold for as long as possible (but not a moment longer) and then transfer them to a different automated mailbox.

The goal is to make the customer feel as though the (computerized) operators are doing their best, but of course they never actually *do* anything. Keep track of the conversations and the record numbers. Keep transferring people. Promise to call back, but never do. Sooner or later, the customer gives up and walks away. (If the firm does their job right, the customer blames himself, at least a little bit, for not being more patient.)

End result? Not only are operator costs saved, but you don't even have to fix any of your products!

Yes, it's a stupid idea. But it's cheap. If cheap is what you want, then go do this. If customer *service* is what you want, maybe it's not such a good idea to obsess about being cheap. Customer service, we see time and time again, is a profit center; it is the cheapest form of marketing.

DAYLIGHT SAVING TIME

History moves in cycles, over and over, to the point where it's sort of boring.

One of the cycles is the way governments and long-lived organizations unite to fight change. It involves pronouncements in the halls of Congress; lobbying by entrenched industries; outspoken demonstrations by fringe religious groups ostensibly representing the masses; controversial court decisions; and, most important, pronouncements that "this changes everything," "it's the end of the world as we know it," "this goes against God's will," and, my favorite, "sure there are cycles, but this one is different."

I'm in the middle of reading *Seize the Daylight: The Curious and Contentious Story of Daylight Saving Time*. An odd topic for a book, something to read after you've read *Salt* and *Cod*, but still fascinating.

Here are some things worth noting about the evolution of daylight saving time:

"The system was invented" by Ben Franklin, but not really. In

1444, the walled city of Basel was about to be attacked. There were infidels outside, and some had infiltrated the town. The guards caught some of the bad guys and learned that the attack was to begin precisely at noon. An alert sentry set the clock in the square back an hour. Brilliant! The infidels inside the city, unaided by their allies, started their diversion an hour early. They were all arrested.

But I digress.

Lobbying for daylight saving time started in earnest about one hundred years ago (just eighty years after time was standardized—it turns out that before trains traversed the Continent, it didn't really matter that the time was different in different towns).

A large-scale lobbying campaign was waged on behalf of changing the clocks as the seasons changed, but it ran into trouble early and often.

Sir William Christie, Astronomer Royal, called daylight saving nothing but special legislation for late risers (he played the "moral failing" card).

Sir William Napier Shaw, director of the meteorological office, said, "To alter the present mode of measuring time would be to kill a goose that lays a very valuable egg."

Nature magazine said, "The advance from local to the standard time of today was a step well thought out, and one that cannot be reversed by the introduction of a new and really nondescript time under the old name."

The secretary of the London Stock Exchange, Mr. Satterthwaite, said the bill would create "a dislocation of Stock Exchange business in the chief business centre of the world."

Of course, many reactionaries with nothing concrete to say merely mocked William Willet, the chief proponent of the change. *Nature* wondered if his next trick was going to be to redefine the thermometer so that the freezing temperature would be 42 degrees instead of 32.

The theater owners united (foreshadowing the future behavior of the Motion Picture Association of America) and worked hard to defeat the bill, saying that if it weren't dark at night, their business would be completely decimated.

Year after year, the bill failed to pass in the United Kingdom. In the United States the story was much the same.

If it hadn't been for the need to save energy during World War I, daylight saving time would never have been instituted—the forces against change refused to accept how much money would be saved by changing the clocks. It turns out that the savings were millions and millions of dollars a year, probably billions by now. Many politicians were against the change on general principle.

The *New York Times* wrote that it was "little less than an act of madness."

My very favorite quote of all comes from Mississippi:

"Repeal the law and have the clocks proclaim God's time and tell the truth!" That comes from Congressman Ezekiel Candler, Jr.

And Harry Hull of Iowa said, "When we passed the law, we tried to 'put one over' on Mother Nature, and when you try to improve the natural laws it usually ends in disaster."

After the law passed, there were court battles everywhere. Battles over state versus federal jurisdiction, for example.

Just something to think about the next time an "emergency" (something that threatens the status quo that must be vanquished before it ends in disaster) overtakes our culture.

DIGITAL DIVIDE, THE NEW

A few years ago, pundits were quite worried about the digital divide. The short definition is that the haves would have reliable, fast access to the Net, which would give them employment and learning opportunities that the have-nots wouldn't be able to find. This would further divide those with a head start from everyone else. Wiring the schools in the United States was one response to the threat of this divide.

I think a *new* divide has opened up, one that is based far more on *choice* than on circumstance. Several million people (and the number is growing daily) have chosen to become the "haves" of the Internet, and at the same time that their number is growing, so are their skills.

THE DIGERATI	THE LEFT BEHIND
Uses Firefox	Uses Internet Explorer
Knows who Doc Searls is	Already has a doctor, thanks very much
Uses RSS reader	RSS?
Has a blog	Reads blogs (sometimes)
Reads Boing Boing	
(or Slashdot)	Watches *The Tonight Show*
Bored with Flickr	Flickr?
Gets news from Google	Gets news from Peter Jennings

Does it surprise you that more than *half* of the hundreds of thousands of BoingBoing readers use Firefox? That's about five times the number you'd expect. It turns out that a lot of these tech-savvy behaviors come grouped together. Someone who has a few of these behaviors is likely to have most of them. (And no, this is by no means a complete list.)

So what? Why should you care if a bunch of nerds are learning a lot of cool new stuff?

Well, five years ago geeks pretty much kept to themselves. They'd be sitting in IRC chat, or arguing about Unix versus Linux, but their obsessions didn't spread very fast and didn't influence the rest of the world outside the tech community.

Today, though, the Net is far more robust and far more ubiquitous than it used to be. And it's the bloggers who are setting the agenda on everything from politics to culture. It's bloggers that journalists and politicians now look to as the first and the loudest.

As a result, odds are that your most connected, most influential customers are part of the digerati. They can make or break your product, your service, or even your religion's new policies. Because the Net is now a broadcast (and a narrowcast) medium, the digerati can spread ideas.

The second thing to keep in mind is that the digerati are using the learning tools built into the Net to get smarter, faster. A new Internet tool can propagate to millions in just a week or two. This means that, unlike the old digital divide, the divide between the new digerati and the rest of the world is accelerating.

So, it's choice time. Several of my colleagues (Tom Peters being a notable example) are jumping in with both feet. Others take a look at the digerati's head start and decide that it's just too much work to catch up.

Try to imagine doing your work today without e-mail. It's inconceivable. I think the tools of the digerati are going to be just as essential soon enough. You can wait until Microsoft issues them all as a dumbed-down package, but if you do, you'll not only miss the nuances and understanding that come from learning as you go, but you'll always be trying to catch up.

If you think that del.ico.us is a better way to enjoy food, you're already on the wrong side of the divide.

I can't decide if I'm really one of us or them; I've got all the tools, but it's still hard work. The good news, though, is that you won't break anything if you try these new tools and commit yourself to understanding the new digerati. Better hurry, though, because they won't wait for you.

DING

I answer all my own e-mail, and sometimes, in my haste to get to all of it, I'm brief. And sometimes, that brevity is confused with shortness or even snarkiness. I'm working hard at doing better.

I was reminded of this when I saw this "ding letter" from Google posted. It says:

We received your résumé and would like to thank you for your interest in Google. After carefully reviewing your experience and qualifications, we have determined that we do not have a position available which is a strong match at this time.

The thing is, there's no salutation. How "carefully" could Google (which states quite clearly that one of their biggest challenges is finding enough great people) have reviewed the résumé if they didn't even bother to include the person's name?

More important, is this letter going to just disappear, or is it going to be used as a marketing tool to help Google find more applicants? What if the letter was a little bit less formal? What if it included links to other firms that are hiring? What if there was some sort of incentive to recommend your friends to Google, or a remarkable way to be reconsidered in the next batch of hires?

Even when you say no, you're marketing.

DISRESPECT

It's been quite a week for disrespect. And it's only Thursday.

Half of my incidents have been business-to-business situations. The other half occurred in places where I was just a consumer.

Looking back, I'm really sort of amazed by two things: First, how visceral the emotions are when I feel as though I've been disrespected, and second, how easy it would be to avoid these situations.

Let me be clear here: Disrespect is in the eye of the beholder. It occurs when someone feels slighted, or demeaned, or undervalued, or lied to. There is no absolute measurement, and, because it's relative, people will surely disagree about whether or not it has occurred at all.

Doesn't matter. If you feel disrespected, then you were.

1. I just spent two hours at the doctor's office. An entire hour was spent in a little room, waiting. No updates, no apologies, nothing. Even after the doctor finally arrived, he acted as though the long wait didn't even happen. Then, when I nicely asked to talk to the office manager on my way out, she took a phone call instead.

2. I spent nine months negotiating a deal with a company where I've had a long and fruitful relationship. This project was going very, very slowly, and not because I was slowing it down. I'd been patient and flexible and was working it through the system. Two days ago, I got an e-mail. It said, in its entirety, "Unfortunately, this is getting way too complex and not worth the effort for either of us. I know that we keep trying to make this work (for months now!) but it's not working for either side. So, I think we should let this go and part friends."

Both have the same elements in common:

All the other person had to do was use a one- or two-sentence apology and the whole thing would have been fine. Almost all the instances of disrespect didn't have to do with the *substance* of the transaction, it was the *style* of it. If the person had accepted some responsibility and acknowledged how I might feel, the outcome wasn't really a big deal.

"I'm really sorry you had to wait. Mr. Wilson's eardrum exploded and we're doing everything we can to help him."

"I know you worked long and hard to make this deal work, but we just can't figure it out. I'm so sorry we wasted your time."

It's really simple: Most of the time, most of your customers will cut you slack if you just acknowledge that the outcome isn't the one they (think they) deserve.

People have a hard time saying they're sorry. If someone feels as though they're treating you correctly (technically speaking), they don't want to apologize. They don't want to acknowledge the feelings of the other side. This is awfully shortsighted. These are words that are worth thousands and thousands of dollars in lost sales and word-of-mouth advertising.

"You must feel terrible about what happened. I know I do. If there were any way I could figure out how to make this better for you, I'd do it." When isn't that a true statement when you're dealing with an unhappy customer?

DO LESS

Years ago, when I was starting my first company, I believed in two things: "Survival is success" and "Take the best project you can get, but take a project." I figured that if I was always busy and I managed to avoid wiping out, sooner or later everything would work out.

Most organizations, large or small, operate from the same perspective. As you add employees, there's pressure to keep everyone occupied, to be busy. Of course, once you're busy, there's a tremendous need to hire even more people, which continues the cycle.

If your goal is to be big, there's no doubt that taking every gig you can makes sense. Pricing for the masses, building the biggest factory, and moving as fast as you can is the very best way to get big. And if big equals successful, you're done.

Many of us have realized, though, that big doesn't equal successful. We're starting to see that fewer women are willing to do what it takes to be a CEO or a senior law partner. Perhaps that's because they've redefined success.

Maybe you need to be a lot pickier about what you do and for whom you do it.

Dan, a real-estate developer I met recently, told me that he does one new investment a year. It's not unusual for his competition to do ten or a hundred deals in the same period of time. What Dan told me, though, really resonated: "In any given year, we look at a thousand deals. One hundred of them are pretty good. One is great." By only doing the great deals, Dan is able to make far more money than he would if he did them all. He can cherry-pick because his goal isn't volume.

Or consider the architect who designs just a few major buildings a year. Obviously he has to dig deep to do work of a high enough quality to earn these commissions. But by not cluttering his life and his reputation with a string of low-budget, boring projects, he actually increases his chances of getting great projects in the future.

How many newly minted college grads take the first job that's "good enough"? A good-enough job gets you busy right away, but it also puts you on a path to a lifetime of good-enough jobs. Investing (not "spending") a month or a year in high-profile internships could change your career forever.

Take a look at your client list. *What would happen if you fired half of your clients?* If you fired the customers who pay late, give you a hard time, have you work on low-leverage projects, and are rarely the source of positive recommendations, would your business improve? Even in our dicey economy, it's pretty easy to answer that one with a yes.

What if you fired half your workforce? Give the very best people a 50 percent raise and help the rest find jobs in which they can really thrive. Unless you produce a commodity like oil or billiard balls, it's not clear that selling more and more to an ever larger audience is the best way to reach the success you seek. When your overhead plummets, the pressure to take on the wrong jobs with the wrong staff disappears. You're free to pick the projects that make you happy.

"Projects." A funny word to have used thirty years ago, but one that makes complete sense today. Thirty years ago, we were still fine-tuning our factories. Thirty years ago, everything was part of the assembly line. Today, though, we're in the project business. Just about all of us work on projects, but the one thing we give very little thought to is which projects we should do.

When I was a kid, the buffets in town proclaimed, "all you can eat!" Now they say, "all you care to eat." There's a big difference. You only get to eat dinner once a day, and most of us are smart enough not to eat more just because it's free. So, as you head through the line, the question you need to ask yourself is, "Would I rather eat this . . . or that?" You can't have everything.

The same thing's true with our business life. We can't have everything. We've tried and it doesn't work. What we've discovered, though, is that leaving off that last business project not only makes our profits go up, but it also can dramatically improve the rest of our lives.

DON'T GO TO BUSINESS SCHOOL

I thought maybe I'd open a business school. This is particularly ironic given my past: No student in the history of the Stanford Graduate School of Business has ever come closer to not receiving an M.B.A. than yours truly.

When I was at Stanford (it seems like decades ago—probably because it was), I thought that the environment there was terrific, and I truly enjoyed some of my classes. But before the start of my second year, I got an irresistible job offer—which prompted me to try to go to school and work at the same time. The classes were in Palo Alto, and the job was in Boston, but, thanks to some help from TWA and a bizarre willingness on my part to fly on the red-eye, I managed to commute for a semester. After that, a kindly professor decided to stop the madness and just give me the rest of my credits, so graduate I did.

Despite my less-than-stellar attendance record at business school, I've since found that teaching business is a blast. I taught a class to second-year students at NYU this year and discovered that aggravating ninety soon-to-be-graduating young people is great fun. I had so much fun, in fact, that I started thinking about what business school is, what it's good for—and what it's not good for at all.

As far as I can tell, there are only three reasons to apply to business school. My new, fictional school, the New Order Business School (NoBS), will focus on excelling at all three.

First, business school provides a tremendous screen for future employers. If you go to Harvard Business School, for example, you are investing in your personal branding, and you are guaranteed a job interview—at the very least—virtually anywhere in the world. When it comes to business, Columbia, Stanford, Wharton, and a few other schools aspire to Harvard's level. And in some industries, they even surpass it.

Just as Internet investors have successfully trained themselves to look past the present and to invest in companies that have a wonderful future, some employers have realized that waiting for someone to graduate from one of these august institutions is a waste of time. Instead of hiring students after they finish classes, why not just hire people as soon as they've been accepted to business school?

The student who drops out of school after getting in but before beginning classes saves about $55,000 in tuition—as well as another $180,000 in opportunity cost. Add to that the stock options and a chance to change the world that much sooner, and you can see why this is a no-brainer for all involved.

At NoBS, we offer a special program for just this sort of student. Basically, it's the most exclusive business school admissions program in the country. We guarantee that only one out of every one thousand applicants will be accepted to our school. And we guarantee that upon being accepted, every single person will receive at least three job offers—each with a minimum salary of $95,000 a year.

The fee to have your application considered is $300. After all, as an admissions-based institution—actually, as an admissions-*only* institution—we have to do a great job, so it's $300 well spent.

There are few classes. There is no degree. You apply. You get in (or, more likely, you don't). That's it. We're done. (Oh, and by the way, the profit margins are huge! But you figured that out already.)

Think about the prestige associated with being the one in one thousand. Think about the pride in knowing that you are one of the few people smart enough, motivated enough, and crazy enough to apply to a school that exclusive. Stuck in a dead-end job? Work like crazy on your GMATs and your essay, and you, too, may be able to break through the clutter of applicants and become a NoBS standout.

The second reason that people go to business school is to build a network. There's a social insurance policy among students. If someone in your class actually becomes successful or lands a powerful job, the rest of you have someone to go to for favors or even cash.

It's sort of astonishing how powerful networking can be. One investor I know gives preference to companies whose staff includes an alumnus of Camp Tahigwa. Employees don't necessarily have to have attended Camp Tahigwa at the same time that the investor did—so long as they know the same camp songs.

At NoBS, we offer a concentrated program, half of which focuses on just this sort of networking. Rather than waiting for networking to occur through random osmosis—through unpredictable events like working on a project together in Cost Accounting 101— students at NoBS gather for two weeks every six months to engage in some intense team building. They row crew. They play chess. They build houses for the disadvantaged. They stay up all night putting a Volkswagen Beetle on the roof of Larry Ellison's home.

The third (and least important) reason to go to business school is actually to learn something. And this is where traditional business schools really fail. The core curriculum at business schools is as close to irrelevant as you can imagine. If you and I were trying to create a series of courses that would all but guarantee that, upon graduating, students would have no useful knowledge about how to do business in the new economy, today's business school curriculum would be a great model for us.

So eliminating the curriculum may be a great idea. But sooner or later the illusion of a thriving, useful institution will fade if a business school doesn't offer any courses. Ask people who are thriving in to-day's economy to name five things that helped them succeed, and they'll probably come up with a list like this one:

1. Finding, hiring, and managing supergreat people

2. Embracing change and moving quickly

3. Understanding and excelling at business development and at making deals with other companies

4. Prioritizing tasks in a job that changes every day

5. Selling—to people, to companies, and to markets

There are other skills that might show up on the list—for example, balancing a life for the long term, working with venture capitalists and other sources of funds, being creative, and understanding the impact of new technologies—but this is a good starting place.

Now take a look at the core curriculum for a $55,000 M.B.A. You'll find virtually no focus at all on any of these five issues. My M.B.A. students at NYU had never taken a selling course, they had never been taught how to give a presentation, but they were experts in cost accounting, in understanding manufacturing efficiencies, and in applying the Black and Scholes Option Pricing Formula.

People in the real world buy how-to books to figure out how to succeed. So the NoBS curriculum includes only courses that are worthy of being the subject of a best-selling book. And whenever possible, the authors themselves teach the courses. (In fact, my facetiousness aside, you can learn 100 percent of the M.B.A. curriculum at home, in a month, just by reading books. I'll go one step further: I can condense an hour of class presentation into ten book pages. If you can discipline yourself to read, you can free up two years of your life for the good stuff!)

The last thing to consider about business school is that in many cases precisely the wrong people attend. Instead of filling their classrooms with people who are too kind to go to law school, business schools ought to find people who are already in the business world, but who are panicking because they don't know as much as they want to know. Instead of looking for people who are working two mind-numbing years at a bank while waiting to get into a top institution, schools ought to seek out entrepreneurs who are champing at the bit to get their businesses started.

There are two kinds of people who don't belong in business school: the talented folks who are in too much of a hurry to spend time studying, and the dull ones who don't have anything better to do.

The paradox, of course, is that the best people aren't prepared to leave their lives behind for two years. They're in a hurry.

So at NoBS, students only need to attend classes for four weeks every six months. The rest of the school runs online for two hours every day. And the M.B.A. is completed in less than a year.

During the four weeks of live stuff, we all fly to some off-season ski resort with excellent food, decent rooms, and an Olympic-sized swimming pool. Classes run from 8:00 A.M. to midnight, three days a week. The rest of the week, students teach one another from real-life anecdotes. Sharing life experiences prepares people for the arrival of unexpected events.

The "faculty" isn't really a faculty at all. There are no Ph.D.s in the bunch—not one. Instead, our teachers are compelling public speakers, the kind of people who get standing ovations. People like Zig Ziglar on selling, Tom Peters on embracing change, or Regis McKenna on public relations.

Sound like a powerful experience? It's totally nonaccredited. There's no bureaucracy. One dean. Drop out if you want. Do it for the learning, not for the grades. Everybody is as motivated as you are. Get it over with in just nine months. Walk out with a great credential and one hundred lifelong friends.

Is NoBS yet another bizarre thought exercise on my part? Probably. Depends on how many of you mail your nonrefundable $300 application fee to PO Box 305, Irvington, New York, 10533. Send it by midnight tonight—before you forget!

NoBS is worth considering. Before you go to business school, before you decide that a fancy M.B.A. is the one thing standing between you and success, you ought to think really hard about why you're going and what you're going to learn.

And that, of course, goes double for any company itching to hire the latest freshly minted M.B.A. Perhaps instead of letting a three-hundred-year-old institution do your screening for you, you should start your own business school. Bring in a hundred kids. Put them through the real curriculum in four weeks. Keep half, and pay the other half a year of severance (or have them lick envelopes until they find another job).

It's easy to forget that business school is a thoroughly modern phenomenon—that it's not rooted in the ancient canons of Shakespeare or even Madame Curie. Most modern business schools were founded in the 1960s. Their time has come and gone. So say goodbye, and mail your $300 to NoBS. That address again . . .

DOUGHNUTS

Today's *New York Times* reports that the Radiant Church in Surprise, Arizona, spends $16,000 a year on Krispy Kreme doughnuts.

The health risks aside, this is smart marketing. (And is there anything wrong with a church doing marketing? Churches have always done marketing.)

Marketing doesn't mean advertising.

ECHO CHAMBER

If you're defining yourself and your business in terms of your competition, you're living in an echo chamber. Companies and organizations don't grow fast at the expense of existing competitors. They grow fast for reasons that have nothing to do with whether your service is 5 percent better or your product is a little more convenient.

There are two ways to grow: by stealing from the competition or by growing the market. The first path is slow and painful and difficult. The second path is where the magic of fast growth kicks in.

You don't beat McKinsey with better consulting advice, you don't raise more money than the United Way by spending it more efficiently, and you don't sell more widgets by offering a slightly longer guarantee.

EGOMANIAC

The other day, my new friend Tucker told me that I was a massive egomaniac.

Aren't all bloggers?

What sort of ego do bloggers have? We spend time and energy and money to post our opinions to the world, and we do it daily, or even hourly, often on topics on which we have no obvious authority.

Ego is the biggest reason that corporate blogging may be an oxymoron. Working for the Man often means that your ego is subsumed by that of the organization, and blogging goes against this. It's one reason that there have been high-profile firings of corporate bloggers. It's hard to have two voices (the writer's and the shareholder's) competing and often conflicting.

"Egomaniac," by the way, is the wrong word. I think that blogging requires you to have a healthy respect for your opinions, as well as the generous desire to share them with others. That's not a negative social trait; if you don't respect your opinions, who will? And if you don't share the ideas you value, you're being selfish, aren't you?

ENTHUSIASTS

Depending on his area of expertise, an enthusiast cares about the answers to the following questions:

"Paddle shift or stick?" "SACD or DVD-A?" "Cherrywood or carbon fiber?" "Pho Bac or Pho Bang?" "PowerBook or iBook?" "Hearthstone or parchment paper?" "Habanero or chipotle?" "Linen or organic cotton?"

I'm an enthusiast. As you may have guessed, I am every marketer's dream. I am an enthusiast in not just one but a bunch of areas. I get magazines with names like *The Rosengarten Report* and catalogs from Garrett Wade.

Enthusiasts are the ones with otaku. We're the ones who care about what marketers are up to. The ones who seek out new products and new corporations, the ones who boldly go . . . (oops, sorry, another enthusiastic topic jumped in there). Anyway, we are the ones who will spread the word about your innovation, tell our friends and colleagues about your new Purple Cow.

It's not just consumer goods. Enthusiasts read the *Harvard Business Review* and get excited about a new consulting firm or a new technique. Enthusiasts read the classifieds at the back of *Advertising Age* to figure out which ad agencies are doing well. And political enthusiasts decide who gets elected president of the United States.

Plenty of marketers have decided that they need to be obsessed with these otaku-filled piggy banks. Some of them have even rented or, better yet, collected permission-based lists of the most profitable subsets of these populations. And yet most of them fail.

I think they fail for the very same reason you often fail in getting the enthusiast in your life the perfect Christmas gift.

Enthusiasts don't want you to hand them a gift certificate. (They'll figure out how to get the money for the thing they really want.) Nor do they want you to give them a gift and say, "The salesman at the store said you'd like this." While you may satisfy our short-term craving for more, you also remind enthusiasts that you're not on the bus. If you're not one of us, you've disappointed us, made us feel marginalized, or, at the very least, made us feel like failures for being unable to persuade you about the joys of our enthusiasm.

Enthusiasts are *enthusiastic*! This means we want to spread the word. It means we want other people to "get it" as well. We want the organizations we buy from to feel like we do, to care as much as we do about the experiences and the products and the processes. We want our friends and fans not just to buy us a stick shift warmer for the Ferrari, but to research it first, to compare the different warmers, to understand the trade-offs and make the same (obvious) choice that we would.

When you take a chowhound to dinner (that's what enthusiasts of good, authentic restaurants call themselves), she wants to know that you care as deeply as she does about the choice—not that you picked the closest restaurant listed in Zagat. When you design a product for a videophile, he wants to know that you've spent as many hours staring at the flat screen as he does.

Visit Steve Deckert's site, Decware, and you'll have no doubt that he's a true enthusiast. It's different than buying from some invisible technology conglomerate. That's one reason it's so easy for little companies like this to do just great with the early adopters with otaku. We buy from him because he's like us. He's one of us.

So, what should you do if you want to sell to an enthusiast, or buy a Christmas present for an enthusiast? She's not going to make allowances for low price or great service or kindness. She's going to be picky. She's going to be aware of the trade-offs. And she's not going to go easy on you. If she did, she wouldn't be an enthusiast, would she?

What you'll need to do, I'm afraid, is become one yourself. If it's important to you to deal with people with otaku, you've got to get some.

FEAR OF LOSS, DESIRE FOR GAIN

I found myself in the mall (gasp) this weekend at a Lord & Taylor and discovered the oddest promotion.

After I purchased $200 worth of stuff, the salesperson said, "You qualify for two gift certificates worth $40. No strings attached. Go upstairs and you can get them right now."

Note: There was no notice before the purchase. No signs, no promises. The certificates weren't designed as an enticement to get me to buy anything.

"Why would they spend 20 percent of revenue and perhaps 50 percent of profit for no reason?" I wondered.

I headed upstairs, waited for two minutes and got my certificates, just so I could let you, my gentle readers, know about this crazy scheme. Walked over to the tie department and bought $39 worth of beautiful ties, marked down from $100 (hey, I'm cheap), and I was done.

On my way out, I passed a woman carrying four shopping bags. Big ones.

Here's her deal: She was on her *fourth* batch of gift certificates. Every time she got $20, she needed to spend it right away. She ended up spending more than $100 each time, so she then went back to get another certificate or two, then needed to spend those, and on and on and on. A quick talk with the gift-certificate-dispensing person confirmed that this was far from unusual behavior. It was a frenzy.

So people "earn" the certificate and, unable to resist the fear of losing what is theirs, they go over and collect it. But now that they have it, it's "free money," so they go and spend it, and the cycle continues.

This is so much more effective than the typical markdown.

I bet it would work even better online. Imagine how it could help shopping cart conversion . . .

FEEDBACK, HOW TO GET

It's not about you.

It's not about you.

It's not about you.

It's about *me* (of course).

Amazon, meaning well, sent me a note offering a $5 gift certificate if I'd answer a short survey about their associates program. Good for them for wanting feedback. Good for them for compensating people.

So, I visit the site and discover not one or three or ten multiple-choice questions.

Sixty-three.

What sort of person sits still for sixty-three multiple-choice questions?

How scientific is the feedback if it's only from the people who answer sixty-three questions?

What concrete action can Amazon take with all this finely tuned statistical nonsense?

Wouldn't it be a lot more useful to just say: "Tell us the three things you like most (or least) about our program and how you would improve it."

Then have a real, live, honest-to-goodness person read each answer and write back.

Invite one hundred people to do the survey. Then one hundred more. A hundred a week for a year. You'd learn a lot.

That's my two cents.

FEEDBACK, HOW TO GIVE

My readers are far more likely to be asked for their input than the average employee. You're frequently required to approve, improve, and adjust things that are about to hit the market. And yet, if you're like most people, you're pretty bad at it.

In the interest of promoting your career, making your day at work more fun, improving the work life of your colleagues, and generally making my life a whole lot better, I'd like to give you some feedback on giving feedback. As usual, the ideas are simple—it's implementing them that's tricky.

The first rule of great feedback is this: No one cares about your opinion.

I don't want to know how you feel, nor do I care if you would buy it, recommend it, or use it. You are not my market. You are not my focus group.

What I want instead of your opinion is your *analysis*. It does me no good to hear you say, "I'd never pick that box up." You can add a great deal of value, though, if you say, "The last three products that succeeded were priced under thirty dollars. Is there a reason you want to price this at thirty-one?" Or, "We analyzed this market last year, and we don't believe there's enough room for us to compete. Take a look at this spreadsheet." Or even, "That font seems hard to read. Is there a way to do a quick test to see if a different font works better for our audience?"

Accurate analysis is a lot harder than opinion because everyone is entitled to his or her own tastes (regardless of how skewed it might be). A faulty analysis, however, is easy to dismantle. But even though it's scary to contribute your analysis to a colleague's proposal, it's still absolutely necessary.

The second rule? Say the right thing at the right time.

If you're asked to comment on a first-draft proposal that will eventually wind its way to the chairman's office, this is not the time to point out that "alot" is two words, not one. Copyediting the document is best done just once, at the end, by a professional. While it may feel as if you're contributing something by making comments about currently trivial details, you're not. Instead, try to figure out what sort of feedback will have the most positive effect on the final outcome, and contribute it now.

Far worse, of course, than the prematurely picky comment is the way too late deal-breaker remark. If I've built a detailed plan for a new factory in Hoboken, New Jersey (and negotiated all the variances and integrated the existing landscaping), the time to tell me you were thinking of relocating the plant to Secaucus was six months ago, not the night before we break ground.

The third rule? If you have something nice to say, please say it.

I've been working with someone for about a year, and in that entire time, he's never once prefaced his feedback with, "This was a really terrific piece of work," or "Wow! This is one of the best ideas I've heard in a while." Pointing out the parts you liked best is much more than sugarcoating. Doing so serves several purposes. First, it puts us both on the same side of the table, making it more likely that your constructive criticism will actually be implemented. If you can start by seeing the project through my eyes, you're more likely to analyze (there's that word again) the situation in a way that helps me reach my goals. "I think it's great that you want to get our quality ratings up. Let's see whether the added people you say this initiative requires are really necessary, and whether beginning your report with staffing needs is the best way to get this past senior management."

The other benefit is that this approach makes it so much more likely that I will come to you for feedback in the future. It's easy to interpret the absence of positive feedback as the absence of any sort of approval or enthusiasm. Finally, being nice to people is fun.

If I haven't intimidated you with my other rules, here's the last one: Give me feedback, no matter what.

It doesn't matter if I ignored your feedback last time (maybe that's because you gave me your opinion, not an analysis). It doesn't matter if you're afraid that your analysis might ultimately be a little shaky. It doesn't matter if you're the least-powerful person in the room. What matters is that you're smart; you understand something about the organization, the industry, and the market; and your analysis (at the very least) could be the kernel of an idea that starts me down a totally different path.

FIFTY STATES, FLAMETHROWERS, AND STICKY TRADITIONS

There are fifty states. This is a problem. If there were five states or five hundred states, programmers would never have been tempted into forcing consumers to scroll through a pull-down menu to enter their state when shopping online.

This means that everyone from Texas or New York or, heaven forfend, West Virginia, has to scroll all the way down in order to buy something.

This scrolling led to a similar "breakthrough" in submitting the name of one's country. Afghanis get a big break (so do people from Andorra) but those in the biggest online-consuming country on Earth have to scroll all the way down to the *U*s.

No wonder so many people abandon shopping carts online.

This is not a riff about how stupid this is.

This is not even a riff about how easy it would be to fix (it's actually easier to add a text field than a pull-down menu).

Nor is it a riff about how useless the precision of a pull-down menu is. Knowing the state is not nearly as important as knowing the zip code, and the scroll-down menu is likely to get you errors, anyway.

No, this is a riff about how bad ideas stick around forever.

The reason is simple: In most organizations, you don't get in trouble for embracing the status quo.

More than a hundred years ago, Kaiser Wilhelm wanted to get rid of his enemies in the German government. He noticed that they were all over sixty-five years old. So he decreed that this was the official retirement age, and it still is.

If you want to see what happens when you challenge the status quo, just say this at a party: "I know how to fix social security. Let's just raise the official retirement age for everyone who is currently under fifty. We'll take it from sixty-five to seventy."

Stand back and beware the flamethrowers. Bad ideas stick around for a long, long time.

FLACK, AS IN PR FLACK

File this under, "They just don't get it."

My contact info is pretty easy to find on my Web site, and as a result I'm getting more and more stuff from PR people. Notice that I'm being really generous and calling it "stuff" instead of "worthless, annoying, time-consuming spam."

The PR folks are used to shoveling loads and loads of outbound stuff in order to get one or two things picked up. That's the way it works in traditional media.

But tell me, please, which blogger out of the ten million is going to run a story with this headline (I'm not making this up):

REFLECTING REACH AND BREADTH OF ITS MEDIA NETWORKS, THE VENDARE GROUP CHANGES NAME TO VENDARE MEDIA

Wow! Now there's something that's interesting and relevant to the people who have a choice about what to read. If your press release is a square peg and all the blogs out there are round holes, that doesn't mean you should send it anyway.

Many in the flack community are trying to turn blogs into just another media outlet. They're not. Instead, they are a terrific home for the remarkable. Make stuff worth talking about first. *Then* talk about it.

FLIPPING THE FUNNEL

In a book called *eMarketing*, which I wrote in 1995, I said something like "There are only four kinds of people: prospects, customers, loyal customers, and former customers." The book was ahead of its time, and I was wrong.

For a book called *Permission Marketing*, which I wrote in 1998, the subtitle was "Turning Strangers into Friends and Friends into Customers." My timing was better, the book was a bestseller, but I was still wrong. Or at least incomplete.

Flipping the Funnel finishes the sentence. Now, I might just be right:

Turn strangers into friends.
Turn friends into customers.
And then . . . do the most important job:
Turn your customers into salespeople.

The math is compelling. Most of the people in the world are not your customers. They haven't even heard of you actually. And while many of these people are not qualified buyers or aren't interested in buying your product, many of them might be—if they only knew you existed, if they could only be convinced that your offering is worth paying for.

But how on earth are you going to get them to know about you?

We're living in the most cluttered marketplace in history. Whether you are selling steel I-beams, scientific glassware, or soccer balls, people are better at ignoring you than ever before. You don't have enough time to get your message out.

Not only that, but you can't afford to interrupt all the people you need to reach. The cost of running an ad that gets seen or an ad that gets clicked on or a billboard that gets remembered is higher than it has ever been. You just don't have enough money to get your message to all the people who need to hear it.

And not only *that*, but you don't have enough people. Your sales force isn't as big as you'd like it to be, and all of your best salespeople are running flat out—without selling as much as you'd like.

But wait.

You have assets that are underused: your friends and your customers.

I define your "friends" as the prospects you've earned permission to talk with—even though they haven't turned into customers yet. And your customers have crossed the Rubicon; they've been converted from total strangers to interested friends, and then all the way to dedicated users of your product or service.

And there's a bunch of them.

You've certainly got more customers than salespeople (at least I hope so). And your list of permission-based friends probably dramatically exceeds your list of customers.

THE FUNNEL

Marketing is a funnel. You put undifferentiated prospects into the top. Some of them hop out, unimpressed with what you have to offer. Others learn about you and your organization, hear from their peers, compare offerings, and eventually come out the bottom, as customers.

If you're like most marketers, you've been spending a

lot of time trying to shovel more and more attention into the top of the funnel. After all, if you can expose your idea to enough people, you can afford to buy more attention, to run more ads, to put more people into the top.

As we've seen, though, the amount of time and money you need to keep that funnel filled can explode your budget pretty quickly.

Here's a quick example. The chart below compares Web traffic at Ford.com (which is supported by more than a hundred million dollars' worth of advertising every year) with Squidoo.com, a brand-new community-driven site. Squidoo is the line on the bottom that moves up, fast.

DAILY REACH (PER MILLION)

squidoo.com ——— ford.com ———

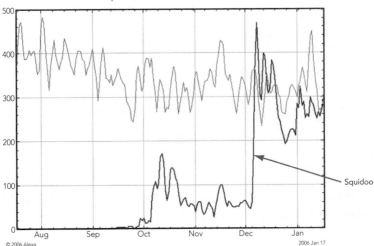

FLIP THE FUNNEL

Here's a different idea:

What if we flip the funnel and turn it into a megaphone?

What if you could figure out how to use the Internet to empower the people who like you, who respect you, who have a vested interest in your success? I call this group of people—

your friends and prospects and customers who are willing to do this—your *fan club*.

A new set of online tools makes this approach not just a possibility but also an imperative for any organization hoping to grow. Give your fan club a megaphone and get out of the way.

THEY DON'T CARE (THEY DON'T HAVE TO)

Most of your friends and customers don't talk about you.

In many cases, it's because they're unimpressed. Somewhere along the way, your organization put profits ahead of relationships. Or you produced something that was just fine, but not remarkable. Or you're in an industry where the customers just don't care that much. (When was the last time you talked about paper clips?)

But what about those customers who are impressed? Whom do they tell? Do they do it often? Do they do it with leverage, or do their goodwill and good words get dissipated quickly?

The challenge you face is that people don't care about you. They care about themselves, which is pretty natural. So someone is unlikely to expend a lot of time and energy and personal branding effort to promote your product—it's too much work and there's nothing in it for them (at least not yet).

Even then, once you overcome those hurdles, your fan club's meager efforts on your behalf (which seem huge) rarely catch fire. Not loud enough, not often enough, too short-lived.

THEN CAME THE NET

Thanks to Al Gore, the Internet changes everything. Now, one person armed with a keyboard can reach millions. One person with a video camera can tell a story that travels around the world. And one person with a blog can sell a lot of computers.

The trick is this: You need to give your fan club some leverage, an amplifier—a megaphone.

DAILY REACH (PER MILLION)

cio.us —— flickr.com ——

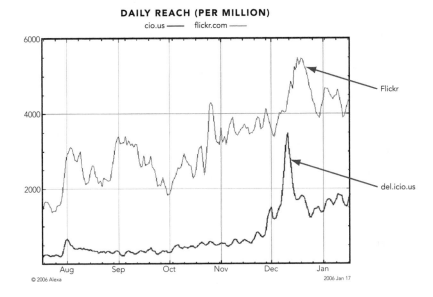

Your former customers, the aggrieved ones, the critics—they've already found the Web. They're the ones who have managed to post play-by-play accounts of your misdeeds and missteps. Unhappy customers are motivated and they're already embracing this medium.

A diligent marketer, however, can make it easy for your fan club to get the word out as well. And to do it in an authentic, uncontrolled, honest way.

It's astonishing to see how quickly this idea has become popular. Two of the most successful information-sharing sites (Flickr and del.icio.us, see chart above) have been growing at an amazing clip.

The easiest way to grasp this is through examples. I'm going to describe three online services that have been around for a year or more and then a new one that I developed and that launched at the end of 2005. All of them are free, effective, and easy to use.

Del.icio.us Tricky name, simple idea. The del.icio.us site makes it easy for anyone to "tag" Web pages. A tag is just a simple set of keywords that people can use to mark a page or an item. Del.icio.us gives its registered users a tool that in just a click or two permits them to bookmark and tag a site.

I did a search on "Sarbanes" because I wanted to find some detailed information on an accounting issue. The bookmarks that had been tagged led me to a site filled with white papers—all written by software and accounting firms that wanted to start discussions about their services with clients.

No, it's not an earth-shattering discovery. But the chance of that site's surfacing in Google is slim—yet because eight people (not a computer) had tagged this page, it rose in popularity and got noticed.

What happens to your site when a dozen of your best customers start tagging your product pages? IBM has perhaps a million or more pages on its site—yet most of them are essentially invisible. If the company made it easy for IT managers and employees to start tagging pages, the most important messages would rise to the top.

For example, IBM has a paper with an in-depth look at the code in the NSA's security-enhanced version of Linux. No doubt this is interesting to a wide range of computer geeks. And no doubt IBM would benefit greatly if everyone who needed to read it, read it. (It's at http://www-128.ibm.com/developerworks/security/library/s-selinux2/ if you're curious.) But not enough geeks will read it because it's buried, and if you don't know to look for it, it's invisible.

If a few surfers tagged it appropriately, though, other surfers would find it. And the word would spread.

The big secret of del.icio.us is that the percentage of users who do the tagging is tiny. Most of the traffic to the site is looking for the tagging done by a tiny minority. This is the essence of online leverage.

Action Item: Figure out who the happiest members of your fan club are (I'm assuming you've already done that). Then teach them about del.icio.us and get out of the way. Sure, some of the tags will point out your lame products or offerings. Some will be more blunt than you'd like. Learn from those, but understand that it's part of the deal.

Blogging (Blogger, TypePad, etc.) My guess is that if you're reading this, you know about blogging. (If you want my free e-book on the topic, it's right *here*.) Although eighty thousand *new* blogs get built every day, it's likely that most of those don't last very long— good thing, too. Faced with a semiblank page, most people write stuff that is either boring, selfish, or indecipherable. Most bloggers quickly lose interest and their blogs wither away.

But if you give people a template, you'll discover that they can thrive. Give them a hole to fill, and fill it they will.

Imagine creating a customer blog where every one of your customers is invited to post a comment. Your post could be as simple as "Today we launched the XR-2000. Comment below and let us know what you think of it."

Yes, you can edit the comments on your blog but, no, you shouldn't delete the negative ones. Get rid of the profanity, the anonymous heckling, and the juvenile, but if you're going to give your users a megaphone, you need to let them use it. If you don't, no one will bother reading.

The real power of blogs comes from the fact that they can be as specific as you like. It's easy to imagine a blog about the quest to create the ideal shade of white at your paint company, or to enable a discussion about a particularly contentious AJAX coding convention. Most of these blogs will be ignored, but some (perhaps more than some) will gain a following and help spread the word about your work.

Obviously, in addition to allowing comments on your blog, the big win comes when fan club members build their own blogs (or when you convert bloggers into fan club members!). The tools are now available to do just that.

Flickr Flickr is a photo-sharing site. It is incredibly easy to post digital photos and tag them. Photos of what? How about your hotel rooms or the closing banquet at your convention? What if you sent digital cameras to landlords who are using your boilers or cleaning products? I have no idea what masses of people will want to take pictures of (or look at), but it's pretty clear that people enjoy expressing themselves.

This phenomenon is moving beyond photos. Google is now hosting videos. The Beastie Boys recently gave fifty video cameras to fans and had them all videotape the same concert. Then all that footage was edited into one film.

In each case, the idea is the same. By making it easy for people to use pictures, you allow a massively parallel publishing operation to take place, spreading the word in ways you could never execute on your own.

Your first instinct will be to upload the photos yourself, to somehow control the dissemination of information. But that just won't work—not on Flickr or on any of these other services, either. The community is too large and too powerful. You can't outperform them; you must join them.

The Sripraphai Story One of the most profitable small businesses in Queens, New York, is a little Thai restaurant named after its owner. Sripraphai sells amazing Thai food. With no advertising, they've managed to keep the place packed, night after night.

The buzz about the restaurant got so loud that the all-powerful *New York Times* could no longer ignore the place—even though it's not in Manhattan. A two-star review (almost unheard of for a restaurant like this) led to long lines—even after the restaurant doubled in size.

So what's the secret? How did she do it?

She didn't. Chowhound did.

Yes, Mrs. Sripraphai created a remarkable restaurant. But the visitors to chowhound.com made the difference. For several years, dozens of us posted about the restaurant. Every single dish was analyzed. Arguments were made for and against the jungle curry. There was no funnel—but many of the diners had a megaphone.

Chowhound.com is exactly the platform a remarkable business needs. Even though the design of the site won't win any awards, the 350,000 people who come every month (looking to read and to be read) are precisely the people who make or break a new restaurant.

Why does it work? Because the people who post are trusted. They have a reputation. They are not anonymous. And most of all, they have real voices, voices filled with authenticity and experience, giving people a reason to trust them. If you like three of my recommendations, you'll likely agree with my fourth.

Unfortunately, chowhound works only for restaurants. Which doesn't do you a lot of good if you sell consulting services or wholesale bananas or books. That's why I was compelled to create a team to build Squidoo. It's a platform that enables people to point to the products, services, and ideas that matter to them. Squidoo is unashamedly commerce based because our world is commerce based.

Squidoo is not social networking. It's social databasing. Here's what we're trying to do.

Squidoo Squidoo is an all-purpose platform for user-generated content. It's designed to make it easy for each member of your fan club to build a page that highlights the best of what you have to offer.

A Squidoo page contains links—links to products for sale, to reviews, to pictures, to videos, to RSS feeds, and to blogs. A Squidoo page, which is called a *lens*, is one person's take on one topic.

A lens on London, for example, could include links to five restaurants, with a quick paragraph on each one. The lens could include a description of a favorite hotel, with a link to the hotel's page about a specific suite. The lens might feature three or four guidebooks for sale on Amazon, some tourist memorabilia on auction at eBay, and pointers to Flickr postings of great sites to visit.

The only thing the pages have in common is that they are built *by* real people *for* real people. Squidoo pages form a social database—a human index of the best stuff on a given topic.

The magic of Squidoo comes from the proximity effect. Every lens is next to every other lens, so the serendipity of exploration kicks in. Squidoo attracts traffic from across the Web—people find a lens they are interested in, and it leads them to another lens, or to a product or a service they didn't know about. The person coming to a lens is exploring—looking for new ideas and solutions—which is exactly where *you* want to be.

The biggest difference between Squidoo and the other social services is that Squidoo adds value by juxtaposing ideas so they coalesce into useful meaning. A Flickr picture becomes popular because it's clever or funny. A blog posting gains an audience when other bloggers decide it's useful enough to refer to on their blogs. But a Squidoo lens works when it presents important information as part of a whole—when it's a piece of the big picture of meaning.

Imagine, for instance, if L. L. Bean made it easy for three thousand of its customers to build Squidoo lenses about dressing their kids for winter. A lens that included links to just the good stuff—the right clothes, fashions, sleds, and outdoor gear—would save a mom a huge amount of time and trouble in online selection. The value comes from the selection and the presentation.

A more sophisticated example: a lens presenting links to six technical articles on data security and cryptology, written by senior IBM researchers. Those articles have been on IBM's Web site all along, but only by presenting them together, along with a narrative that makes it all clear, can the lensmaster offer a page that's worth looking at.

Here are four ways I can see using Squidoo to give your fans a megaphone:

1. A blogger (take David Meerman Scott, for example) encourages his readers to view his lens highlighting his favorite posts and his books, thus surfacing the good stuff for new readers. That lens drives traffic to his site, which increases downloads of his e-book, which leads to more lens traffic, and on and on.

2. An online seller of tropical fish makes it easy for customers to build lenses in which they each profile the contents of their aquariums, including links to various species and to photos from Flickr. If only 1 percent of his customer base (rabid fish fans!) take him up on this, he's increased his Web exposure by a factor of one thousand. For free.

3. A site with an online content strategy uses lenses to expose that content. So, for example, Martha Stewart could build a lens about cookies (www.squidoo.com/cookies), making it far easier for someone who is not already a Martha fan to discover content she didn't even know she was looking for.

4. A corporation "adopts" a nonprofit and challenges customers and employees to build lenses on a wide variety of topics—with all the proceeds* benefiting the charity.

5. (And a bonus): A company asks every employee to build a lens about the business or about a favorite product the company offers. The lens would include new ways to look at the item, or dream about it, or use it. The lens could point to blogs or newsclips or photos.

For more Squidoo, visit:
www.squidoo.com/partnerships

---

*Proceeds? Yes, there are proceeds. Every lens earns a royalty for a charity or its creator. The royalties come from a share of the ads that run on the site as well as from directly earned affiliate revenue. An example? If a movie lover builds a site that refers to Netflix, and Netflix records a new member as a result, the person who built the site—the lensmaster—earns as much as $10. Build enough lenses and drive enough traffic, and it can add up.

ON COMMITMENT AND INVESTMENT

The thing about these flipped-funnel techniques is that they don't cost you any money (in fact, they could generate revenue). As a result, many businesses skeptical of things that are new and inexpensive don't take swift action. They may assign a junior person or dabble with something in their spare time and see what happens. We've seen this movie before—it's hard to take action when you have the biggest opportunity, but seemingly a lot easier when it involves investing millions to catch up.

What a shame.

Watch a company that's intending to advertise during the Super Bowl. The $3 million for airtime is a fraction of the expense and effort they put into the commercial. The company and its agency will spend months planning a commercial. They'll hire a fancy director and Equity actors and build a set in South Beach with waves crashing in the background. The sales force will be prepped, brochures will be created. The company will probably even build a hospitality tent at the game itself, flying in big buyers from around the country—on a private jet.

All so the company can spend millions on an ad that probably won't work.

Funnel flipping is a bit different. Different in that it clearly works and that it doesn't cost much. But it takes even more commitment. It takes a substantial emotional investment at the top (hence this riff, which you can find as an e-book by typing "Flipping the Funnel" into your favorite search engine), as well as consistent, measured effort by everyone involved.

The first time you invite fans to install the del.icio.us toolbar, they might not do it. The first time you e-mail people a link to build a Squidoo lens, they might ignore you. And the first time you read a comment on your blog that embarrasses you, you'll be tempted to quit.

All good reasons to keep going.

The fact that it isn't trivially easy for big organizations (or small ones) to embrace this approach is exactly why it's working. Being first matters. Being first in a substantial way, with a real online presence, matters even more.

I'm confident that over the next nine months, one organization after another will empower its fan club to speak up, to be noticed, and to spread the word. The question that remains is: Who will go first and create a lasting impression, and who will be timid and fall behind, perhaps permanently?

ISN'T THIS A CLEVER SPIN ON WORD OF MOUTH?

A recent article in the *New York Times* reported on the Word of Mouth Marketing Association (WOMMA) and its recent convention in Orlando. The theme of the article (not surprising since it ran in its advertising column) was that somehow, WOM was a replacement for advertising. The article implied that frustrated advertisers could see an end to their troubles because word of mouth was here to save the day.

I don't think most marketers have a clue about how word of mouth can help them. They think they need to *use* word of mouth, to manipulate it, to pay for it, and put it to work.

I may be in the minority, but I think it's a lot more organic than that. I think consumers of all kinds are too smart. They're not going to get fooled into shilling for a company that manipulates them into it. When the megaphone becomes a shortsighted corporate initiative, it's gotta fail.

The alternative lies in being authentic. In creating products that are genuinely worth talking about. In going out of your way to invest in experiences that people choose to share. Then, yes, by all means, make the tools available. Amplify the happiest fans. But without the kernel of truth you've got nothing but a short-lived packaged-goods campaign.

WHAT NOW?

It starts with this big idea: *Can you buy into the fact that you can empower your fans to speak up?*

Once you are willing to make that commitment, the tactics are simple and straightforward. You can publicize the tools, build the affiliate links, create the RSS feeds, and start down the road to embracing your biggest supporters.

Of course, after you do that, you'll need to make ever more remarkable products and services—so your fans have something to talk about.

FLUFFERNUTTER

I was dishing out some Marshmallow Fluff yesterday (this is a *great* product) and I saw the recipe for a Fluffernutter on the back. What did *that* invention net them? It's almost as good as putting baking soda in your fridge. Suddenly, there's a reason for every household with kids to have Fluff in stock, all the time. The Fluffernutter turns it from a dessert topping into a daily staple.

Do you think you could invent a new use for your product?

FOG CITY CHOCOLATE

I was visiting San Francisco today, and passed (they were closed, alas) Fog City News. They have one hundred kinds of chocolate. They offer coupons for free chocolate to anyone who signs up to receive them by mail (and they'll send you as many as you volunteer to hand out to your friends).

How Purple.

The thing is, it's just a newsstand. A newsstand with one or two small tables devoted to the passionate pursuit of a hobby. And those little tables sell a lot of newspapers.

FREE PRIZE

The Free Prize is the experience of service at the Ritz-Carlton, when what you paid for was a good night's sleep.

The Free Prize is the change-counting machine at Commerce Bank, when what you needed was a checking account.

The Free Prize is the line at Al Yaganeh's soup stand, when what you came for was the soup.

The Free Prize is the milk carton that housed the first ten thousand copies of *Purple Cow*.

The Free Prize is the way you feel when you open the little blue box from Tiffany's.

The Free Prize is in the look on the face of the valet when you drive up in a Hummer.

The Free Prize is the lighting and ceiling of the new Boeing 77e.

The Free Prize is the lighted keyboard on the new Mac Power-Books.

The Free Prize is the way it smells inside a bakery.

The Free Prize is the line to ride Space Mountain at Disney World.

The Free Prize is the container that Method dish soap comes in.

The Free Prize is the exterior design of the Maytag Neptune dishwasher.

The Free Prize is the thunk that the relays make when you turn on the Mark Levinson amplifier (which costs $4,000).

The Free Prize is the way you can pack cigarettes against the side of the package before you smoke them.

FUNCTIONALITY

On Amazon, you can now search the *contents* of the books, not just the titles. This innovation cost the company millions of dollars and years of effort. Why bother? Because *functionality is the new marketing*.

How did Amazon get so big and so profitable and so important? Not by interrupting people who don't want to be interrupted. By interacting with people. Interactions are a million times more powerful than interruptions.

THE FUTURE ISN'T WHAT IT USED TO BE

Sadly, the future ain't what it used to be. We've gotten used to smaller dreams and harsher reality. Here's to unreachable goals!

Remember rocket cars? When I was growing up, the best way to evoke the future was to depict one or two people (no families, no station wagons!) flying about in a bubble-topped rocket car. It was straight out of Tomorrowland, and it was apparently the consensus that this was to be part of our future. But now, sadly, rocket cars are gone—along with commuter flights to the moon, robot servants, automatic food-making machines (programmed to create any dish that you could imagine), and invaders from Mars.

For a long time, our future was described by science-fiction authors. Arthur C. Clarke invented the communications satellite. Isaac Asimov developed the robot. Robert Heinlein was responsible for "waldoes," those automated gloves that scientists use to manipulate dangerous items by remote control. These objects all became real (on some level) during the lifetimes of the people who created them as pure fantasy. Ironically, one of the reasons it was so easy to invent the future then was that it felt so unlikely. You didn't have to worry about the implementation details required for a space station because, of course, no one was actually going to build one. For half a century, our vision of the future was driven by magazine covers, novels, movies, and television.

Somewhere along the way, the future changed. Reality caught up with us, and we discovered that there weren't really men on the moon, that robots wouldn't really take over the Earth, and that making a computer talk was a little different than making it think.

At the same time that our bubbles burst, we discovered that some areas were growing far faster than we ever expected. Technology was on a tear, and it took all of our energy to keep up with it. We stopped talking and thinking about the distant future and started talking about tomorrow. And because tomorrow was just around the corner, a lot of the poetry and guts went out of our vision. After all, anything you imagined might actually happen.

The future became boring and predictable. The computer chip revolution (the power of a computer doubles every eighteen months) meant that there was always another tech miracle nearing fruition. Don't like this handheld organizer? Well, in just a few months, there will be a thinner, lighter, more powerful, cheaper version. Now, instead of talking about the big conceptual breakthroughs that could lead to levitation or particle transmission or ray guns, we worry about when Escient will finally upgrade its operating system. (It's been more than a year!)

Our dreams, alas, have been handed over to the M.B.A.s. And frankly, the M.B.A.s are pretty bad at dreaming. During the Internet boom, newly minted M.B.A.s from the top schools lined up to take jobs at the latest dot-coms. With their very limited three-year ability to look ahead, the M.B.A.s were sure that this was the next big thing and were eager to give it a try.

The M.B.A.s made the Internet trivial. They dreamed small dreams—and most of those weren't even realized. When IPOs were hot, the time horizon was short; now IPOs are not, and the time horizon is (if possible) even shorter. Last April, when the NASDAQ went south, the new M.B.A.s went with it. A January 2001 *New York Times* article talked about how unstylish dot-coms have become with top M.B.A.s. No surprise there! After all, the chances of cashing out anytime soon have dramatically decreased.

If you are an investor, now is the time to discover where those M.B.A.s are going—and then short the stocks in that industry. The increasingly limited horizon that businesspeople are using is going to cause us all trouble soon.

Without a big, hairy, audacious goal, it's too easy to be distracted by momentary setbacks. If your goal was to go public by the year 2000, you've already failed. However, if your goal is to connect every person on the planet with instant digital communication (a plan worthy of some of my favorite science-fiction authors), then you're well on your way—IPO or not.

Harry Harrison is a big thinker. He is the guy who wrote the book that became the movie *Soylent Green*. In the film, Charlton Heston lives in the distant future and discovers that the leaders of Earth have been dealing with overpopulation in a not-so-palatable way: They turn dead folks into a tofulike substance called Soylent Green and feed it to people. Hey, it didn't taste good, but it worked!

I'm hopeful that no one is working on that project, but here are some big, hairy, audacious goals that we ought to use to restore our view of the future:

1. A device that converts changes in the ambient temperature into electricity

2. The ability to transport matter through teleportation

3. A cell phone chip implanted in the ear so that you can talk to anyone without making a sound—by subvocalizing

4. Farming in the ocean

5. Efficient solar cells that generate "free" electricity

6. A solution to global warming

7. Antigravity devices

8. Vaccines and cures for all chronic degenerative diseases

9. Permanent contact lenses with variable telephoto lenses

10. Effortless, effective birth control

11. Food that eliminates the need for livestock

12. Behavior modification for criminals that would eliminate the need for jails

13. Faster-than-light travel beyond our solar system

14. Time travel (forward and backward) or, at the very least, nonfiction "movies" made by time-traveling cameras

15. Personal submarines and vacation homes located at the bottom of the sea

16. Processes that reverse decades of pollution at EPA Superfund sites

17. A worldwide force field that disables handguns and nuclear weapons

18. Computers that really and truly think

Some of these ideas are nonsense, clearly impossible, and not worth working on. But so were ICQ chat, travel to the moon, and the fax machine.

What is the point of these visions? I've intentionally tried to paint some unreachable goals, just as Isaac Asimov did with his vision of smart, kind, and useful robots. Technological change is accelerating, and frankly, our daydreams just aren't keeping up with it. Do we really need to double the speed of a computer just so we can play Donkey Kong faster?

When a computer is fast enough, why won't it be conscious? Or couldn't a fast-enough computer scan my brain and know what I know and act how I do? And if it could, why couldn't I just send that data structure to a meeting in Hong Kong or to another planet?

The Jetsons was fun to watch, largely because we knew that such a future was far away, imaginatively fanciful, and likely impossible. Yet as I write this, Dennis Tito has just returned from a week in space— our first space tourist. And he did it less than forty years after Hanna and Barbera invented Elroy, Judy, George, and Jane, his wife. So, what are you working on?

GMAIL

Gmail was Google's big chance to change the fabric of the anonymous Web. What if Google decided to make a Gmail account cost $1 a year instead of giving it away for free? And what if you had to use a valid credit card to pay for it?

And further, what if your Google e-mail address had to include your real name?

And what if a violation of Google's antispam rules (I'm assuming they'd have some) would cost $20 per incident?

Suddenly, Google mail would become the gold standard. People would happily let it through the spam filters. You could trust it. People would become suspicious of anyone who used any other online e-mail service ("What, you're afraid of validating your account?").

That's what I would do.

GRANDMOTHERS UNDERSTAND THE NET NOW, EVEN

Yes, it's only been ten years. Ten years since the popularization of the Internet as a tool for the masses.

And despite our memories of the crash of 2000, here are ten reasons why I believe that there's about to be a significant flourishing of Net companies and business successes, not to mention extremely cool things for the rest of us:

1. *Penetration* There are fifty times as many people using the Net as there were ten years ago. Fifty times is a multiple you don't see every day.

2. *Bandwidth* It's easy to forget how horrible modem surfing was. The prevalence of high-bandwidth connectivity means that surfing is a far more natural, frequent, and altogether better experience.

3. *Tools* You can launch almost any online service with almost no custom programming. Changethis.com demonstrated to me how straightforward this has become. This also means that finding the world's greatest programmer is no longer a critical component for *most* services.

4. *Servers* When Google can offer a gigabyte of storage at no cost to users, it's proof that server space is essentially free. You may recall that just ten years ago, a three-gig hard drive cost $3000.

5. *WiFi* The next generation of WiFi will be faster, but, more important, it will also have a vastly improved range. Which means, for example, that all of downtown San Francisco will offer free WiFi. With ubiquity will come cheap machines that dramatically increase the number of surfers, and put those surfers most everywhere.

6. *Multimedia* The Web is still stuck in an ASCII world, but not for long. Add a few million video cameras, fifty million cell phone cameras, every song ever recorded, every TV show and movie ever made, and the contents of most any scholarly book and it gets interesting fast. Sure, the lunkheads at the RIAA and MPAA will make up lies to try to stop it, but the cosmic jukebox meets the real-time surveillance camera is going to happen.

7. *Grandmothers* It is no longer necessary to explain to the average American (of any generation) what this "Internet thing" is. Google has made the world safe for entrepreneurs. Don't underestimate how important this is.

8. *Teenagers* The Yahoo! generation is now getting driver's licenses! These are kids who have grown up without encyclopedias or videocassettes or LPs. These are kids who have completely and permanently integrated the Net into their lives and are about to go to work and to college.

9. *Venture capital* Fred Wilson has more than a $100 million to invest in great Net companies. So do a dozen or more other (less talented) venture capitalists. Given that it takes far less money today (see #10 and #3) than ever, this means the search for money is not the challenge.

10. *The death of TV* (It wouldn't be a Seth Godin riff if I didn't mention the death of TV, would it?) You know what killed the first crop of stupid $100 million Internet consumer service start-ups? Advertising. They all believed that they needed to spend millions to build a brand. Today, we've got proof—every single (no exceptions!) Internet success is a success because they spread an ideavirus. It's not TV ads. It's word of mouse.

Hyperbole alert: Forgive me, please, if I've used too many absolutes. No, servers and bandwidth aren't *free*. No, TV isn't totally *dead*. It's all part of projecting a few steps ahead. But you already knew that.

GRASS (NO, NOT THAT KIND)

Do you have a lawn?

You know, the wasteful green expanse in front of your house? That kind of lawn.

It turns out that lawns were virtually unknown in the United States until after 1850, and were invented in the United Kingdom not too long before this.

The reason for a lawn? To demonstrate wastefulness. A lawn tells your neighbors that you can afford to waste land, waste water, and have a team of servants to keep it all pretty (visit http://www.american-lawns.com/history/history_lawn.html for all the gory details).

The marketing of lawns is true marketing. Not interruptive clever ads, but an idea that spreads and sticks. Just like Starbucks. Or e-mail. The challenge facing industries and organizations is to create ideas that have the marketing built in.

You don't have a front lawn so your kids can practice soccer. You have one so your spouse won't yell at you for embarrassing the family in front of the neighbors.

Happy mowing.

GUILLOTINE OR RACK?

My first job was cleaning the grease off the hot-dog roaster at the Carousel Snack Bar near my home in Buffalo, New York. Actually, it wasn't a roaster. It was more a series of nails that rotated under a lightbulb. I also had to make the coffee and scrub the place clean every night. It very quickly became obvious to me that I didn't have much of a future in food service.

I didn't have to make many decisions in my job. And the manager of the store didn't exactly look to me to initiate change. In fact, she didn't want anyone to initiate change. (My suggestion that we branch out into frozen yogurt fell on deaf ears, as did my plea that it would be a lot cheaper to boil hot dogs on demand than to keep them on the rack under the lightbulb all day.)

Any change, any innovation, any risk at all would lead to some sort of terrible outcome for her, she believed.

After I set a record by breaking three coffee carafes in one shift, my food service career was over. I was out on the street, unemployed at the tender age of sixteen. But from that first job I learned a lot— and those lessons keep getting reinforced.

Just about every day, I go to a meeting where I meet my boss from the snack bar. Okay, it's not really her. But it's someone just like her: a midlevel corporate worker who's desperately trying to reconcile the status quo with a passionate desire to survive. My boss didn't want to jeopardize her job. She viewed every day and every interaction not as an opportunity but as a threat—a threat not to the company but to her own well-being. If she had a mantra, it was Don't Blow It.

In her business, she faced two choices: to die by the guillotine, a horrible but quick death, or to perish slowly on the rack—which is just as painful a way to go, if not more so, and guaranteed to leave you every bit as dead. But in her nightmares, only one of those two options loomed large—the guillotine.

I have to admit it. I have had the same dream.

Have you ever spent a night worrying about what your boss (or your stockbroker or a big customer) is going to say to you at that meeting the next morning? Have you ever worried about some impending moment of doom? That's fear of the guillotine.

But almost no one worries about the rack. We don't quake in our boots about a layoff that's going to happen two years from now if we don't migrate our systems before our competition does. We're not afraid of stagnating and dying slowly. No, we're more afraid of sudden death, even though the guillotine is probably a far better way to die.

Recently, at the invitation of the president of a company, I visited its operation in Chicago. This company is a household name, a financial-services giant. And its people know that the Internet represents a huge threat to their future.

When I get there, people are so earnest. They've all done their homework. They all take notes and ask questions. At first, it seems as if they're doing everything right to prepare for the future. They've got an Internet task force, and it reports directly to the president. It's a high-profile gig: Lots of senior people are on this team, and virtually every department in the company has a representative on it.

The team is busy hiring consultants, building prototypes, creating business models, and generally working hard to get the company in shape for the next century.

I give my talk, and team members invite me to sit in on a presentation by the company's top marketing person. We sit down in a huge conference room, with a fantastic view of the lake, a silver tea set on a sideboard, and custom-printed yellow pads placed in front of everyone.

After the presentation—which sounds all too much like state-of-the-art Internet strategy circa 1996—they ask me what I think.

I look around, and that's when I realize that every single person in the room is waiting for me to say the same thing. They want to hear, "Hey, you guys are totally prepared for the Net. Don't worry about it." They want to hear, "Hey, this Web thing isn't a threat to your business model. You don't need to change a thing." They want to be told that everything will be fine.

And the really sad and amazing thing is that they don't care if I'm wrong. The idea that their company could end up like Waldenbooks or CBS or Sears or any other big, dumb company is just fine—as long as they don't have to change *now*.

What was going on here? I had just met a group of smart, aggressive, well-compensated people who control billions of dollars in assets and one of the best brand names in the world. Yet they knew they were going to fail, and they couldn't do a thing about it. They had all bought into a system in which it's just fine to fail on the big stuff—as long as little failures don't happen now.

Let's be honest.

Nobody likes change.

HEINLEIN

"There has grown in the minds of certain groups in this country the idea that just because a man or corporation has made a profit out of the public for a number of years, the government and the courts are charged with guaranteeing such a profit in the future, even in the face of changing circumstances and contrary to public interest. This strange doctrine is supported by neither statute or common law. Neither corporations or individuals have the right to come into court and ask that the clock of history be stopped, or turned back."

I liked reading Robert Heinlein when I was a kid. Maybe I should start again.

HERSHEY (NO KISSES)

Hershey, Pennsylvania, is the epicenter of cheap chocolate. More than that, though, it demonstrates a really important principle about design, style, and the quest for the remarkable.

Hershey Park is roller-coaster heaven. There are wood coasters, metal coasters, coasters that get you soaking wet, and coasters for kids. If the point of an amusement park is to offer lots and lots of rides, Hershey Park has it down.

But spending even an hour at the park is fatiguing. It's not just boring, it's actually demoralizing. Part of this is due to the huge crowds, but hey, it's a business and they make their money selling tickets, so they're entitled . . .

More than ten years ago, Philip Crosby changed the world of manufacturing with his provocatively titled book *Quality Is Free.* The thesis of the book was that it's actually *cheaper* to make stuff right the first time than it is to fix things later.

In other words, you can make a profit by making your product better. While this seems to be common sense today, it sure wasn't then. We were manufacturing junk, because it was fast and we thought it was cheap. The Japanese taught us that it was even cheaper to make stuff that worked.

Well, here's the corollary: *style is free.*

Let me give you some examples from Hershey Park:

Every ride has a few signs you're expected to read before you get on. The signs are a necessary expense, but that doesn't explain why they are so ugly. For example, every sign about safety is WRITTEN IN ALL CAPITAL LETTERS, WITH TIGHT LINE SPACING AND AN UNATTRACTIVE, HARD-TO-READ FONT. Other signs are in gold, in green, in black. Every sign, just about, is different from every other.

The cost of making each sign attractive is precisely zero. Same amount of ink, same amount of wood. Yet if more people read the signs, injuries would decrease, lines would move faster, and Hershey would make more money.

While we're on the topic of signs, I did a count, and there are (this is true, you can check it out) more than hundred different typefaces used on official park signage. Standing in one spot in "Mining Town," I saw more than forty.

It's like there was a horrible accident at the type foundry down the road. Imagine reading a book or driving on a highway or operating a car that had more than forty typefaces displayed simultaneously.

This decentralized, disrespectful method of communication quickly turns into *no* communication.

The same sloppiness extends to the choice of foods served, the menu designs, the uniforms worn by employees, and on and on.

My favorite (hmm, maybe not favorite) moment came just before we crawled away, defeated. In the midst of all the chaos, a six-piece brass band (including a small tuba) marched by, playing the theme from *Hawaii Five-O*.

Why one brass band? Why here? Why *Hawaii Five-O*? I have no idea.

In *Purple Cow*, I talked about my take on being remarkable. Remarkable is necessary to marketing today, because unremarkable products don't get talked about, they just fade away. The opposite of remarkable is "very good," at best.

Trying hard doesn't make you remarkable. Doing a good job doesn't make you remarkable. What makes you remarkable is being amazing, outstanding, surprising, elegant, and noteworthy.

Hershey is actively spending money (on million-dollar rides and brass bands) trying to be remarkable, and they are barely ending up as very good.

There is no style at Hershey. It's not that it's *bad*—there are plenty of examples of bad design that have ended up being so distinctive that they became good (McDonald's, for example). No, it's that they are lazy, or bureaucratic, or stuck. Hershey doesn't feel like Disney. You won't remember it after you leave. You won't talk about it. You couldn't describe most of the experience even if you tried. There's no parallel to give you a mental map of what you just saw. No hierarchy of what's important and what's not. Nothing to look at when you're not rocketing at a hundred miles an hour.

The funny thing is that this thinking is consistent. The Hershey hotel is just as *ungupatch* (What a great yiddish word! It means a thrown-together mess, and the last syllable rhymes with "botch.") as the park. And the candy the company makes is boring, nonremarkable, and distinctly unstylish. Compare this to the fictional Willie Wonka or the very real Scharffen Berger company.

Does Hershey make money? Sure they do. They're still profiting from their great timing in being the first company to produce a mass-market chocolate bar at precisely the right moment, and profiting further from running TV ads back when TV ads actually worked. But both those moments are long gone, and it's a downhill ride from here.

So what's the lesson? If you run a Web site, does it look like Hershey Park? If you run a retail establishment or any sort of consumer experience, is it as deadening and boring as Hershey Park?

Why am I picking on Hershey? Because they are well known and it's obvious and I probably won't hurt their feelings. But the very same lack of design and style is probably happening at your shop as well.

Design isn't expensive. It's actually free. The Apple Store is the un-Hershey. Here's a company with so much style that it occasionally gets in the way. But not at the store. At the store, you can use any three square feet as the DNA to make an entirely new store—and it would be totally consistent with the original. Just a glance around the store tells you where you are and what it means.

So what? A huge percentage of visitors to an Apple store don't own a Mac before they walk in . . . and do when they leave. The store isn't just a place to exchange cash for computers, it's a place to create a genuine, emotional branding experience, one that lasts. It's so cool, people come back with their friends.

Are the design, the lighting, the carpeting choice, the layout—all that stuff—expensive? Nope, they're free. Apple had to carpet and build out the store anyway, and the cost is in the thinking and the guts, not necessarily in the fixtures themselves.

Hershey built a much hyped store in Times Square. It's one of the most efficient (in sales per square foot) stores in the world. You can find the same candy at the drugstore down the street, but Hershey's prices are three or four times as high. They realized that they can sell the process, the souvenirs—the experience—by embracing design.

Disney World may not be your favorite place (nor is it mine) but one incredible statistic tells the tale. Every year, more than 20,000 brides choose to have their wedding there.

Think many people got married last weekend at Hershey Park?

HOTELS AND THE CHEAP FORTUNE COOKIE

Dragging my butt, disheartened by the new "we don't care, we don't have to" economy, I showed up at the W hotel in San Francisco. Other W hotels hadn't blown me away, but this place was across the street from my speaking gig and the booking agent put me here, so no big deal.

I walked in with diminished expectations.

Two extremely attractive people behind the counter looked up. The guy said, with a genuine smile, "Welcome." And it all started to change.

These people were actually trying. Because they wanted to, not because they had to.

I got to my floor. The turn-down-the-bed person handed me a crisp fortune cookie as I walked past her on the way to my room. My room had an Etch A Sketch on the desk, a cool CD softly playing on the stereo, and very neat toiletries in the bathroom. Extra cost, maybe $3.

I called for a wake-up call. A truly nice person answered the phone, not a computer. They also asked if I wanted breakfast soon after I woke up (at 4 am!). I did. Net profit for having a person answer? $15.

There is no perfect experience. But this was great storytelling, storytelling with authenticity from caring people. It restored my faith (at least a little) in what organizations can do.

I CHANGED MY MIND YESTERDAY

Actually, I changed it a lot.

As alert readers know, I've been holed up all summer, working on a new project that will debut this fall. We've got an exceptional team of people, and the invention process has been refreshing, fascinating, and completely energizing.

Which corner of the cube is closest to you? Can you make it flip?

Yesterday was the second day of a marathon eleven-person meeting. We started at point A and worked our way all the way to point Z, considering the features, strategies, and stories of everything we're building. And I watched myself change my mind not once but quite a few times.

I don't know how it is for you, but for me, when I change my mind something chemical happens. I go from one mental state to another and I can feel something flip. What's interesting (and particularly relevant to you and to your customers) is that a person can easily insulate himself from this flip. If you don't *want* to change your mind, odds are you won't.

Too often, we spend a lot of time trying to persuade people to see a different point of view, but the person is not persuaded. If the person you're talking with (or marketing to) sets out to *not* change her mind, it's very unlikely that any other outcome will occur.

I recently needed to fly to Buffalo. The flight was full and I was on standby—second on the list. It was a cheap flight and I really needed to get to my meeting in Buffalo. I decided that it was worth $200 extra to me to get on board this flight. All I needed to do was persuade two people to give up their seats and I'd be fine.

New airport rules don't make this easy—once you've got a seat assigned, they won't let you take the next flight—but it turns out that if someone ahead of you on the standby list gets a seat on the plane but decides against it, that's permitted. So I camped out and waited for the standbys to get called.

The first person, about twenty years old, obviously a student, gets called. All I had to do was persuade her to give up her seat. The next flight out (for which she has a ticket) is in ninety minutes. "Hi," I say, calmly taking $100 in cash out of my pocket. "I'll pay you a hundred dollars to take the next flight—the one you're already on—so I can take this one and make my meeting."

Now, my guess is that this woman has rarely made $65 an hour to sit in an airport and watch TV or read a novel. But that's precisely what she turned down without a moment's thought. She smiled, said no thanks, and got on the plane.

The next two guys to clear standby had precisely the same reaction. I didn't get on the plane.

My guess is that I could have offered $1,000 and it wouldn't have mattered.

Why? Why is $1,000 so worthless at the airport and so valuable when a beggar asks for a quarter or when you cross the street to save a dime on a hamburger?

Here's why: Because for two hours, the people on the standby list had been imagining that they'd make that earlier flight. They had fallen into the human trap of believing that mental effort can magically impact external events. It worked! All that hoping got them on the flight.

So, when the thing they'd been dreaming of actually happened, they were sold on taking it and watching their wish come true. They'd worked hard to get on this flight! They had earned it. There was no way a short conversation with me would change someone's mind. Not because my offer wasn't good, my presentation was deficient, or I wasn't credible. No, because they'd already decided and they weren't open to changing their mind.

This phenomenon is absolutely critical inside your organization. There's no point whatsoever in having a meeting designed to elicit change if the attendees are insulated against changing their minds. Assuming that your co-workers are open to change is a mistake. It's essential that you go through exercises designed to loosen up the flip muscle.

When was the last time you changed your mind in a conference room? Ironically, the setting and tone of a conference room create precisely the atmosphere where people are uncomfortable flipping positions. Business meetings (and sales calls) are custom-made for failure. People walk in and are reminded that this is the place to stand your ground, this is the place where good arguments carry the day and build careers, and weak-kneed flip-floppers hurt their careers. A conference room is an arena, and people come armed and ready to support their ideas (and the status quo).

My recommendation? As a group, start by changing your (everyone's) minds about something astonishingly simple, obvious, and unimportant. Establishing a pattern in which people flip (no flopping, just flipping) is the first step toward creating an atmosphere where things actually get done.

And what about outside your organization? How on Earth are you going to sell something to someone when you don't get to meet them, don't get to pick the conference room, don't have the leverage to insist on change?

Well, you can argue against human nature or you can follow a two-part strategy:

1. Sell to people who are already in the mood to flip. Pick an audience that for all sorts of external reasons is open to changing their minds, such as people who just moved to a new town, just started college, just got a new job, or just bought a new car. The value of these groups is well understood, but still underestimated. People who are reading a magazine about new ideas are a lot more receptive to new ideas than those rushing to catch the commuter train to work.

2. Start a cascade of small flips. Apple argued for years that people should abandon the Windows platform and switch to the Mac. It's better. It's faster. It's cooler. It's proven. No dice. Mostly because Windows users refused to even consider switching. *But,* when it came to music, getting someone to flip to an iPod from a Walkman was a lot easier. And then, gradually, as people open up to flipping the other electronics in their life, Apple has a voice in that conversation.

I'm hoping I can get you to change your mind about changing minds. If you're one of those folks who's predisposed to change, ask yourself the following questions before you try to persuade anyone of anything:

Is this person in a situation (emotional, professional, even organizational) where they are predisposed to flip?

And, *how can I get them to make a tiny flip? And then another one?*

Being right isn't the point. Being persuasive doesn't seem to matter much either. Being right, being persuasive, and being with the right person when that person is predisposed to change their mind—that's when things happen.

JETBLUE

Have you noticed how the audio experience changes the way you feel at the airport?

In a crowded terminal, when the folks making gate announcements start yelling or talking fast or acting panicked about a full flight, it makes everybody uptight.

What if the airlines realized that the product that they sell isn't the plane, it's the idea of a safe and comfortable (maybe even fun) trip. What if every announcement was prerecorded by Clint Eastwood or J. Lo? Or if all the in-flight announcements were as funny as the one I heard today. ("JetBlue, your snacks are being handed out by Tom, who's single and looking for love. Hey, if you marry him, you can fly free!") Even simpler, what if every announcement was calm, slow, and easy to understand? That's free, but it's worth noticing.

Dutch Boy reinvented the paint can. JetBlue could reinvent what you hear when you travel.

JOBS FOR PURPLE COWS

A friend of mine is a world-class lawyer, with a great background in copyright, deal-making, and intellectual-property issues. She has a stellar résumé and could get a cog job in about two seconds. Except that she doesn't want to do that. She wants to work for a fast-growing, interesting organization with flexible hours. And she's willing to take a 60 percent pay cut to do so.

In the current system, there's no place for her (or for you, for that matter) to let the right person know that they ought to rethink the way they're allocating their payroll and their services budget and take advantage of this opportunity. *This is ridiculous.*

There's no other similar expense in a corporation that is totally demand based. Companies don't post a note online saying, "We're thinking of replacing our phone system, please let us know if there's some new technology that we don't know about" or, "Our charity currently uses a traditional system to do fund-raising but we're auditioning automated online systems. Please send a properly formatted brochure. . . ."

In fact, companies most often change strategies when new devices and great salespeople make a successful pitch for them to change.

Well, if the single most important thing a business can do is hire amazing people, why shouldn't the hiring process be more flexible and built around the people, not the slots?

Why does a job show up in the classifieds, already defined, just waiting for the perfect peg for that existing hole?

At this point, I'm supposed to point you to some amazing Web site that is people-centric, not job-centric, and talk about how smart bosses from around the globe are using it to scout for great people. How an eBay-like revolution is changing this huge marketplace. I can't, so I won't.

Sure, there are résumé-driven sites, but this doesn't matter. The bosses aren't there. The culture hasn't shifted yet.

But it will.

Why not tear this riff out, attach it to a letter (not a resume!), and send it off to the place that needs you? If two or three or ten people did this, it might not matter, but if thousands of people started auctioning off their skills in the way it ought to be done (recognizing that you, not the factory, are where the value is) it could become a movement.

A JOB STRATEGY THAT MAKES YOU A LOSER

I've been thinking about the paradox of finding a job, and it seems completely broken to me.

Consider a few facts:

1. The traditional way to get a job is to send a boring résumé in response to as many posted jobs as you can. Your résumé will be scanned, sorted, and, if it doesn't stand out too much, a person might look at it.

   Then you go for a job interview and try to be as coglike as possible in your malleability and desire to fit in. If random acts are working in your favor, you get the job.

2. Then, the big Fortune 1000 company that hired you complains that all their people act like cogs, don't care enough, aren't creative in solving problems, and don't push the status quo.

3. Then, the big Fortune 1000 company realizes that as long as they've got interchangeable cogs, they ought to just move jobs offshore, because that's cheaper; or, the company doesn't do that, succumbs to Wall Street pressure, and either cheats on their numbers (and gets caught and tanks) or doesn't cheat (and gets bought or folded and tanks).

Something's wrong here.

Let's start with one assumption that has changed in just a generation. You might think that big companies are the backbone of our economy. In fact:

It turns out that 100 percent of all job growth is now coming from small companies (under five hundred employees). In fact, the big companies are shedding jobs, not adding them.

That wasn't true for our parents. It's true for us.

Also true: More likely than not, the best jobs, the most interesting jobs, and the most secure jobs are found in small organizations.

Conclusion: Fitting in to get a job for the big guy is a bad strategy for everyone.

JOURNALISTS

More than twenty-five million bloggers are now tracked by some of the online services.

That's 8 percent or so of the active online population, and since it seems as though the number is doubling every month or so, this is becoming significant.

Remember how you used to curse journalists? Curse them for being lazy, or hyperbolic? How about this headline from today's *Independent* (U.K. newspaper):

FIRST NIGHT: CLINTON TAKES TO THE STAGE
FOR THE ULTIMATE SELL

Ultimate? What makes it ultimate? A $30 book is hardly the ultimate sell, right?

But choosing words, choosing headlines, choosing photographs—it all adds up. When the *New York Times* admits that it colored its reporting the wrong way regarding Iraq, we're talking about a big side effect: thousands of people dead.

Now, everyone with a blog is a journalist. When you run a post accusing a politician of having no personality, for example, you're indulging the public's desire to elect a dinner partner, not a president. When you chime in on the day's talking points, you're a tool, not a new voice.

So, we come to the moment of truth. Now that anyone who

wants to be a journalist *can* be a journalist, are the ethics going to get better . . . or worse?

I'm an optimist most of the time, but on this issue, I'm afraid I'm a realist.

JUSTIN AND ASHLEY

According to recent government data, Justin and Ashley are the two most common names given to children of Hispanic parents in New York.

For Asian parents the story is different: Name number one is Emily.

Names are a funny thing. Now, naming a company Google or Squidoo or Blueturnip in the dot-com world isn't weird. It's the equivalent of naming your kid Michael.

A recent government study found that distinctly ethnic first names got fewer callbacks on otherwise identical résumés. Fair? Of course not. Not surprising, though, either.

Standing out is not the same thing as being remarkable. Standing out can just as easily get you ostracized. I don't think being Purple is the same as just being different.

LATER IS NOT AN OPTION

My friend Kim reminded me of something I told him fifteen years ago: "If you're going to do it, do it now."

The new marketing requires less planning and more interaction, more now and less later.

So pick up the phone or write the copy or design that page in Photoshop. But waiting for later is pointless.

LOCAL MAX, HOW TO AVOID THE

My guess is that you've been wrestling with your Local Max.

If your organization or your career is stuck, it may just be because of this chart.

Everyone starts at that dot at the bottom left corner. You're not succeeding at this point, simply because you haven't started yet.

Then you try something. If it works, you end up at point A.

A is where you see direct results from your strategy and hard work. A is the job you get after investing in an M.B.A. A is the sales you do after running an ad.

Of course, being a success-oriented capitalist, that's not enough. So you do more. You push and hone and optimize until you end up at the Local Max. The Local Max is where your efforts really pay off.

So you try even harder. And you end up at point B. Point B is a bummer. Point B is *backward*. Point B is where more effort doesn't return better results anymore. So you retreat. You go back to your Local Max.

And that is where most people stay. Most people get stuck at the Local Max because changing strategy in any direction (this is really a 3D chart, but I've flattened it to the page) leads to poorer results.

You've got a very good job as an art director. To do better, you'd either have to move to another firm, move to another town, switch careers, or go back to school. All of these options have costs and very uncertain returns, so you stay where you are.

You have a hundred competitors in an industry that is a self-described commodity. You use the same tactics your competition does, because if you change your pricing or fundamentally alter your marketing outreach, you get punished in terms of sales or profits.

You've got a summer camp with eighty kids in it. If you want to grow, you've learned the hard way that hiring one or two more senior staff people won't work, because you can't afford them. So you stick with what you've got.

The lie of Local Max is this: The chart is incomplete. It really looks like this:

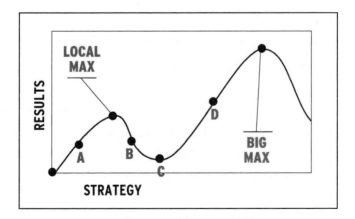

You'll discover that the Local Max isn't actually a suitable place to stop trying, especially when you realize that the Big Max is not particularly far away.

The problem is that to get to the Big Max, you need to get past point C, which is a horrible and scary place to be.

There were ten thousand single-location hamburger restaurants in the world when Ray Kroc decided to build the giant McDonald's franchise. Anyone could have done it. No one did. Because everyone who tried had to go through point C to get there. It took Colonel Sanders more than a decade of pain to get through point C.

Of course, it's not just about growing sales or revenues. The Big Max/Local Max paradox affects everything from education to non-profits to politicians. If you have a "Max," whatever you're measuring, the odds are you're actually dealing with a Local Max, not the big one.

If your market is changing, this idea is even more important to understand, because changing markets are continually surfacing new Big Max points, and the only way to get to them is to go through the pain (yes, it's painful) of point C.

You can't reinvent yourself or your organization until you deal with the fear of point C, and that's hard to do without talking about it. I think the benefit of the Local Max curve is that it makes it easy for you and your team to have the conversation.

LOCAL MAX, HOW THE NEW MARKETING CHANGES THE

The obvious question, after you've had the conversation with your team about points B and C and the pain of getting to the Big Max is this: How do we get to work to find the really big thing?

The good news is that the new marketing makes it easier than ever before.

The cost of inventing, prototyping, manufacturing, and especially advertising a new product, concept, service, or organization is a tiny fraction of what it used to be. In some industries, you can do it for 1 percent of what it used to cost.

Sooner or later, your team needs to embrace this fact.

What this means is simple. You can take the cash and the

momentum you get from being at the Local Max and invest a fraction of it so that a new team, a smaller team, a team without traditional constraints, can go ahead and launch something new. Something that disrupts the market, that even competes with the mother ship.

And if it's your career we're talking about, the same thing is true. You don't have to get a formal M.B.A. or quit your job to start a profitable business or sideline. You can use the amazing tools that exist without having to wager everything.

There are two mistakes that satisfied Local Max folks make:

1. Believing that they can get to the next Max in a linear, pain-free way

2. Believing that the best way to get there is with brute force (more products, more salespeople, more ads, more buildings, more staff . . .)

In fact, the opposite is true.

The more you coddle your new team, the harder it will be for them to find the new Max.

This isn't the scary bet that involves all your money or your full-time job. This is the scary bet that involves intellectual risks and going way outside your safety zone to see what happens when you disrupt the status quo.

MCDONALD'S COCKTAIL PARTY

Stephanie Howard from Leo Alliance, Inc. sends me this clip from *AdAge:*

NEW YORK (AdAge.com)—Declaring that mass marketing no longer works and that "no single ad tells the whole story," Larry Light, McDonald Corp.'s chief marketing officer, said McDonald's has adopted a new marketing technique that he dubbed "brand journalism."

Speaking at the AdWatch: Outlook 2004 conference at the New York Sheraton Hotel and Towers, Mr. Light described the concept as one marking "the end of brand positioning as we know it." He went on to say that effective marketing should use many stories rather than employing one message to reach everyone. In effect, he declared that McDonald's was abandoning the universal message concept.

"Any single ad, commercial or promotion is not a summary of our strategy. It's not representative of the brand message," he said. "We don't need one big execution of a big idea. We need one big idea that can be used in a multidimensional, multilayered and multifaceted way."

He went on to define brand journalism, which he also referred to as a brand narrative or brand chronicle, as a way to record "what happens to a brand in the world," and create ad communications that, over time, can tell a whole story of a brand.

My take? Yay for Larry for realizing that monolithic marketing is broken.

I worry, though, about two things:

1. Changing the marketing without changing the underpinnings of the business is almost always a bad strategy. If all the people, the systems, the real estate, the factories, and the menus are organized around monolithic marketing, slapping a little brand journalism on top isn't going to work very well.

2. The marketer doesn't get to run the conversation. It's not really brand journalism that's happening, you see. It's a *brand cocktail party*! You get to set the table and invite the first batch of guests, but after that the conversation is going to happen with or without you.

I have four irreverent ideas for McDonald's:

1. Start your own brand of lightly sweetened, caffeine-free iced tea. Use 10 percent of the sugar they put in Coke. Generate four times the profit. Create a brand you can own. A way to significantly impact the health of the world. Phase out Coke completely. Take profits to the bottom line. Tell a different story.

2. Offer a free DVD of the award-winning *Super Size Me* documentary with every iced tea sold. (No, I'm not kidding.)

3. Challenge every store to offer something new and local and remarkable on the menu. Diversify times one hundred.

4. Bend over backward to host meetups (visit www.meetup.com for details) in your stores. Keep offering free WiFi. Sponsor soccer teams and the Girl Scouts and the local astronomy club. Put chessboards on the place mats. Use the real-estate advantage to create a place where people congregate.

"MCJOB"

The people who put together the dictionary have really annoyed the folks at McDonald's. Apparently, they've decided that "McJob" is a word. A word that signifies a menial, easy-to-get, follow-the-numbers job. A job you ought to quit when you can.

McDonald's, no surprise, is outraged. But that's a mistake on their part, caused by confusing two things: what customers think, and the truth as they (McDonald's) see it.

If people call a burger-flipping job a McJob, then of course it belongs in the dictionary. If everyone thinks your ball bearings cause brake linings to seize up, then they do, regardless of what the truth of the matter is.

You don't get the privilege of deciding what people will think. If they think it, then their truth is already established.

The challenge of marketing is to get ideas to spread. Twelve years ago, Douglas Coupland used the word "McJob" in his book *Generation X* because he knew everyone would understand what he meant. Twelve years later, McDonald's is angry because it's inaccurate. Of course it is! So what?

If you're not happy with the story consumers are telling themselves, the issue is the story itself—the story you are spreading.

MAIL, THE CHECK IS IN THE

Some lies that people will tell in order to maintain the status quo:

1. Canadian pharmaceuticals are dangerous.

2. Piracy is killing the ongoing creation of music and movies (notice I didn't say anything about the movie and music *businesses*).

3. Dental work lasts forever.

4. A bottle of Evian is dangerous to airline security and must be surrendered.

5. The Microsoft monopoly pays dividends to all users (like the benefits we get from Internet Explorer, for example).

6. You can't start a business without venture capital or a big bank loan.

7. Working hard for your boss and following instructions is the best way to get ahead.

8. We need to spend taxpayer money on support for traditional factory farming.

9. It's impossible to make a fuel-efficient automobile that Americans will accept.

10. Who you know is more important than what you do.

It fascinates me that we're so gullible, that people will embrace patently false ideas if it helps them deal with their fear of change.

"MAYBE," GETTING PEOPLE NOT TO SAY

Susan Storms belongs in the Salesperson Hall of Fame. I was lucky enough to have Susan on my team at Yoyodyne Entertainment. In 1998, I sent her to Seattle to make a sales call on a very well-known company. As often happens when you're selling a new idea, there was a lot of resistance to what Storms had to offer. And as usually happens when the company that you're calling on is run by a visionary, there was a lot of confusion among the people with whom Storms was meeting. They were all worked up, trying to guess, or second-guess, what the boss would do. No one wanted to make a commitment one way or another. All they had to offer was "maybe."

Ordinarily, a meeting like this doesn't lead to much at all. It's a wasted day. It's a sleepless night in yet another hotel room. It's $900 spent on a round-trip airplane ticket for no good reason. You just figure that it comes with the territory, and chalk it up to the usual cost of doing business.

But, as I said, Susan Storms is a great salesperson. She was so sold on our product, so sure that this potential client needed the solution that we were offering, that she refused to take "Well, maybe, but not now" for an answer.

So she reached into her briefcase and took out a sheet of paper. Then she turned to the group and said, "Folks, I'm excited about this opportunity. And I'm so sure that it's right for your company that I flew across the country to present it to you." She paused and slowly sipped her Odwalla juice. "You've heard my presentation. You know how this product could change the way you do business. If you were to decide that this isn't right for you, I would totally understand. If you were to decide that you want to go ahead with this right now, then that would be fantastic."

Then she stopped, looked the senior manager in the eye, and asked, "What would you like to do? Go forward or say no?"

And the manager repeated his weasel words: "Well, we really have to look at this more closely and run it by some people, and then we'll get back to you."

Storms knew that they'd do no such thing. She knew that they were severely limited in their zoomwidth—that this was a company that couldn't find a way to try new things, even if these were really just old things slightly adjusted to take advantage of new opportunities. She knew that the manager's response was a time-honored technique in severely zoom-challenged companies, and that he was looking for a way to make her go away without really making any decisions. So she turned the paper over.

"Here's the thing," she said. "This is obviously a time-sensitive program, and if you don't commit today, then we're going to have to offer it to one of your competitors. But that could cause all kinds of trouble for all of us. I mean, what if your boss calls my boss later and wants to know why we aren't working with your company? So all I need you to do is initial this sheet of paper that says that you heard the presentation and that you decided *not* to take advantage of our offer." And she handed the paper to the guy from Seattle.

Now, all the paper said was that his company had listened to the idea, had decided that they weren't interested, and that it was fine to take the idea to a competitor. Simple enough. Guess what? He refused to sign it!

Saying yes was a risk. Saying no was a risk. Signing the release was a risk. In his mind, every single option meant some sort of change. Rather than seeing this as an opportunity to zoom—to do the same thing as usual, only different—he saw it as a threat to his position at the company. So he did the one thing that he could do without having to take a risk: He threw Storms out of the meeting.

No, Storms didn't get the sale. And she didn't get the guy's signature either. But that's okay. Because she got the story—and she taught us all a lesson about how to make change happen (or not happen) in organizations.

The acknowledgment that no decision today actually means no was a brilliant device on Storms's part. Perhaps a braver manager would have viewed this as an opportunity rather than as a threat. Dealing with change ultimately does make you confront one thing: dishonesty. And dishonesty—intellectual dishonesty, decision-making dishonesty, not-willing-to-face-the-music dishonesty—is the greatest enemy that a company can have. We disguise it as waiting to get more information or looking for more input. In fact, the real deal is that we're not willing to look the situation in the eye and make a decision, right or wrong. And so companies and individuals put off acknowledging what they already know and acting on it. They don't commit to a decision until they have to—even if they've already made the decision in their minds, and a delay in making it official means spending more money, making mistakes, and staying up all night to catch up.

I wonder what Storms would have done if Neil Goldschmidt, former U.S. secretary of transportation, had been sitting in that seat instead of that chicken middle manager. I've heard that while attending the University of Oregon, Goldschmidt was considering joining a fraternity. The big climax to a fraternity's rush period is the "hot box," at which members of the frat get a potential pledge into a room, surround him, and put pressure on him to join.

Goldschmidt was in a hot box. One frat brother dramatically lit a match, held it in front of Goldschmidt's face, and told him, "You've got until this match burns down to decide: Are you pledging or not?"

Goldschmidt blew out the match and left the room.

It actually took more guts for Goldschmidt to say no than to say yes. But saying either one demonstrated a level of bravery and an ability to zoom—a kind of character and self-awareness that's sadly lacking at most companies.

The great managers are the ones who make changes when there isn't yet an emergency. We remember that Barry Diller invented the made-for-TV movie. Or that Bob Pittman persuaded his bosses to back that crazy MTV idea. Charles Schwab got online early, while Merrill Lynch waited until there was a stampede.

The risk-averse "Hall of Shame" is so large that it needs its own campus to house all of the enshrinees. Several publishers turned down *The Bridges of Madison County* because no editor would go out on a limb and back it. IBM couldn't find a quorum that would back the idea that later became the Xerox machine. In the old days, risk-averse managers knew that they'd never get in trouble for ducking a tough decision. In fact, it might even have been the fastest ticket to a promotion: It's one sure way to keep all of the dirt off your feet. But these days, if you can't make a decision, you're out of the action. Any decision is likely to serve you and your company better than no decision at all. And knowing why you think what you think is the fastest way to get even more involved with the quick-moving chain of events that epitomizes life in the new economy.

MAYBE-PROOFING YOUR ORGANIZATION

Is it possible to manufacture little emergencies so that everyone in an organization has to say yes or no? Is it possible to create match-lighting-decision situations, when simply sitting there inertly isn't an option? Is it possible to create a "maybe-proof" company?

Some of the best project management that I've ever seen has happened in companies that use the "red/yellow/green" system. It's based on a very simple, very visible premise: Every single person in the division of a company that's launching a major new initiative has to wear a button to work every day. Wearing a green button announces that you're on the critical path. It tells everyone that the stuff that you're doing is essential to the product's launch—that you're a priority. If you don a yellow button, you're telling your co-workers that you're on the periphery of the project, but that you have an important job nonetheless. And wearing a red button sends the signal that you have an important job that's not related to the project.

When someone with a green button shows up, all bets are off. Green buttons are like the flashing lights on an ambulance, or the requests of a surgeon in an operating room: "This is a life-or-death path," green buttons say, "and you'd better have a damn good reason if you're going to slow me down." When a person wearing a yellow or red button meets up with someone wearing a green button, that person understands that it's time to make a decision: "How can I help this green button get on with the critical job?" Or, at the very minimum, "How do I get out of the way?"

Of course, people can change their button color every day, or even several times during the course of a meeting. But once you adopt the button approach to project management, several things immediately become clear: First, any company that hesitates to make people wear buttons because it's worried about hurting employees' feelings isn't really serious about the project—or about creating a culture in which decisions get made. In fact, if you duck the buttons, you'll just keep ducking other decisions. Second, folks don't like wearing red buttons: They'll work very hard to find a way to contribute so that they can wear a green button. And there are plenty of people who are totally delighted to wear a yellow button. Third, the CEOs, project leaders, and team leaders can quickly learn a lot about who's accomplishing what inside of a company.

Are you itching to work at a red/yellow/green company? Would it turn you on to wear a green button to work? Would it make you take an important—if painful—look at your own decision-making style if you were issued a button each day that signaled your decision-making readiness?

There's a lot of focus in fast-moving start-up companies. At the beginning, just about everyone wears a green button. And when someone like Susan Storms visits one of those companies, it's no trouble at all to get someone to sign a sheet of paper saying yes or no. In the heat of a start-up, people know what they know. Right, wrong, or sideways, you will find no maybes there!

But pretty soon, the culture of the company starts to change. Slowly at first, and then faster and faster, the environment shifts. People get hired for good reason: to add value to the status quo. Then the company stops zooming and starts taking root. People freak out when you ask them to wear a red button. A red button is a threat! They can't handle the idea of a simple sheet of paper that puts them on record—on any record! Facing a lit match that makes them declare their intentions is an agonizing experience.

So here's the real question: Are you ready to maybe-proof your company? A simple yes or no will do.

MEASUREMENT INCREASES SPEED

No one is perfect. And no company can avoid every mistake. But why do companies make mistakes and then do nothing to remedy them?

Let me propose five reasons:

1. The people who make the policies don't actually work in the field.

2. The people in the field aren't given the ability to influence management without appearing to be troublemakers.

3. Customers aren't encouraged to speak up, and their suggestions are ignored.

4. It's easier to make a policy than to undo it.

5. Business is complicated and unless you come up with a clever way to measure the impact of a decision, it's often difficult to tell if it's a good idea or not.

I thought of all of these reasons as I flew from one airport to another over the last few weeks. My heart goes out to the folks working in the airline industry—they are brave and stalwart people, and they deserve far more credit than they get. I also completely support our efforts to make flying safer. That said, I think the airline security issue is an amazing analogy for what's wrong at most companies (your company?).

First, it's obvious that most of us aren't encouraged to speak up about security at the airport. To do so is to be a troublemaker or even unpatriotic. Just as a company can build a culture that makes it hard to criticize a decision from headquarters, it's been made clear to us that experts are in charge and we should shut up and support any efforts to stop "bad guys" from flying.

But the experts *aren't* in charge! Many of the changes that are implemented are nothing but superstitions. One person decides that nail clippers are dangerous but ballpoint pens are not, and airports all over the country begin to confiscate nail clippers. There's no system in place to measure whether or not this policy is effective, whether or not it is worth the thousands of hours and millions of dollars it costs to enforce. And without a way to measure the effect, we can be confident that the policy will last a long time.

Today's *USA Today* says that a whistle-blower is accusing the FAA of failing to follow up on security tests and ignoring bad results when they do perform tests. Has that ever happened at your company?

Because there's no consistent measurement, we also discover obvious discrepancies across the system. At the airport in Montrose, Colorado, your shoes are x-rayed and you need to remove a fleece sweater (*if* it has a zipper). In New York, however, shoes are fine, as are sport coats and fleeces of any kind. At one airport, the guards confiscated all Duracell batteries but allowed much larger laptop batteries through. Why? Because of superstition. Because there was no measurement system. Because the person who invented the policy wasn't involved and hadn't discovered whether it was working or not. It seems pretty obvious to me that if it's important to x-ray shoes in Colorado, it's important to do it in New York.

One last example and one suggestion: In Los Angeles, I discovered that you can't walk through security with an open bottle of Poland Spring water in your hand. You have to take a sip to prove it's not acid or something. But why wouldn't a bad guy just put the bottle in his carry-on? I know, I'm not supposed to ask because that would be undermining the system, but come on!

And my suggestion? Here you go: Let's put an e-mail address on every X-ray machine in the country. Have it say, "Do you know how to make security screening better? Drop us a line!" Now, imagine hundreds of thousands of very smart businesspeople, all travelers, many of them security experts or consultants or whatever, constantly upgrading the system by feeding back advice, detecting errors, or increasing consistency.

Imagine that both the person making the suggestion and the operator reading it would get a bonus every time a suggestion made it through the system and was put into action. I could send a note praising the speed, thoroughness, and kindness of the woman who patted me down or describe three ways to make the system at West Palm Beach go more smoothly. The system would evolve—fast. Hey, it might even work at your company!

Why is an obvious idea like this (evolving quickly using feedback loops based on data) so hard to swallow? Because managers like to make decisions. Because managers like to be right. Because employees have been trained to want the managers to make the decisions, and to want stability in the policies they work with.

As our world moves faster, we need to evolve faster. If we don't, the competition will.

MEDIOCRITY

Why settle?

It's not expensive to make a world-class dinner roll. There are only a few ingredients, the recipe is straightforward (but not easy), and the ingredients don't cost a penny extra.

Mediocre rolls are easier and more predictable. Once you figure out how to make a mediocre, tasteless, soggy roll, you can do it over and over again. Mediocre rolls can be baked by anyone, with very little care. And no one would ever go out of their way to purchase or consume a mediocre roll.

So why do we settle? Why bother being in the food business if you're going to serve something you can't possibly be proud of? Is making that extra dollar so important that all pride goes out the window?

Part of the curse of Wall Street is that enough is never enough. So short-term thinking sets in. Too many companies believe that their owners (the stockholders) would rather have them make schlock and alienate customers to turn a little extra profit—even though it's clear that this strategy virtually always leads to their doom.

The real story here, though, has nothing to do with the stock market. It has to do with our willingness to settle for product that just isn't that good—at the same time that we vote with our dollars to buy things and experiences that are exceptional.

MINNESOTA ISN'T AKRON

Halfway through a recent trip to Minnesota, I realized how delighted I was by the experience.

In addition to extremely nice people, inspiring architecture, a vibrant arts community, and surprisingly good food, there's a vibe in the air about the work people are doing. This placed is filled with organizations that are working hard to create stuff that's remarkable.

What a radical difference from so many other places I've visited recently, areas full of strip malls and low-grade office parks, with disheartened people following scripts and trying to cut costs. These are consumer- and business-focused marketing organizations that have decided that the best way to make a buck is to race to the bottom, to be the cheapest or the fastest to market. No need to worry about a worn carpet or an industrial waste product with side effects. These are the people who cut corners during the day so they can make enough money to buy what they like at night.

I found the same contrast up in the air. American Airlines is racing to the bottom as fast as it can. The staff has given up. No smiles, no service, no effort. Saving money is the order of the day. JetBlue, on the other hand, continues to strive to get to the top, from the free WiFi offered at JFK in New York to the terminal they want to build there to the snacks (they even suggest mixes—created by taking say, animal crackers and pretzels and mixing them up—even though it means people are taking twice as much).

So, I think I understand what happens when you win the race to the top. You end up with a healthy, motivated workforce that's focused on adding creativity and joy to your products. You end up with profits and market share and a community that's glad you're there.

What happens, though, when you win the race to the bottom?

MISSION

Typical mission statement: "To satisfy our customers' desires for personal entertainment and information through total customer satisfaction."

Mission statements used to have a purpose. The purpose was to force management to make hard decisions about what the company stood for. A hard decision means giving up one thing to get another.

Along the way, when faced with something difficult, many managers just avoided the issue and created mission statements like the one above. A mission statement that says everything says nothing.

MONOPOLIES AND THE DEATH OF SCARCITY

Why can't Nike charge $500 for sneakers? Because there are easy substitutes. In almost every industry, consumers have countless choices. And unless a product is truly unique, they can take their money elsewhere.

The media business has always been different. At its heart, the media business is actually about the prospect of becoming a monopoly—and about getting paid a lot more than your products cost to make. Not too long ago, if a couch potato wanted to watch TV, there were only three channels she could choose from. If a moviegoer wanted to see *Butch Cassidy and the Sundance Kid*, there was only the William Goldman version, and she had to buy a ticket to see it.

The point is this: The media business was built on scarcity. Scarcity of spectrum. Scarcity of hits. Scarcity caused by copyrights and limited shelf space. Consumers hate scarcity. But you and I know that monopolists love scarcity. When consumers have fewer choices, a monopoly thrives.

Scarcity made it easy to get fat and happy. But almost overnight, the scarcity on which media monopolies are built has begun to disappear. All of a sudden, there are about a billion channels available on the Web. There's a movie theater in any home with a DVD player. Amazon has infinite shelf space, so retail market power is now a myth. It's hard to charge take-it-or-leave-it prices when the consumer can just leave it.

And you need to care about this if you've ever tried to advertise something or interrupt someone. Because without a monopoly to buy attention from, you're going to have a much harder time.

There is no scarcity of spectrum or retail space. And now there's no scarcity of easy ways to duplicate something that has already been purchased. It's easy to share with friends (and strangers). The result: Just because media companies enjoyed an eighty- or ninety-year-long ride doesn't mean that it will last forever. It's over.

The government has a long history of trying to help monopolists. And try as it might, in every single case, Congress has failed. Why? Technology, capitalism, and consumer demand destroy just about any monopoly that can be destroyed. Legislation can prolong the pain, but sooner or later, the monopoly loses. The fascinating lesson is that once the monopolies disappear, they're almost always replaced by markets that are more profitable for more companies (and better for more consumers) than the old monopolized market ever was.

Look at the music business for a second. Here's the good news: Artists can make a record with hardly any cash. Online retailers have infinite shelf space. There are thousands of Internet radio stations that sap the power of a small number of program directors. Near instant file sharing can help spread a great song across the world. (Check out www.cdbaby.com to see this system working wonders.)

Why isn't this a scenario for tremendous commercial innovation?

Isn't it possible that there will be more music, at lower cost, for more consumers? Isn't it likely that many people who would never have made an album will do so now?

There are plenty of winners in this new world. Rickie Lee Jones wins when she can self-publish her new CD (the CD that she really wanted to publish, not her overproduced live-hits Warner Bros. CD) at www.rickieleejones.com. If she sells twenty thousand copies, she's way ahead of where she might be if Warner Bros. had published it. Better still, Jones and her team could build an entirely new and different business, where the music is free but the concert tickets cost money. With a million fans around the world (enrolled in her e-mail fan club, even), she could sell out concert venues anywhere on the planet.

Or consider this possibility: I might be wrong! Maybe there's no way at all for her to make a fortune. Perhaps she needs to get a day job. Is that going to force her (and thousands who would like to be her) to retire? Somehow, I don't believe that sucking the money out of the music business will eliminate the musicians. I do believe, though, that it will change the middlemen.

You're not going out of business tomorrow. The structures that you have built and perfected are going to stick around for a long time. But it's not going to get better, more profitable, or more fun. It's only going to get worse.

Unless you start playing by different rules.

MOUSE FLAVOR

I'm spending the weekend feeding the cat across the street while my neighbors go hither and yon. If you don't already believe that all marketers are liars take a look at this promo copy for Fancy Feast cat food:

> Fancy Feast Gourmet cat food is finely ground and smooth, like pate offering a taste and texture to please every cat's discriminating

palate. Choose your cat's favorite flavor from our 11 different flavors, for complete and 100% balanced nutrition every day.

Did you know that cats had discriminating palates? When was the last time a house cat starved to death? Remember, these are animals that capture, torture and then eat small rats.

Do the cats know that there's gravy in the chicken? Do they care about the paté-like texture? Hey, if cat food was really for cats, it would come in mouse flavor.

It's pretty obvious who expensive cat food is for, and it sure isn't cats. (One flavor is even "grilled." Grilled!)

And baby food isn't for babies, and life insurance doesn't work until you're dead and . . .

MYTHS

There are plenty of myths that have far outlasted the data that proved them to be wrong. (The Earth is flat; heavy objects fall faster than light ones; and Noah's Ark all come to mind.) The most expensive myth around today, though, could be the $220 billion spent on unmeasured advertising every year—in the United States alone.

Randall Rothenberg is almost always right, and he's correct again when he states that entire media companies are about to bite the dust because advertisers are just now (fifty years later) realizing that almost all ad money is wasted. But now, they can tell which part works.

Myths make people emotional, of course, and there's bound to be plenty of angst before the advertising argument is settled. Ultimately, it's a simple challenge: Do you want to bet your future on a process that's getting less effective every day?

NAMING

Greg Harrington writes, "I've been thinking quite a bit about a topic lately—how to best name a business—and in looking for some ideas, I've reviewed several of your books, but don't find anything in the way of a thorough treatment of this topic."

Here's what I think. First, the main point: a brand name is a peg on which people hang all the attributes of your business. The *less* it has to do with your category, the better.

If you call yourself International Postal Consultants, there's a lot less room to hang other attributes. Some names I like? Starbucks. Nike. Apple.

Second, please pick a real English word, or a string of them. Axelon and Altus are bad. JetBlue, Ambient, and Amazon are good.

Third, be sure it's easy to spell *and* pronounce. Prius is a bad name. I can't tell anyone to buy a Prius because I'm embarrassed I'll say it wrong.

Fourth, don't obsess about getting a short Web name. If you want to name your venture capital firm Nickel (a great name, imho), then you could have www.NickelVenture.com and that would be fine. The only way this turns into a problem is if the current owner of the URL is a competitor (which won't happen if you pick a nonobvious name, as I recommend in #1 above).

If you follow these pieces of advice, you'll discover that there are literally millions of names available to you. (Lemonpie, for example, is perfect for a scuba tour company. So are Orangepie, Melonpie and Kiwipie.) You will have far fewer trademark hassles. You will have no trouble coming up with a cool name that means nothing and is easy to hang a good brand upon. And you'll have fun.

But don't forget to come up with a great tagline. "Lemonpie, the easy way to learn scuba," for example.

P.S. A couple more tricks:

1. Use a stock-photo CD and find cool pictures that fit your name *before* you pick the name. If you can find a bunch of $30 images that work well with a name, grab the pictures, *then* the name.

2. Don't listen to anyone else. All your friends will hate it. *Good.* They would have hated Starbucks, too (you want to name your store after something from *Moby Dick*!?). If your friends like it, run.*

NAMING, THE NEW RULES OF

For a long time, I didn't like my name. I spent more than thirty years spelling both my first and last name in school and on the phone. It didn't help that I had a little trouble with my *S*s when I was a kid.

Of course, now I think it's fantastic that my grandfather overruled my mom when she wanted to name me Scott. (I think he had an issue with the branding of a type of toilet paper, but that's a different story.)

"Scott" is a tough name in the Google world. "Mark" is even tougher. "Michael" is probably toughest of all. Do a Google search on "Mark" and who knows what you'll find. "Seth," on the other hand, will get you right to me.

We went through a lot of hoops in naming my new company, Squidoo. I realized as I was explaining the process to a friend the other day that the same logic applies to any product or service or company in our bottom-up world, so here goes:

A long time ago, the goal of a name was to capture the essence of your position. To deliver a USP, so you could establish supremacy in your space just with your name. International Business Machines and Shredded Wheat were good efforts at this approach.

*Written in June 2003—two years before the sequel, below.

It quickly became clear, though, that descriptive names were too generic, so the goal was to coin a defensible word that could acquire secondary meaning and that you could own for the ages. That's why "JetBlue" is a much better name than "Southwest" and why "Starbucks" is so much better than "Dunkin' Donuts."

"Naming companies" flourished, charging clients hundreds of thousands of dollars to coin made-up words like "Altria."

Then domain names came along. Suddenly, people are charging (I'm not making this up) $300,000 for goggles.com. The idea was that if you could grab a good domain name (there's only one goggles.com in the entire world), then people could easily find you.

I think many of these rules have changed, largely because of the way people use Google.

If you want JetBlue or IKEA or some other brand, you're just as likely to type the brand name into Google as you are to guess the domain name. In essence, we've actually added a step in the process of finding someone online. (How else would anyone find del.ico.us?)

This means that having the perfect domain name is nice, but it's *way* more important to have a name that works at technorati.com and on Yahoo! and Google when someone is seeking you out. Sort of a built-in search engine optimization strategy.

If you pick the right name, a unique name, a name that is easy to remember and spell—*and* one that's likely to put you at the top of the search engine results when people type it in—you've just bought yourself a reliable stream of prospects.

Flickr is a good name. So is 37signals. The design firm Number 17, however, is not. Answers.com, About.com, Hotels.com, and Business.com are all fine URLs, but they don't work very well if someone forgets to put the ".com" part in. Do a Yahoo! search on "radar" and you won't find the magazine or the Web site in the making, and do a search on "simple" and you won't end up at the very expensive simple.com domain.

Think about that for a second. You could spend a million dollars to buy simple.com, but when someone types "simple" into a search engine, they don't find you.

If you're trying to be noticed as a blogger, calling yourself Doc or Scoble or Seth is a much simpler way to establish a platform than calling your blog Mike's Blog.

Sound obvious? Of course it does. But books still get titles like *Chip Kidd, Work: 1986–2006, Book One.*

Back to me and my Squidoo adventure: So, that was the first task, finding a name that came up with close to zero Google matches. The only English-language matches I found for Squidoo were for a style of fishing lure (we bought six gross).

If I had a choice between a killer domain name with a generic word in it or a great word that led to a less-than-perfect domain, I'd take the great word every time.

The second thing that's happening with the explosion of made-up, unique names is that the very structure of a word now communicates meaning. The architecture of the sounds matters. Web 2.0 names often have missing (or extra) vowels. The "oo" double *O* is a great way to communicate a certain something about a Net company.

"HRKom" doesn't sound like the same kind of company as, say, "Jeteye." This is all very irrational, artsy fartsy stuff, but it's also important.

Altria and Achieva and Factiva and Kalera all sound like companies invented by naming firms. Which is a fine signal to send to Wall Street, but nothing you'd want to name your kid or your Web 2.0 company. The structure of a name is at least as important as what the name says.

The shift, then, is from what the words *mean* to what the words *remind* you of. The structure of the words, the way they sound, the memes they recall all go into making a great name. Starbucks is made of two words that have nothing at all to do with coffee and the reference to *Moby Dick* is tenuous for most of us. But over time, the shape of the letters, the way they sound, and the unique quality of the word make it close to perfect.

So, using the fantastic NameBoy service (www.nameboy.com), I found thousands of available domains that managed to sound right and were unique. It took more than a month. Along the way, I almost bought FishEye.com but the owner (who has a charter boat in the Cayman Islands) wasn't budging.

The last thing I want to tell you is this: After you find a name that works in the Google world, a name that is easy to spell and remember and is structured in a way that supports your story, then you need to sell the name *internally*. There are two things you should keep in mind when dealing with your organization:

1. Don't use a placeholder name while you're out looking for the real name. People will fall in love with the stand-in, which is not useful. Find your name, use that name, and that's it.

2. Don't listen to what your friends and neighbors and colleagues tell you about a name. We had a placeholder name (yikes), I had to change it, and everyone hated the new name. For weeks! But now it feels like it couldn't be anything else.

   The entire point of "secondary meaning" is that the first meaning doesn't matter at all (especially since you picked a name with no meaning to begin with). Over a surprisingly short time, your unique word, especially if it sounds right, will soon be the one and only word.

THE NEEDLE, THE VISE . . . AND THE BABY RATTLE

Most ventures that want to grow do some sort of marketing. And that marketing can be divided into two things that work. And one that doesn't.

The needle uses simple physics to work. Apply pressure to a tiny, carefully selected area and you're going to get penetration.

That's why a ninety-two pound nurse can give you a flu shot—the tiny surface area of the tip of the needle has no trouble slipping into your skin.

Permission marketing is about the needle. The right person, the right message, the right moment. Anticipated, personal, and relevant messages that get through to the person you need to reach.

The needle doesn't happen all at once. You need to have the right combination of reputation, product, and prospect.

The vise uses a different principle of physics to work, but it works as well. The vise is about providing increasing amounts of pressure over the entire area. And because of the nature of a screw, you can create huge amounts of pressure over time without overexerting yourself. Get your hand stuck in a vise and you'll see what I mean.

The vise approach works, for example, with Starbucks, or with the local doctor's office or in grassroots politics. Show up often enough, be in enough places, engender enough support from one individual after another, and sooner or later, your investment in spreading the word pays off.

What doesn't work? What doesn't work is the annoying baby rattle.

Babies will occasionally get quite energetic in using a rattle to get attention. But then they get bored and move on to other techniques. Sooner or later, they come back to the rattle, frustrated that nothing seems to work.

Most marketers, and just about all struggling marketers, are rattlers. They try some gimmick or technique or product, focus on it for a little while, then lose interest and move on. After a while, out of frustration, they come back to retry, just to prove to themselves that they're doing everything they can to get the word out.

"Hey!" the blogger says, "I built a blog just like that Dummies book says, but it's not paying off. Let's do a podcast instead." And then on to the next thing.

The best marketers, of course, use the needle and the vise at the same time. They don't assault, they don't demand; instead, they earn attention. And they apply their marketing pressure so consistently and in such a measured and relentless way that sooner or later, they profit from it.

One commercial Web site I know is spending millions tightening its vise. Unfortunately, the offer and the site design is so confused (and unappealing) that it's unlikely they can make the system pay. If they figured out where to apply the pressure, what offer would appeal, how to reach the right person in the right way, their leverage would triple.

The ironic thing is that ad agencies have been backed into a corner and mostly do rattling. It's the high-cost, high-profile, high-risk part of marketing, and the kind that rarely works. What a shame that some of the smartest people in our field aren't allowed (by their clients and by their industry's structure) to get behind the scenes and change the product, the strategy, and the approach instead of just annoying more people with ever louder junk.

NEVER, DO THE

Here's a neat way to invent a new Purple Cow.

Figure out what the *always* is. Then do something else.

Toothpaste always comes in a squeezable tube.

Business travelers always use a travel agent.

Politicians always have their staff screen their calls.

Figure out what the always is, then do exactly the opposite. *Do the never.*

NO!

"I've worked out a series of no's. No to exquisite light, no to apparent compositions, no to the seduction of poses or narrative. And all these no's force me to the 'yes.' I have a white background. I have the person I'm interested in and the thing that happens between us."
—Richard Avedon

Do you have a no?

NO SUCH THING AS SIDE EFFECTS

Barry Schwartz pointed out to me that I shouldn't talk about side effects. Marketers who are inauthentic and shortsighted hide the side effects of their products from purchasers. This fraudulent behavior inevitably comes back to haunt them. But Barry points out that these aren't really "side effects."

There's only effects.

When you make something or sell something, it affects the world around it. Some of those effects are desired. The others, the negative ones, are unintended, but they are still real. These bad effects are just as important as the good ones. And smart marketers are honest about them.

ONLY

Is your organization the only?

The only all-rock radio station in Hempstead?

The only organic bakery in Toledo?

The only church that offers its believers true salvation?

The only magazine that brings readers a particular type of story?

The only consultant that can teach people how to increase a certain type of productivity?

A few years ago, the walls of "only" started to crumble. I can buy organic bread online, or frozen, or pick some up at the Whole Foods market. I can tune in to music ten different ways. I can learn everything I want to learn without ever subscribing to a magazine again.

Only is very comforting. Only eliminates competition, provides price insulation, and boosts my ego. Only, alas, is in short supply these days.

The challenge of being remarkable is being fast enough and brave enough to embrace the new, not just to rely on being the only.

OPEN BIG

We all want to open big. We want our product launches to be instant successes. We want the résumés we send out to be reviewed in one day, we get called the next day, interviewed the third, and we're in a corner office by the end of the week. This mentality persists in almost every aspect of life, in everything from consulting services to receiving a report card in first grade.

In Hollywood and in book publishing, marketers spend 100 percent of their time on the big open. Same with trade show launches of new products. We want an event, a debutant party, something that causes a tremor.

The new marketing, it appears, doesn't work that way.

My first book sold very few copies. My first blog post had very few readers. But, day by day, an audience can grow.

Permission Marketing, a book I wrote more than *seven* years ago just went back to press at the publisher and continues to sell. *Unleashing the Ideavirus*, which you can get for free online or in a handy paperback edition, came out in 2000, but it took until 2005 before there was enough critical mass for the marketing industry to launch an organization around the ideas in it.

The bottom line is that it is way easier to start things than it used to be (opening a movie big costs a tenth of a *billion* dollars, while opening a blog costs about twenty dollars). The natural, user-driven networks that make a product succeed or fail rarely fire all at once. *But the snowball effect online is far more powerful than the old-world scream-and-dream approach.*

So, what does this mean to you?

Make something worth making.

Sell something worth talking about.

Believe in what you do because you may have to do it for a long time before it catches on.

Don't listen to the first people who give you feedback.

Don't give up. Not for a while, anyway.

OPRAH'S SHOW?, HOW MUCH WOULD YOU PAY TO BE ON

What would happen to your organization if you had a solid ten minutes with Her Majesty? How much benefit would you receive if you were able to tell your story to millions of people on television? Of course, you can't pay to be on Oprah, but if you could, no doubt you would.

This simple thought exercise exposes a paradox that we're finding online.

Should authors get paid to put their work into Google Print, the online service that lets you search for information inside a book?

How do you measure how much to invest in a blog?

The persistent reporter who spoke to me the other day wouldn't stop asking the same question: "What percentage of your annual sales are directly attributable to your blog?" Perhaps you've heard the same question from your boss. Proof is what they seek! Management doesn't want to invest in new media without understanding what the short-term payoff is. Authors don't want to "give away" content without proof that it'll pay off.

But they'd all pay to be on *Oprah*.

That local paper, the one that struggles to make its subscription and newsstand bottom line every day, wants you to register before you can read an article online. And they want to know a lot about you (your gender, your date of birth) before they will allow you to pay attention to their site.

The same company that runs ads hoping you'll buy a newspaper that costs more to print than it does to sell puts up roadblocks to keep you from reading online.

Wait.

"Pay attention" are the key words. The consumer is already **paying**. They're paying with a precious commodity called attention. Instead of fending them off and holding them back, perhaps the newspaper ought to be making it easier for them to give their precious attention away.

A quick gut check will probably confirm what many of us truly believe: The number of channels of communication is going to continue to increase. And either you'll have a channel or you won't. Either you'll have access to the attention of the people you need to talk with (notice I didn't say "talk at"), or you won't.

So, the real question to ask isn't, "How much will I get paid to talk with these people?" The real question is, "How much will I *pay* to talk with these people?"

OPTIMISM

Take a quick look at just about any news source covering the business world and you're likely to be either frightened or depressed. Seems like everyone is a crook. What are these people thinking? Is capitalism doomed?

Personally, I'm betting on small companies. Small companies are where the people doing the work are also making the decisions. I'm endlessly optimistic about the capacity for human beings to make money solving problems for one another. It's only when we create a new sort of royalty—an unelected ruling class—that these companies seem to get into trouble.

I can't wait to see the new stuff that's being invented in someone's garage right now.

OPT-IN

I've fought this battle so many times, I'm a little weary of it, but hey, here goes:

Opt-out=spam. Opt-out takes advantage of laziness, inertia, and infoglut to inundate people with stuff they don't want. Opt-out is no way to build a great company. If you advertise, you should never buy opt-out ads. They don't work so well, and, more important, you're going to annoy people.

I'm ashamed of this. Most online businesses have news and offers that people will willingly read. That's the path to go down. That's the way to build sustainable, profitable businesses. Opt-out is a mistake. It's too bad, really.

OSTRICH

Have you ever eaten ostrich?

I missed my chance when I gave up poultry as the last land animal in my diet.

My guess is that you haven't had much ostrich either.

It turns out that there was a huge bubble in ostrich farming (yes, they have bubbles off the Internet, too). Once a few clever breeders realized that the world would go crazy about ostrich meat (and don't forget the eggs), there was money to be made selling breeding ostriches.

So, you bought two ostriches and a bunch of land, and soon you'd have some baby ostriches. You sold those ostriches for $20,000 or more each—to other people who wanted to breed ostriches. Do this for a few generations and pretty soon there would be plenty of ostrich meat available (and the breeders at the top of the pyramid would be rich indeed).

You can guess the punch line. The breeders sold their ostriches to other breeders, and soon there were plenty of ostriches but, in the end, restaurants didn't want to sell the stuff because people didn't really want to eat it.

A Blogads survey says that more than 20 percent of blog readers are also blog writers. Imagine a world where 20 percent of the people who *read* novels also *wrote* novels. Let's hope we're not breeding ostriches. We're so busy *writing* that maybe, just maybe, nobody who shows up is going to actually spend the time to read! As a parting shot, here's a quick blurb from one ostrich site:

"The ostrich industry is the fastest growing agricultural business in the world. With the vast array and almost unlimited supply of products and services that we have available, your opportunities to resell these products has never been better."

OXYMORONS, JUST ABOUT

Every single article about podcasting mentions Adam Curry (which makes sense, since it was his idea). And every article ever written about Adam Curry mentions that he was once an MTV video jockey (we're talking almost 100,000 Google results). For no good reason.

And, every single article about Google (until recently) included the phrase "And employees eat lunch in a cafeteria where the food is prepared by a former chef for the Grateful Dead" (we're talking 25,600 matches.) For no good reason.

What they have in common is pretty obvious: oxymorons. It's a jarring juxtaposition of facts that no one expects but is pretty easy to remember. Oxymorons make it easy to tell stories. Do you have one?

PAINFULLY SIMPLE

I lost the keys to my Toyota Prius (actually, someone stole my shoes when I was skiing on a snow-covered bike path, and my keys were in my shoes, but that's another story altogether—why would someone steal my shoes?).

Anyway, I go to Google and type in "replacement key" and "toyota prius." A quick check along the ads on the side of the results screen shows that the second one, www.autopartswarehouse.com, has paid a lot to offer me a solution.

I click.

It takes me *not* to the parts for my car, but to the parts for all Toyotas (even though it matched on the word "Prius"). I enter "Prius" and it takes me to another menu. No keys listed here.

I do another search, for "keys."

This is what I get:

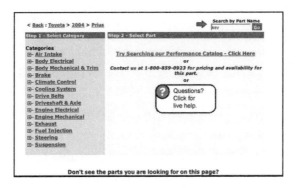

So, in fact, they *don't* have keys for the Prius.

There are two problems here. The first is that the company is too lazy to buy just the right keywords.

The second is that the Web guys at the company are probably not the same people as the folks who are buying the ads. If they were, the entire online buying experience would be centered around me and my need for keys, not them and their need to accurately describe the hierarchy of their store.

Let's assume for a moment that many businesses are going to grow or disappear based on how well they find the needles in the huge haystack of Web searches . . . and that accomplishing this means efficiently turning that first clickthrough into a sale. If that's true, then there needs to be a much more measured, more customer-centric approach to turning mild interest into a completed transaction.

This isn't technically difficult (do a search on Google keyword-matching options and you'll see). It's also not particularly time-consuming.

What's tricky, and the reason everyone doesn't do it, is this:

You're probably still working under a retail mind-set.

The retailer builds a store. She stocks it. She arranges the shelves. She runs ads in the local paper and waits for people to come in who are "just looking."

This is not what happens online (and this applies to fund-raising and just about anything, not just clothes or car keys).

Online you don't have one retail store. You have fifty thousand retail stores.

And you know what the customer is looking for *before* they walk in! So make sure that they are sent to the right store.

And if a store isn't working well, close it and start over.

P.S. If you're a Google shareholder (I don't trade stocks) then this is really good news for you. Why? Because once companies increase their conversion efficiency, they'll probably be willing to pay 400 percent more than they pay now for the right words.

PARSLEY

I had breakfast with my friend Jerry today. We ate at Naples 45 in New York. I ordered the $12 omelet.

This is what I got:

(I know I asked for no potatoes, and it's true that the muffin didn't come with a bite already in it.)

Who eats the garnish? No one does. What a waste, right? But once it's gone, you notice. You notice that there wasn't a sprig of parsley or even a strawberry on the plate. It's a vivid reminder that you were just ripped off.

All of us sell parsley. Sometimes, in the race to cut costs and increase speed and figure out how to fight off Wal-Mart, it's easy to decide to leave off the parsley. No focus group ever asked for parsley!

Right next door to Naples 45, a little café serves breakfast with a smile. And garnish. That's my stop next time.

PERMISSION

I stumbled into a bookstore of a major chain yesterday. I couldn't help myself—I bought five books. As I finished checking out, the clerk said, "Can I have your e-mail address for our newsletter?"

By reflex, I just said no. Too much spam, not enough trust, no real need to read their newsletter. Then, of course, I got curious. "Do many people say no?" I asked.

"In fact, almost everyone does," she said. Obviously, asking wasn't her idea.

In the old days, when permission was new, all you had to do was ask. Now, it seems, it's not so easy.

What if she had said instead, "Hey, look at this! You just qualified for a twenty-dollar gift certificate. Want them to e-mail it to you? You also get a list of special books six times a year. . . ."

That's a totally different offer, right? That's an offer about *me*, not them. Something I can use right now. A definite promise of what I'm going to get (and not get) by e-mail.

PEZ AND LITHUANIAN LANGUAGE RECORDS

The other day, I found myself sitting next to Robert Klein at *Spamalot*. When I was a forlorn teenager, I would spend hours listening to his comedy albums. I memorized his bit ("every record ever recorded . . . we drive a truck to your house"). I resisted the temptation and did not recite it for him on Saturday, though I still know it by heart. "Lithuanian Language Records!"

For a long time, I figured that the inevitable was just about to happen. That every record ever recorded would find its way online and if you had a big enough hard drive, you could have them all.

Mark Fraunfelder at Boing Boing points us to the Tofu Hut where you can find a painstakingly created directory of hundreds of sites pointing to almost a million MP3s, all free.

I no longer believe that you can have every record ever recorded. I now know for certain that by the time they drive the truck to your house, a thousand new records will be made.

When everybody can make everything, the amount of clutter reaches a whole new level. When everybody can make everything (do a Yahoo! search on handmade custom Pez dispensers, for example), then the whole idea of clutter at such an overwhelming level changes the way you need to think about supply and demand.

Warner Bros. is now an anachronism in a world with too much music.

PIGEONS, SUPERSTITIOUS

What happens when your boss starts to think like a pigeon?

B. F. Skinner was right: You can make a pigeon superstitious. Just put it in a cage and arrange for food to appear at regular intervals. Whatever the pigeon happens to be doing just as the food arrives—spinning around, bobbing its head, whatever—it will keep doing, over and over again, in the hope that the dance caused the food to appear. The pigeon will assume a cause-and-effect relationship that doesn't really exist.

That's what a superstition is: a compulsion to take an action that has no actual influence on the desired outcome. Pigeons are superstitious, and I'm afraid that most of us are as well. There's plenty we do—plenty we've always done—that has nothing to do with what actually works. But once we've made up our minds, we're like pigeons. We don't want to change our behavior, regardless of how much data we see to support a new and better alternative. It's easier to be superstitious, easier to hope that the food will just slide out of the dispenser when we spin around and around.

We don't expect a pigeon to wise up and change its behavior. But what about your boss? Have you ever had a boss who said, "I've looked at all the best thinking on (insert issue here: factory expansion, layoffs, global warming, stem cell research, foreign trade), and I'm going to change my mind; my old position was wrong, and this is what we should do instead"? Or is your boss, well, more like a pigeon?

I've got nothing against pigeons. The problem comes when people in power are superstitious—when superstitions become part of the operating system for major companies and other important institutions.

People in power usually want to stay there. And one way they think they can do this is by enforcing rigid adherence to a set of principles that they believe are responsible for their organization's success. By requiring employees to abide by these superstitions—better known as company policies—rather than examining the facts, they build organizations that appear streamlined. In fact, they're doomed.

You can think of these managers as examples of the current crop of fundamentalists who are appearing all over the world—including the world of business. These people are characterized, I believe, by two traits. First, they live according to a large body of superstitions. Second, they believe that they are right and everyone else is wrong. They believe that they have found the one and only truth, and they can't abide changing old rules in light of new data. *Fundamentalists decide whether they can accept a new piece of information based on how it will affect their prior belief system, not based on whether it is actually true.*

It's much easier to effect change if you don't have to overturn a superstition first. For example, nobody questioned the law of gravity. That's because there wasn't a competing theory of gravity built into the dominant social systems of the day. No one was threatened by gravity, so it was quickly accepted as fact. One of the reasons why e-mail took off so fast was that it didn't try to replace the phone or the mailman. It was a third method of communication, something new. But finding a place to grow where there isn't already a prevailing superstition is rare.

When I meet someone who's willing to disregard an obvious truth just because it conflicts with his worldview, I wonder about his judgment. I wonder what other truths he's willing to ignore in order to preserve his superstitions. When such a person is in charge, I do more than worry. I think that we're obligated to start pointing out superstitions at work, in politics—anywhere we find them. Superstitions are the final vestiges of prescientific humankind, and they make the workplace (and the world) a scary one.

The problem is that challenging someone's faith (when it's killing your organization) is also a scary thing. Here's a possibly useful insight: When we know what to call this aversion to rational change, it's much easier to deal with it. In a meeting, we can say, "Are we superstitious about closing this plant and hiring people to do software instead? Or is there an actual analysis that will help us decide?" We can sit down with a co-worker or a client and talk not about what we irrationally believe, but about the facts that suggest that we should try doing things a different way.

My dream is that we'll discover our obligation to spot the fundamentalists and call them on it. Regardless of the organization—a nonprofit, factory work group, or political party, it doesn't matter—we now have no choice but to point out the difference between rational thought and pigeon-minded superstition.

PLACEBO AFFECT,* THE

Everybody already knows how powerful the brain is. Take a sugar pill that's supposed to be a powerful medicine and watch your symptoms disappear. Have a surgeon perform fake bypass surgery on your heart and discover that the angina that has been crippling you vanishes.

The placebo effect is not just for sick people anymore.

Why do some ideas have more currency than others? Because we believe they should. When Chris Anderson or Malcolm Gladwell writes about something, it's a better idea because *they* wrote about it.

Even as our culture of ideas and marketing enters its Long Tail, open-source, low-barrier, everyone-has-a-blog era of mass publication, we still need filters. Would your iPod sound as sweet if everyone else had a Rio? Would your Manolo Blahniks be as cool if everyone else were wearing Keds?

Arthur Anderson audited thousands of companies, and those audits gave us confidence in those companies, made them *appear* more solid, which, not surprisingly, *made* them more solid. Then, after the

*The knack for creating placebos.

Enron scandal, the placebo effect disappeared. Same companies, same auditors, but suddenly those companies *appeared* less solid, which made them less solid.

The magic of the placebo effect lies in the fact that you can't make it work on yourself. You need an accomplice. Someone in authority who will voluntarily tell you a story.

That's what marketers do. We have the placebo affect. Of course, we need to convince ourselves that it's morally and ethically and financially okay to participate in something as unmeasurable as the placebo effect. The effect is controversial and it goes largely unspoken. Very rarely do we come to meetings and say, "Well, here's our cool new PBX for Fortune 1000 companies. It's exactly the same as the last model, except the phones are designed by frog design so they're cooler and more approachable and people are more likely to invest a few minutes in learning how to use them, so customer satisfaction will go up and we'll sell more, even though it's precisely the same technology we were selling yesterday."

Very rarely do vodka marketers tell the truth and say, "Here's our new vodka, which we buy in bulk from the same distillery that produces vodka for eight dollars a bottle. Ours is going to cost thirty-five dollars and come in a really, really nice bottle, and our ads will convince laddies that this will help them in the dating department [nudge, nudge, know what I mean, nudge, nudge]."

It would be surprising to meet a monk or a Talmudic scholar or a minister who would say, "Yes, we burn the incense [or turn down the lights or ring these bells or light these candles] as a way of creating an atmosphere where people are more likely to believe in their prayers," but of course that's exactly what they're doing. (And you know what? There's nothing wrong with that.)

It's easier to get people to come to a meeting about clock speed and warranty failure analysis than it is to have a session about storytelling.

We don't like to admit that we tell stories, that we're in the placebo business. Instead, we talk about features and benefits as a way to rationalize our desire to help our customers by allowing them to lie to themselves.

The design of your blog or your package or your outfit is nothing but an affect designed to create the placebo effect. The sound Dasani water makes when you open the bottle is more of the same. It's all storytelling. It's all lies.

Not that there's anything wrong with that.

In fact, your market insists on it.

PLANE, THERE ARE TWO WAYS TO CATCH A

The first method of catching a plane, which happens to be more common, is to leave on time, do your best to park nearby, repeatedly glance at your watch, and then start moving faster and faster. By the time you get to security, you realize that you're quite late, so you cut the line ("My plane leaves in ten minutes!" you shout). You walk fast. As you get closer to your gate, you realize that walking fast isn't going to work, so you start to jog. Three gates away, you break into a run, and if you're lucky you barely make the flight.

The second way is to leave for the airport ten minutes early.

The easiest way to deal with change and with all the anxieties that go with it is not to deal with it at all. The easiest thing to do is to allow the urgency of the situation to force us to make the decisions (or take the actions) that we'd rather not take. Why? Because then we don't have to take responsibility for what happens. The situation is at fault, not us. The beauty of the asymptotic curve is that at every step along the way, running ever faster for the plane is totally justified. The closer we get, the more we've invested ourselves. The more we invest in making our flight, the easier it is to justify running like a lunatic to make it.

Years ago, I published a directory of law firms. No fewer than 70 percent of the firms sent their payment the night before it was due, by FedEx. Eight of the firms sent their payment by messenger—at an expense that was equal to about 10 percent of the entire cost of their listing. Obviously, there was no need to waste all that money. Law firms spend millions every year on last-minute deliveries because, like most of us, they confuse urgent with important.

Urgent issues are easy to address. They are the ones that get everyone in the room ready for the final go-ahead. They are the ones we need to decide on right now, before it's too late.

How can you tell if you're too obsessed with urgent?

Do senior people at your company refuse to involve themselves in decisions until the last minute?

Do meetings regularly get canceled because something else came up?

Is waiting until the last minute the easiest way to get a final decision from your peers?

Smart organizations ignore the urgent. Smart organizations understand that the most important issues are the ones to deal with now. If you focus on the important stuff, the urgent will take care of itself.

A key corollary to this principle is the idea that if you don't have the time to do it right, there's no way in the world you'll find the time to do it over. Too often, we use the urgent as an excuse for shoddy work or sloppy decision making. A quick look at Washington politics (under any administration) is an easy way to understand how common this crutch is. No responsible business (or diligent family) would spend money and resources the way our government does when faced with an "emergency." Urgent is not an excuse. In fact, urgent is often an indictment—a sure sign that you've been putting off the important stuff until it mushrooms out of control.

You will succeed in the face of change when you make the difficult decisions first. It's easy to justify running for your plane when it's leaving in two minutes and you're only five gates away. It's much harder to justify waking up an hour early to avoid the problem altogether. Alas, waking up early is the efficient, effective way to deal with the challenge. Waking up earlier may seem foolish to the person lying in bed next to you, but when you enjoy the benefits of a pleasant stroll to the gate, you realize that your difficult decision was a good one.

Organizations manage to justify draconian measures—laying people off, declaring bankruptcy, stiffing their suppliers, closing stores—by pointing out the urgency of the situation. They refuse to make the difficult decisions when the difficult decisions are cheap. They don't want to expend the effort to respond to their competition or fire the intransigent vice president of development. Instead, they focus on the events that are urgent at that moment and let the important stuff slide.

A quick look at the gradually failing airlines, retailers, and restaurant chains we all know about confirms this analysis. They're all content to worry about today's emergency, setting the stage for tomorrow's disaster. Better, I think, to wake up an hour early, make some difficult decisions before breakfast, and enjoy the rest of your day.

PLEASE DON'T MAKE ME FEEL SO STUPID

I just got a Polar heart rate watch. This thing is supposed to let me track my heart rate as I exercise. It's clearly a remarkable product in that it changes the way you think about something you do for half an hour a day. But, alas, it's having a lot of trouble reaching consumers beyond a small subset of the world of people who actually exercise. Why?

Well, maybe this quotation from the astonishingly poor manual gives you a clue: "While using an exercise set, you can see all the same information as in the BasicUse mode." Or how about, "Exe. Time-> RecoHR/Reco Time->Tot. Time->Limits1->InZone/Above/Below 1 . . ." (all punctuation is recorded as written)?

I'm ashamed that I can't understand how to use this product. So ashamed that I won't mention it to my friends, nor will I evangelize it to others.

What could Polar do? How about a totally obvious quick-start mode that turns off 90 percent of the features and just makes the watch work!

PLEDGE WEEK

I hate pledge week on National Public Radio. It bothers me that the otherwise intelligent people who run the station believe that they can hold it hostage while we buy back our right to listen. I mean, I've got plenty of other things to do in the car. I can listen to "Waiting for Godiva" from the new band Sauce or even, heaven forfend, switch to another noncommercial radio station. Hey, if I've got XM or Sirius, I could switch to a hundred other noncommercial stations. I need a pretty exceptional reason to listen to commercial radio (notice how they put the word "commercial" *before* the word "radio").

Anyway, as much as I hate pledge week, I'm wondering if there's something to it.

The problem with the NPR model is that they don't have a way of discontinuing their broadcast to someone who doesn't pledge. In other words, there's no way to turn you off if you don't pay.

Online, we all know that banner ads are virtually worthless (and they sell for as little as a tenth of a penny per banner) and now the sites we use are upping the ante in order to make a living. They're working to interrupt us with pop-ups, pop-unders, and various other distractions. Of course, they need to (and deserve to) make a profit, so more power to them.

The thing is, it's still not very profitable for them. They realize that they can't *totally* hold us hostage with various advertising come ons, or we'll switch to another site. In their perfect world, their media company would have no competition and we'd have to watch several full-page ads (just like TV or radio) before we could get back to our regular programming.

Fortunately, it's not a perfect world, and as a result the media companies make little or nothing on every single visit we make to their sites. But we, the users, are annoyed nonetheless.

What if, just maybe, we learned a quick lesson from NPR, but without the free rider problem.

Slashdot is now offering a service where you get no ads for about $5 a month.

Yahoo! sees more than 100 million users a month. Can you imagine how profitable they'd be if we all just paid them $5 and never again had to see the Classmates.com ad? Never had to click on "close window" in order to get back to our e-mail . . .

I'd pay. Would you?

PODCAST, WHY I DON'T HAVE A

A few times a day, people ask when I'm going to have a podcast. My answer is probably not too soon.

The good news for podcasters is that users' ability to hear podcasts is dramatically increasing. Forty-eight hours after they built podcasts into iTunes, the number of podcast listeners increased by more than one million.

There's a bunch of bad news, though.

First, you can't browse a podcast. Which means that you won't know what you like until you get it. That means subscribing in many cases. This is, of course, good news, because subscribers are more loyal than browsers. But it's mostly bad news because it means that very few podcasts are going to be heard by large numbers of people.

Example: If there are one thousand blogs and one thousand readers, sooner or later every blog will be sampled by every reader. *But*, if there are one thousand podcasts and one thousand listeners, it's unlikely that you'll be sampled by more than ten or twenty listeners. Why? Because the cost of sampling (time invested) is too high. Once your needs are met, you'll stop listening.

Problem two is that listening is a real time commitment. I can surf three hundred blogs in the same time it takes to listen to just one podcast. That doesn't mean podcasts are bad. In fact, they're far more powerful than blogs in eliciting and selling emotion. But it does mean that it's going to be harder to find a big audience.

Which leads to the last bit of bad news: You can put up a blog post in two minutes, but it takes an hour to make a podcast. So, creators will want either big audiences or big money if they're going to invest in the medium. And both are hard to see coming anytime soon.

My two cents.

POILÂNE, REMEMBERED*

Lionel Poilâne was the world's greatest baker. He was also an extraordinary personality, a visionary entrepreneur, and a kind and thoughtful man.

I was supposed to have lunch with him in a few weeks—and lunch with Lionel was always a treat. Lionel embodied just about everything I've been writing about for the last few years. He was remarkable. His bread was standard fare at just about every two- and three-star restaurant in Paris—because it was different. He was roundly criticized at first (he refused to bake baguettes, for example), but the extraordinary

---

*I wrote this in 2003. And I still mention Lionel, with his picture, in every single public speech I do. Thanks, Lionel.

qualities of his bread (and his sparkling personality) won over the critics. We don't have enough gutsy entrepreneurs in the world, and now we've got one less.

On my first visit with him (I was the weird American tourist who refused to leave the shop without some raw dough I could turn into a sourdough starter back home), he invited me to breakfast, gave me a tour of the world's largest collection of bread cookbooks, and pumped me for Internet advice. I think of him every time I put a piece of bread in my mouth or see a really stylish, cool new business idea.

I'll miss Lionel.

POLKA

This sign is right next to the escalator at the convention center in Milwaukee.

It doesn't cost much, but it transforms the mundane into the memorable. That, and you get to hear polka music for your entire ride.

PROGRESS?

What an amazing world we live in. Information flying about at the speed of light. Cures or treatments for many major diseases. Airplanes. Food for many, if not most. Cat food that tastes like pâté.

It almost feels churlish to complain.

But here's the deal: Almost everything is lousy.

Sure, it's way way better than it was. Sure, it's a miracle.

But is anything as good as it could be?

Maybe a cup of Starbucks coffee or a bowl of cereal. But almost everything else needs a lot of work.

That canoe could weigh half as much. There's no reason to wait an hour to get on an airplane. Software development should be twice as fast at half the cost.

And what's with the layout of this keyboard? They came up with a keyboard a century ago, decided it was good enough, and then stopped! Holy carpal tunnel, Batman.

I've got a few chapters' worth on this topic, but here are my two main ideas:

1. Humans tend to work on a problem until they get a good-enough solution, not a solution that's right.

2. The marketplace often rewards solutions that are cheaper and good enough, instead of investing in the solution that promises to lead to the right answer.

This all sounds pessimistic. Are we doomed to inefficient products, unreliable computers, overpriced services, and new devices that last for a while and then just break?

I don't think so. I think that the open nature of the Web and the hypercompetitive environment of worldwide competition are pushing things in two different directions at the same time. First, toward hypercheap, sort of junky stuff that discounters and others want to sell in volume. And second, the relentless pursuit of better (RPB). The RPB is the opposite of good enough. It's not Jack Welch's Six Sigma nonsense, through which engineers codify mediocrity. It's a consistent posture of changing the rules on an ongoing basis.

David Neeleman, CEO of JetBlue, was talking recently about the way he's running the airline. By any measure, it's good enough. Hey, it's far and away the best airline in the United States. But he's not even close to settling. He riffed about turning one out of three bathrooms on every one of his planes into a ladies-only bathroom. What a great idea. Low cost. Fast. And embracing the RPB.

I asked him why he doesn't raise the price on the 20,000 seats JetBlue runs between New York and Florida (every day). If he raised it $10, he'd make an extra $11 million a year in profit! Without losing a customer.

He said, "We could always do that later. Right now, it keeps us focused and hungry and efficient to do it for less."

PROMOTIONS

Readers will know how fond I am of promotions, and I believe that the Web is the greatest promotional device ever.

Well, Amazon made me smile today. There, with no fanfare, at the top right-hand corner of the page is a little gold box.

Click on it and it shows you a special offer. You can either discard it (forever—you can't go back) and go on to the next one (there are five a day) or buy it on the spot.

I was hooked. I looked at all five. I'll go tomorrow to look at more.

The key is that the offers have to be both relevant and honest. It's not an offer if it's not a lot of money saved. If it's for something I'm not interested in, it's a waste. If it's just promotional hoopla, it's not going to work. Instead, it needs to be special.

The cool thing is that once this works (and I think it will) then manufacturers ought to be willing to pay a bunch to participate. And my guess is that Amazon will likely pass some of the money on to us, the never satisfied consumers.

My only tweak: I'd let people e-mail an offer to a friend if they don't want it.

P.S. I stopped going back. The offers weren't "real" enough. Not enough relevance, not enough savings. My guess? It is too hard for the manufacturers and distributors to think about this program. Sure, they understand Price Club or even Woot.com. But when you talk about offering exceptional values to thousands of microcommunities, they jam up.

PROSTITUTION

Why does it bother us so much when marketers try to subvert the ideavirus process and buy their way into our lives?

The massive marketing engines of the car industry have decided to run roughshod over the idea of authentic viral marketing and they're working hard to manufacture faux ideaviruses as fast as they can.

When you run into someone with "Scion" tattooed on her forehead, it's odd. When you realize that person got paid to do it, you feel used. Maybe it's just me, but I think there's a huge difference between the famous Honda cog movie (or the BMW movies) and the manipulative Scion campaign. In the first cases, the car companies built something worth talking about. In the second, the manufacturer just bought the conversation.

Why does it bother us? Precisely because it feels so intentional. Because it represents an unwelcome intrusion, a display of power. It's a lot like spam, in fact.

With more than 55,000,000 downloads to date, the BMW campaign is a success by any measure. It's hard to imagine that Scion can afford to buy enough buzz tattoos to make a difference. If permission marketing is about dating, then buying these conversations is about nothing more than prostitution.

P.S. What about bzzagent.com? Yes, they get paid to help start conversations. But a key part of their business model is that they *don't* pay the sneezers themselves. The bzzagents work for free. It needs to be that way for it to work.

Is it a fine line? You betcha. So is dating, for that matter! The magic and the art comes in creating remarkable products that don't cross the line—products that are simply worth talking about, not paid conversations.

PROVINCETOWN HELMET INSIGHT

Yesterday, I had a minor epiphany. More of an insight, actually.

Biking in Provincetown (a beautiful day, capping a Yoyodyne wedding weekend, which is more than you wanted to know), I mentioned to my wife that every couple we passed (straight, gay, lesbian, didn't matter) had synchronized their helmet habits.

Either both wore helmets, or neither did.

At first, I attributed the Provincetown Helmet Insight (PHI) to some sort of subtle evolutionary cue. People must be attracted to people with a similar sensibility about helmets. If you were a foolish daredevil, perhaps you could sense that trait in a potential mate. When you both got to the bike store, voilà, you'd see that you both made the same choice regarding a helmet.

Further research at the store (including some surveillance and an interview with the manager) demonstrated that this was a bogus theory.

It turns out that what actually happens is this: A couple stands at the rental desk and the person at the counter says, "Do you want helmets? They're a dollar each." One person starts to answer, but glances at the other. Then a subtle form of bullying starts.

Usually, one person says, "No, I don't think so," and the other, who was about to say yes, is intimidated enough to say instead, "Me neither." Sometimes, it works the other way. "Oh, we'd never ride without helmets," says one, and the other agrees.

So?

So this is actually what happens to your product and to your service every single day. *This* is the moment of truth whether you sell securities or consulting or yoyos or motel rooms. One person hesitates, the other leads, and the decision is made. In a nanosecond, all your marketing and all your advertising and all your sales work is over.

What can you do about it?

Well, for a cheap and basic product like bike helmets, the answer is pretty simple. I'd create momentum via peer pressure. "Here are two helmets," the salesman says, as he hands the helmets to the two renters. "They only cost a dollar each and almost everyone wears them. It's the smart thing to do."

Now, since *both* riders are already holding the helmets, it's easy for the helmet-inclined to take the lead. All she has to do is try it on (a natural thing to do) and the discussion is over. The salesperson is using the PHI to his advantage.

I think the same thinking works when selling a $2 million consulting contract, though. The idea of working with individuals on the buying committee before the meeting, of getting each one to give you the benefit of the doubt, of discovering their favorite features or testimonials, person by person, and then organizing that information for the committee is just like handing over the helmets. If it's easier for each person to say, "Sure, why not?" than it is to say, "I don't think so," then you've got the PHI on your side. Just one little push at this high-leverage moment can have a huge impact.

PROXIMITY EFFECT, THE

Imagine a book publisher being upset because her company's books were being shelved right next to competitive books on the same topic.

In fact, books sell far better at bookstores than they do at trade shows or supermarkets or taverns. That's not news to you, I hope.

What about blogs? Blogs are far more widely read now than they were a few years ago when there were just a few blogs to choose from. And people visiting Technorati (which indexes millions of blogs) are far more likely to discover and read a blog than someone who stumbles onto a blog link on, say, eBay.

And tuna? Tuna sells best in the fish store, lying next to the other, lesser fish on ice.

Too often we're beaten down by comparison shoppers and companies issuing RFPs and commodity buyers who won't take the time to hear our story. Too often, frustrated marketers believe that they'd do better if they just didn't have any competition.

In fact, the proximity effect can work in your favor. It usually does if your product or service is special. The proximity effect gives the consumer confidence. It creates a category where no category existed before. It lets you sell the difference, as opposed to the whole thing.

At a bar, you don't have to sell vodka—the drinker already wants vodka. You should only have to sell why your vodka tells a better story than the other guy's vodka.

Online, this effect is profound. Search engines add value when they present a collection of choices, because your proximity to your "competition" for the reader's attention benefits both of you.

PURPLE

I did a phone seminar with Soundview yesterday. Got plenty of questions at the end, and I promised to answer some of the extras. So here goes:

How can the Purple Cow be used in a service industry, i.e.: mortgage banking? It's unclear that most mortgage brokers have tools available to them to differentiate their business. In other words, it's not the remarkable opportunity it used to be.

I think you win once you can offer a package of remarkable elements that embody the core of what you do, but add enough value that by themselves they become worth talking about.

Frequent-flier miles, for example, have nothing to do with flying and everything to do with choosing an airline. That doesn't mean you should offer frequent-flier miles. It means that you have a problem that needs a nonlinear sort of solution.

What suggestions do you have for a job candidate? How do you use your Purple Cow approach to market yourself to potential employers? The first thing to remember is that you can't be Purple at the last minute. You need to be Purple *before* you start looking for a job. That means doing a remarkable job at work (hence the amazing referrals you'll get for internal jobs) and with clients (hence the unsolicited job offers). People who are remarkable in the way they deal with customers and clients and co-workers rarely find themselves unemployed for long.

The second thing is to fight the temptation to print one thousand résumés and to submit yourself to the cattle call (no pun intended) that is the typical job search. This won't work. You'll get an average job if you do that. Instead, focus on the people with an otaku, the folks who are searching for a truly special hire. If you're that person, it'll happen. What usually occurs, though, is that average people are pretty desperate and try to persuade the hiring person that they are in fact remarkable. They end up not getting the job because their references (yours are attached to your résumé, right?) belie their assertion.

So, it's not an easy answer, but it's this:

be remarkable

build a network of people who truly want to hear from you

. . . and you'll find the job you seek.

Good luck!

What can large established brands do to make themselves remarkable? There are plenty of brands like Hershey, American Express, Maxwell House Coffee, et al. that are selling huge quantities of product and keeping lots of factories busy and people employed. How can they further increase their tonnage? —Chuck at Ogilvy Well, the good news is that these big brands have the cash flow and the market power to get over the hump and create new cows to replace their fading ones (American Express, for example, might be a fine brand, but most of what they offer is hardly remarkable). If they want to grow, they must figure out how to invent something that's on a different trajectory than their existing brand.

The problem is that the organizations rarely if ever have the guts to promote and reward people who will champion remarkableness and permission marketing. That's because both strategies start with the (correct) assumption that the marketer is not omnipotent. Most brands with power insist that they can control the conversation and that they can sell average stuff to average people. Maxwell House should have been Starbucks. Procter & Gamble should have been Method. American Express should have been PayPal.

So, if I were the agency of record, I'd push to do more than just make more ads for the same old stuff. Instead, I'd push to be involved in product development, not just advertising. Ad agencies know how to do this right if they'd only try.

I work for a technology publication that has led the market for the last few years based mostly on quality content as its competitive advantage. Now that our market is becoming more saturated, it has become more of a struggle to keep subscriptions on the rise. What is your opinion regarding competing on quality now that more of our competitors are doing the same? What steps can we take to making our quality product more remarkable? A great question! My answer is that we need to keep redefining quality. At the beginning, quality signifies being remarkable. Over time, quality comes to signify something boring, within boundaries, made to spec.

I'd redefine quality at your organization to mean "new, fresh, Purple Cow stuff that clients and users want to talk about." *Rolling Stone* (which is and was "quality" journalism by most measures) fell into the trap of becoming predictable in a big way.

How do you find the sneezers? Do you think that offering people discounts will help you get at the sneezers? Actually, I think the sneezers find you. They find you because you hang out where they hang out. If you're launching a product that doesn't have a natural hive of sneezers, that's really hard, but generally good marketers are clever enough to find the right nexus. Starbucks didn't open their first shops in rural South Dakota, even though storefronts are cheap there. Apple opens their stores using similar thinking. Software guys realize that a post to Slashdot is worth more than ten ads in *Time* magazine and Steven Spielberg doesn't hesitate to visit science-fiction conventions.

QUALITY

In industries under siege from external change (and I count music, books, airlines, pharmaceuticals, IT, telecommunications, etc.), you'll find that the extra fees extracted by the legacy companies *do not* go toward quality. They go to prop up the status quo.

That's why CDs cost $18 and why JetBlue is the best airline in America.

QUESTION, THE WRONG

For the last six years, people in big media have been asking me one question: "How will new media work for the big advertisers?"

While it's human nature to be selfishly focused on *your* issues, there is a bias implicit in the question that's fatal to the entire discussion. The question shouldn't be, "How do we use this different media to replace the media [for big advertisers] that's broken?"

The right question is, "How does this new media change the game for all the players?" How does it move upstream and influence everything from what gets made to who makes it to how much is charged, etc?

Can the world of blogs help Budweiser? Only on the margins. The world of new media is not the place to launch the next one-size-fits-all megabrand, nor is it the place to shore a flagging brand like that up.

Instead of new media's helping to promote the next megafilm from Disney or Julia Roberts, it allows movies like *Wal-Mart: The High Cost of Low Price* to be made.

Instead of promoting brands like Budweiser, the new media permits that very same megabrewer to launch brands that tell a much more vertical, more focused, more powerful story to a smaller group of people.

Instead of promoting mainstream political parties and mainstream political ideas, it provides donations and vocal support to the fringes.

I don't think new media leads us to products that are better or more healthful or honest, necessarily. I think it clearly leads us to products (and stories about them) that are far more focused. Not only is there no cost to specialization, but there's now a benefit to it. Focus is no longer expensive. Mass is.

RECIPE?, DID YOU FORGET THE

I drink a lot of tea. Herbal tea, in fact. Tons of different kinds. It occured to me that on the side of almost every package of tea, the company gives you the recipe. The recipe for how to make a cup of tea.

Is there anyone who doesn't know how to make tea? Among those who don't know, does anyone think to look for a recipe on the box? If it's not there, do they look it up in a cookbook?

There's not enough attention to go around. Don't waste a drop.

REINFORCEMENT

"Godin reinforces what good marketers know."
—*New York Times*

I'm flattered! I wasn't sure I knew what every good marketer knows. I guess I do now. After all, the paper of record said so. But, assuming that you're like me and the rest of the people I know (which means you haven't figured out everything there is to know about marketing yet), here's a list to get you started.

- Anticipated, personal, and relevant advertising always does better than unsolicited junk.

- Making promises and keeping them is a great way to build a brand.

- Your best customers are worth far more than your average customers.

- Share of wallet is easier, more profitable, and ultimately more effective a measure of success than share of market.

- Marketing begins before the product is created.

- Advertising is just a symptom, a tactic. Marketing is about far more than that.

- Low price is a great way to sell a commodity. That's not marketing, though, that's efficiency.

- Conversations among the people in your marketplace happen whether you like it or not. Good marketing encourages the right sort of conversations.

- Products that are remarkable inspire conversation.

- Marketing is the way your people answer the phone, the typesetting on your bills, and your returns policy.

- You can't fool all the people, not even most of the time. And once they catch you, people talk about the experience.

- If you are marketing from a fairly static annual budget, you're viewing marketing as an expense. Good marketers realize that it is an investment.

- People don't buy what they need. They buy what they want.

- You're not in charge. And your prospects don't care about you.

- What people want is the extra, emotional bonus they get when they buy something they love.

- Business-to-business marketing is just marketing to consumers who happen to have a corporation to pay for what they buy.

- Traditional ways of interrupting consumers (TV ads, trade show booths, junk mail) are losing their cost-effectiveness. At the same time, new ways of spreading ideas (blogs, permission-based RSS information, consumer fan clubs) are quickly proving how well they work.

■ People all over the world, and of every income level, respond to marketing that promises and delivers basic human wants.

■ Good marketers tell a story.

■ People are selfish, lazy, uninformed, and impatient. Start with that and you'll be pleasantly surprised by what you find.

■ Marketing that works is marketing that people choose to notice.

■ Effective stories match the worldview of the people you are telling the story to.

■ Choose your customers. Fire the ones that hurt your ability to deliver the right story to the others.

■ A product for everyone rarely reaches anyone.

■ Living and breathing an authentic story is the best way to survive in a conversation-rich world.

■ Marketers are also responsible for the side effects their products cause.

■ Reminding the consumer of a story they know and trust is a powerful shortcut.

■ Good marketers measure.

■ Marketing is not an emergency. It's a planned, thoughtful exercise that started a long time ago and doesn't end until you're done.

■ One disappointed customer is worth as much as ten delighted ones.

Obviously, knowing what to do is very, very different than actually doing it.

Irony alert: Since the inspiration for what I've written here has been misinterpreted a couple of times, I want to clarify that the *New*

York Times wasn't trying to be nice when they said what they said. Even though it seems nice to you and me, they didn't mean it that way. And this list didn't appear in the *Times*, it was inspired by their attempt to be snide. Thank you.

RELAX . . . , I MEAN, WORK ON THE DIFFICULT

Relax. Don't work so hard. Take a little time off. Chill out!

To understand why this is the best advice for bosses and workers alike, you need to hear about the Kalihi-Palama Public Library in Honolulu, Hawaii.

The Kalihi-Palama Public Library is open until 5:00 P.M. most days. Years ago, when the only way to research stuff was by asking people (as opposed to using the Web), this was a vitally important fact to me and to many people on the East Coast. Why? Because in those days, if you happened to find yourself working away on a proposal at 10:00 P.M. New York time, the library in Hawaii was still open. You could give them a call, and a librarian would happily answer your question, regardless of how obscure it was.

One of the least-savory by-products of the new economy has been an almost complete disregard for sleep, family, and personal time. Macho companies marching toward IPOs pride themselves on their army of totally committed employees, who are all too happy to endure sleepless nights and to take showers at the office.

When I was working on my first product launch about twenty years ago, a team of forty of us stayed in the office all night and all day for about a month. We slept on the floor (when we slept at all) and only left the office for an occasional shower. And if I remember correctly, the showers were pretty occasional.

We made our deadline (just barely—we had to bribe the UPS

man with champagne in order to get the last one hundred units off of the assembly line) and saved the company. I remember the perverse pride we all took in our insane dedication. The camaraderie that we developed during those late nights lasts to this day.

But it almost cost me my girlfriend (I ended up marrying her, which is definitely the good news here), and it definitely cost me my health: I was sick for six months afterward.

If you're shaking your head in understanding or agreement, then we need to talk. *There is no correlation at all between success and hours worked.* People who run huge corporations, superpower governments, and insanely profitable, tiny proprietorships are all working fewer hours than you are. It's time to stop the madness and reset your internal clock.

I think the sleeplessness started when we all moved off the farm. Sure, there are a few weeks a year of really long hours on a farm, when you had better get the crops in or they'll die. But there's a limited amount of stuff to harvest, and bringing in ever more migrant workers and putting in even longer hours isn't going to pay off in a linear way. Sooner or later, you run out of corn.

It wasn't that way in factories or in mines, however. That kind of grunt work had a simple mantra: Work More, Get More. You lived off the sweat of your brow, and the more your brow sweat, the more you got. Even better, getting your employees to work longer hours made you more money—without the sweat (at least not yours).

Understandably, the workers of the world united. They realized that while management got more, they really didn't. Hence, the forty-hour workweek.

Suddenly, in came the new economy, entrepreneurs, freelancers, free agents, speed to market, first-mover advantage, IPOs, and cutthroat competition in a winner-take-all world. The workers got their wish: They got to feel like owners, and all bets were off.

Be careful what you wish for, because you just might get it. Check your e-mail. There are people sending you messages at midnight or at

4:00 A.M. One of my closest friends regularly calls me from work at 9:00 A.M. my time, here in New York, which would be fine, except that she lives in California. The original Macintosh team may have gotten the finest massages and the best catering, but they worked like dogs for more than a year.

One company in Silicon Valley often schedules important strategy meetings at 6:00 P.M. Of course, by that time, most people are running late, so the meetings start at 7:30 or 8:00. That accomplishes a few things: First, only the really dedicated hard-liners show up. The folks who don't really care are at home hanging out with their families, cooking dinner. The true loyalists—at least, according to company culture—are still at work. Second, everyone is tired and punchy, which ensures that crisp, analytical thinking will be in pretty short supply. And third and most important, even the diehards are beginning to think about going home, so there won't be much dissent unless the decision about to be made is really dumb or really important!

Of course, even if you're not at work, you stay in touch. You use your PDA to check your e-mail in a taxi. You make sure that your cell phone has a headset so you can talk while you're driving the family to the Grand Canyon for vacation.

For a while, it seemed as if all of this made sense. It seemed as if working longer hours made your company move faster and that moving faster made your company successful.

Well, now that the NASDAQ has cooled off and we've seen that maybe, just maybe, the new economy does not favor the speed-to-market, first-mover-advantage, IPO, winner-take-all mind-set, it's time to reevaluate this work ethic. But ironically, instead of getting us to challenge the myth of the grindstone, the NASDAQ hiccup has made a lot of people too scared to act smart.

What's smart? The fact is, the companies that made good decisions a year ago or even five years ago are thriving today. Their stock may be down, but the companies are still on course.

Alas, among those that failed to make the right decisions, the strategy is apparently not to step back and start making the best decisions but to work even harder, ignoring the fact that companies may be working hard on the wrong things!

Some folks think that their boss, their boss's boss, or Wall Street wants to hear, "Well, we'll just keep our heads down and work even harder." Wrong! I think the problem is that people are not saying, "We learned from that mistake. Here are the smart decisions that are going to take us where we want to go now."

There's a huge difference between working in a mine or a factory and doing what *you* do for a living. In the old days, people made stuff. *You don't make stuff. You make decisions.*

And the thing about making decisions is that you don't make better decisions when you work longer hours. You don't write better code when you work longer hours. You don't create better business development deals, make better sales pitches, or invent cooler interfaces when you work longer hours either.

Let's face it: The current marathon work culture is nothing but an excuse to avoid making the hard decisions.

Think about the last time you faced a deadline at work. Odds are, you made the deadline—but just barely. Now imagine that the deadline had been one day later. You still would have made the deadline. Your work would have been just as good. And the words "just barely" would still be associated with the project.

It's an old saw, but it's still true in the new economy: Work expands to fill the time allotted for it.

If you allot twelve hours to work every day, you'll spend twelve hours. But are you going to make more decisions? Better decisions?

Let's do a little history exercise. Imagine five success stories from the past decade. Think of companies such as Cisco, Palm, Yahoo!, Starbucks, and JetBlue.

Now list six decisions that each company made that turned it into a success. Are there six things that each one decided to do that transformed it from an ordinary company into an extraordinary success? There might even be fewer than six things.

Everything else these companies did around those decisions is just commentary. Yes, there were important operations happening to make those decisions valid. But those operations weren't the key to those companies' successes. As strategist Gary Hamel says, in the future, business model innovation will be a key success factor.

And it's not just fancy corporate-strategy stuff. Great programmers know that 80 percent of a software project's success or failure is determined by the decisions made during the first four weeks of systems architecture. Get that part right, and you won't be fighting an uphill battle for the rest of the project.

Talk to any truly successful lawyer—the kind with great clients, a great reputation, and plenty of cash. You'll find that the secret of her success isn't pulling an all-nighter the night before a client meeting or a big trial. The secret is understanding the key issues and making decisions about how to act on them. Nobody ever hired a law firm because he was impressed with how well-stapled the memos were.

Now think about your company. Are people so busy implementing, defending, building, and pulling all-nighters that they are short-changing the time that they ought to be spending making decisions?

Take a look at the future. When you write your company's history two years from now, which decisions will have really mattered? What were the key moments that led you to create such a success?

That's what you should spend your time on. Getting those decisions right is far more important than answering your 103rd e-mail or hacking that last piece of code.

At *Reader's Digest* in the 1950s, Lila Wallace used to walk from office to office and say, "It's a beautiful day. Turn off the lights and go home." And it was 4:00—P.M.! Maybe if you left the office once a week at 4:00, the decisions that you would make the next day would be a lot better. Go home. Have dinner with your family. You'll be glad you did.

My recommendation: If your current job environment is one where the only way to avoid getting fired is to work all the time, then hey, get fired. Even under the current regime, the unemployment rate is still less than 6 percent, and if you're smart enough to be reading this book, well, there are plenty of jobs out there that reward you for being smart—not for digging the most coal.

RESPECT AND THE FULLER BRUSH MAN

The Fuller Brush Man knew what he was doing. In the old days, Fuller's door-to-door salesmen learned a basic rule: After you ring the bell, take a step or two backward. That way, the woman of the house won't feel intimidated opening the door for a stranger.

It wasn't just a tactic, though, it was a strategy—one designed to help the company grow by treating people with respect, in contrast to rival salesmen who were taught to jam a foot in the door.

Imagine the Fuller Brush Man trying to make a living today as a telemarketer or a spammer or any of the high-pressure salespeople who jam their electronic feet in people's doors. He'd last about three minutes. He's not selfish enough, not eager enough to steal the customer's time. It's a shame, but in the battle to make our businesses grow, we've forgotten how to respect the people who pay our bills.

We're making those people—our customers—angry. In our race to make as much money as possible, as fast as possible, we have learned to use people and resources as fast as we can. We've lost sight of what it means to treat customers with respect. We also disrespect our shareholders, our employees, and our government—but it's all part of the same problem.

And we're running out of time to do something about it. Ironically, the obsolete tactics of the Fuller Brush Man may be exactly what we need to turn it all around.

The amazing thing is that respect doesn't cost anything. Taking two steps back after you ring the bell isn't just free, it's profitable. Instead of spamming the globe, market to people who *want* to hear from you. It's not just good manners, it's profitable. Everyone wants to be treated with respect—all the time. In fact, when we treat people with respect, they're more likely to do what we want.

Some will tell you that treating people with respect is just an old-fashioned notion. Business ethics may be an oxymoron—is respectful marketing the same? Don't we need to call people at home during dinner or trick them with fine print in order to make a profit? ALL SUITS $299 (AND UP) is what the sign at one clothing store said. And the fine print inside the parentheses was *very* fine. They were tricking you into the store, hoping you'd buy a thousand-dollar suit—by mistake. How does that pay off?

In fact, I believe that the only way to make a long-term profit is by respecting people. There's growing evidence that the old, shortsighted ways of making a profit are becoming less effective. People are fending off marketing assaults with TiVo and Telezappers. More than twelve people a *second* signed up for the Federal Trade Commission's Do Not Call list on its first day. Consumers are voting with their pocketbooks, choosing to visit the retailers that treat them with respect, not avarice.

Some marketers may understand how strip-mining consumer trust is costing them, but most don't want to take two steps back to the good old days. Instead, they're fighting the wrong fights. They're getting ready to sue TiVo, because the device makes it too easy to skip commercials. They're faking the headers on the spam that they send out to get past filters. They're lobbying Congress to stop the Do Not Call list.

But when a business spams, it has made its lack of respect clear. When an airline puts the "gotcha" into the fine print of a full-page ad, it's disrespecting consumers' intelligence. Running a business that can survive only by deception and disrespect is not our right—our right is to realize our dead-end path and pick a better, more respectful business.

I believe that it's all about to come crashing down on slash-and-burn marketers. Consumers (especially the business-to-business buyers) are growing smarter, cagier, and more sophisticated. They won't sit quietly as marketers steal their time and attention and money. Ask yourself a simple question: If all of our customers were well informed, would we do better—or worse? For many companies, the answer is grim. McDonald's was stung when it was caught slipping beef flavoring into its supposedly all-vegetable french fries. And Kmart went bankrupt for the contempt it showed consumers, telling shoppers, "Hey, it's cheap. What do you expect?"

Karl Marx (probably being quoted for the first time ever in a marketing book) asked a simple question. "Who benefits?" This is, I think, the key question. Companies that work to benefit their customers will have no trouble treating the newly picky consumer with respect. It's a natural by-product for marketers who aim to serve. Those who work to trick and coerce their customers, on the other hand, have everything to lose and very little to gain.

RIFTING

After the death of Walt Disney the man, something happened to Walt Disney the company. Walt Disney was a three-time rifter. He was one of the few people who have successfully managed to find a rift in the continuum of life, to bet everything on it, and to make a profit by doing so. And he did it three times.

What's a rift? It's a big tear in the fabric of the rules that we live by. It's a fundamental change in the game, one that creates a bunch of new losers—and a handful of new winners.

Most people who build important businesses build them on a rift, usually one that they find by accident, and usually only once. Sometimes, after they've succeeded once, they fool themselves into thinking that they're so gifted that everywhere they look, they can see a rift. But Disney was different: He really was rift gifted. After all, he found one three times.

First, he noticed early on that movies would change the world of entertainment. Realizing that there would soon be a huge demand for family-oriented entertainment, he pioneered the development of the animated movie, perfecting the form with *Snow White and the Seven Dwarfs* (1937). The film marked the birth of a huge organization that would grow to dominate this new marketplace.

Unlike most folks who are lucky enough to catch a rift at the right moment, Disney didn't just declare himself a genius, collect his stock options, and relax. Nope. He looked for another rift—another change in the rules that he could turn into an opportunity.

That second rift came in the form of the automobile. Disney realized that the car was going to change the way that the American family got its entertainment. He believed that a strategically located, extravagantly designed theme park could reinvent family travel. And he was right. So, beginning with California's Disneyland in 1955, he built another huge organization around this rift—and it has dominated the theme park industry ever since.

Once Disney was into this rift thing, he saw a third opportunity: television. Although many people regarded television simply as in-home movies, or as radio with a screen, Disney saw in it an entirely different medium. So, with properties like the Mickey Mouse Club, he set out to build a third organization, one that would produce a never ending stream of content for this market.

Walt Disney was a three-time winner, someone who saw huge opportunities and who mobilized an entire organization to take advantage of them. Someone who combined clarity of vision with tenacity of purpose. Unfortunately, since Disney's demise, his company hasn't really displayed that same rift-hungry attitude. The motto of most rifters ought to be WWWD: What Would Walt Do? I often wonder what Walt would have done with the Internet. Or with cable TV. Or with home shopping, home video, and DVDs.

Another one of my favorite rifters is Steve Jobs. Jobs is already much celebrated, but several of his successful rifting moments are still worth a look. Here are three:

First, he realized that personal computers could serve as a tool in the home as well as in business, and he was smart enough to find the right people to build the Apple I and II. At the time, there were no headlines about how brilliant Jobs was, but he paved the way for every single desktop computer in existence today.

Jobs's second rift was actually more difficult to catch, because it wasn't an obvious one. Realizing that the graphical user interface that was developed for the Xerox Star could permanently change the way that computers worked, Jobs took a huge risk and introduced the Mac. Most entrepreneurs and virtually every large company would have laughed at the sheer hubris of it: to get lucky once and then to risk it all on a rift as narrow as this! Of course, we know what happened with the graphical user interface.

Jobs's third rift was one that Disney would probably have jumped on. Jobs saw that computers would forever change the way that animated movies are made. And Pixar, the production company behind *Toy Story* and *A Bug's Life*, was his bet on that rift.

The surprising thing is that just about anyone could have caught any of those rifts and built hugely successful companies out of them. Jobs didn't know anyone in Hollywood—and he didn't need to. His success wasn't about connections or reputation or access to capital. In fact, being part of the company that sold the Apple II actually hindered his ability to launch the Mac, because his shareholders and employees fought the idea for years. No, Jobs succeeded because, like all rifters, when he saw an opportunity, he was single-minded in his focus and in his desire to take advantage of it.

My mom was also a rifter, though you've probably never heard of her. She saw and took advantage of two rifts that were probably bigger in scope than even Disney's, albeit more prosaic in execution. First, a few decades ago, she saw that society was not only permitting women to go back to work—but it was also encouraging this behavior. Some women were going back to work because they needed the money; others were doing so because they wanted mental stimulation and social interaction.

Taking advantage of an opportunity that this rift created, my mom started hiring paid and volunteer workers for her nonprofit gift shop at the Albright-Knox Art Gallery, in Buffalo, New York. Her overeducated, underpaid, superdedicated workforce had extremely low turnover, was responsible for essentially no "shrinkage" (internal shoplifting), and displayed astonishing customer service skills.

She was at the forefront of reinventing the way that museums and other institutions staffed and ran their stores. Not content to have a little shop that sold a few postcards each day, owners of such shops turned their businesses into full-fledged, lucrative enterprises.

My mom then foresaw a rift that would change the retail business forever: People were no longer buying things only when they needed them. Instead, they were now shopping for fun. The experiential retail environment—stores that were destinations for people who were bored with TV—became an incredibly profitable phenomenon for almost every nonprofit museum store in the country. By watching for such rifts and then taking advantage of them, my mom was able to fundamentally change the marketing equation for her industry.

Was my mom the first person to notice these two rifts? Not at all! But she was a pioneer in acting on each one. And she did it with confidence and without hesitation.

So why doesn't everyone do this? If Disney and Jobs and my mom can become successful rifters, why can't you and your colleagues do the same? What stops existing companies from grabbing hold of rifts? Why didn't an established coffee company like Maxwell House foresee a rift in the way that adults would spend time and money? (If you don't drink alcohol or it's the middle of the morning, where do you go to hang out?) Why was a start-up called Starbucks able to see that rift? Industry by industry, we're seeing more and more start-ups catching up to—and then destroying—the old-guard market leaders.

Why do companies have to be destroyed before the way that we serve various markets can evolve? Why don't the existing players see a rift when it's right in front of their eyes and jump into it? One reason why companies and individuals hesitate is because they don't know how to zoom. Big, successful companies aren't organized around the concept of change, and they don't reward people who want to change the way that they do business. To them, change is bad, change is evil, change is to be feared. They have enough trouble coping with shift—but rift? Forget about it! You can't just cope when there's a rift. Coping is out of the question. A rift appears out of nowhere and waits for rifters to find it, grab it, and exploit it. And companies that resist zooming and insist on merely coping will always be the last to see and to profit from a rift.

But there's also an underlying architectural problem. Market leaders will always be willing to make incremental changes that please customers, employees, and shareholders. (At the very least, they want to have the support of two out of the three constituencies.) Installing air bags in cars was a smart move on the part of car companies, but it had nothing to do with a rift. Putting Federal Express tracking information on the Net was great for you, me, and the beleaguered operators at FedEx, but it didn't fundamentally change the shipping business.

The problem for established companies is that when faced with a rift, they have to make a choice. They can't please all three constituencies. And, faced with that fact, most companies just say *maybe*. They wait. They hope that the rift will go away quietly. They confidently project that the start-ups that are jumping into the rift are overvalued, overhyped, and sure to fail.

Sometimes the old guard is right: Sometimes a rift isn't a rift at all. But, as Disney and Jobs and my mom demonstrated, if you take advantage of all potential opportunities (and that's exactly what the venture capital community has done with the Internet), you might find a rift—and step into it before someone else does.

A three-step guide to rifting for entrepreneurs, employees, and CEOs:

1. Make sure that it's really a rift—and not just a hiccup. A rift is characterized by a fundamental change in one of the basic rules of the game. You can usually expand the first rip in the fabric by discussing it in hypothetical terms: "What if the transaction cost of auctions became zero?" or "What if everyone had a television?"

2. Answer every objection with "Why?" And repeat that "Why?" until you get to the core of your hesitation. Then you'll know what's really causing the discomfort, and you'll be able to deal with it.

3. Maybe-proof your organization when it comes to rifts. Require someone, anyone, in the company to sign a piece of paper that says, "I heard about this rift from so-and-so, but we're not going to do anything about it, and here's why." Allow people not to sign the paper, but require those people to give the unsigned sheet to their boss, thereby passing the buck—all the way to the president of the company, if necessary. It will only take about a week for the president to become acutely aware of the opportunities that the company is not taking advantage of.

Walt Disney, Steve Jobs, and my mom have shared the secret of rifting. My mom taught me how to rift, and now I'm passing on the secret—no, the responsibility—to you. Go rift!

RIGHT THING, DOING THE

Let's say an influential U.S. senator accuses your database company of having, "an egregious security gap that risks making millions of Americans the unwitting victims of identity theft."

And let's say he shows pictures and data from personalities ranging from Arnold Schwarzenegger to Paris Hilton. Hey, even celebrities are at risk!

Would your response be to issue a written statement saying, "[our] terms of use restricting access go beyond federal law and current industry standards."

What was the meeting that generated that statement like? Do the people at this company really believe that consumers care one bit about "current industry standards" or even "federal law"? Did they think the issue would go away?

And most important, didn't just one person in that meeting say, "Hey, we're people with identities, too. Let's do the right thing. Let's announce that we'll correct the security problem within three weeks?"

RINGTONES

Ringtones, it turns out, are now a sizable portion of all music purchases for certain users. Weirder still, in addition to their willingness to spend money on tones, people are even subscribing to a magazine about them.

It's called *The Ringtone Magazine*.

This is a little jarring on a lot of levels. But it's pretty clear that we're down to buying what we want, not what we need!

RSS

If you're near a computer, put the book down for a second, go over to Google and look up "RSS." Take a few minutes to learn about it. Go ahead. I'll wait.

I think there are two blog/RSS frontiers worth considering, whether you manage a project, a church, or a brand.

The first is the idea of the microblog. Ed Brenegar was asked to help a small group of people understand word of mouth and turned it into a blog. The idea is that you find a tiny (or huge) group that wants to hear from you regularly. Then you use the direct connection that RSS offers and combine it with a blog to drip essential information to people over time. I did the same thing when I produced a musical for an elementary school. I made a blog for the parents to use to keep up with news about the play, with the schedule and photos of each rehearsal.

Blogging doesn't have to mean talking to anonymous strangers.

The second idea is what BasecampHQ.com is doing. This is project management software that uses RSS to alert the people who need to be alerted whenever something is up. They can ignore it the rest of the time.

RSS is like e-mail, except there's no spam, the loop is closed, there's a far wider range of available media, and, best of all, recipients can configure a host of readers to present the info in the way they want to view it. Thinking like this led to podcasting, and it's going to lead us in a bunch of new directions now.

RULES, PLAYING BY THE

Market leaders make up the rules. They establish the systems and the covenants and the benchmarks that a market plays by. And yes, a market leader can be a church, a political party, or a nonprofit.

If you play by those rules, you will almost certainly lose.

After all, that's why market leaders make rules. They establish a game that they can win, over and over again, against smaller or newer competitors.

The alternative is both obvious and scary: Change the rules.

Newcomers and underdogs can only benefit when the rules change. The safe thing to do feels risky, because it involves playing by a fundamentally different set of assumptions. But in fact, dramatically changing the game is the safest thing you can do if you want to grow.

SAFE IS RISKY

I had two brushes with higher education this past week.

The first was at a speech I gave in New York. There were several Harvard Business School students there, invited because of their interest in marketing and exceptional promise (that's what I was told, I think they came because they had heard that Maury Rubin would make a great lunch!).

Anyway, they asked for my advice in finding marketing jobs. When I shared my views (go to a small company, work for the CEO, get a job where you actually get to make mistakes and do something, not just give an opinion) one woman professed to agree with me but then explained, "But those companies don't interview on campus."

Those companies don't interview on campus. Hmmm. She has just spent $100,000 in cash and another $150,000 in opportunity cost to get an M.B.A., but . . .

The second occurred today at Yale. As I drove through the amazingly beautiful campus, I passed the Center for Asian Studies. It reminded me of my days as an undergrad (at a lesser school, natch), browsing through the catalog, realizing I could learn whatever I wanted. Not only could I take classes but I could start a business, organize a protest movement, live in a garret off campus, whatever. It was a tremendous gift, this ability to choose.

Yet most of my classmates refused to choose. Instead, they treated college like an extension of high school. They took the most mainstream courses, did the minimum amount they needed to get an A, tried not to get into trouble with the professor or face the uncertainty of the unknown. They were the ones who spent six hours a day in the library, reading their textbooks.

The best part of college is that you can become whatever you want to become, but most people just do what they think they must.

You've graduated now, but nothing has changed. You have more freedom at work than you think (hey, you're reading this on company time!) but most people do nothing with that freedom but try to get an A.

Do you work with people who are still in high school? Job seekers only willing to interview with the folks who come on campus? Executives who are trying to make their boss happy above all else? It's pretty clear that the thing that's wrong with this system is high school, not the rest of the world.

Cut class. Take a seminar on French literature. Interview off campus. Safe is risky.

SALES

. . . in just one easy step: *Make something people want to buy.*

In 1998, when I first got to Yahoo!, I was excited. All my life I'd been selling media. Sometimes I failed slowly, other times I barely succeeded. I was pretty good at it, if you compared me to everyone else in the field, but it was by no means easy.

The Yahoo! guys were different, though. Where it took my staff and me months or even years to make a million-dollar sale, Yahoo!'s sales force was doing five- or ten-million-dollar deals every week or so. They knew the secret. They were supertalented, highly trained, and very motivated. That's what I figured, watching from the outside in. They were killing us and I wanted to know why.

So, after I sold them my company, I found myself at Yahoo!, playing for the winning team, and I was invited to go along on a sales call. I was vibrating in my shoes with anticipation.

You've probably already guessed the punch line. It was one of the most inept sales presentations I'd ever seen. A lousy PowerPoint. A noncharismatic, nonempathetic salesperson who faced the wall and read the fine print on the slides aloud. At the end of the presentation, he mumbled something about being able to take a check.

A few minutes later, the prospect handed over $4 million.

Yikes!

Sometimes it seems like the very best stuff sells itself. That explains why some car dealerships have waiting lists and sell stuff for a premium, while others look like ghost towns.

Sometimes, salesmanship is overrated. What matters more is real marketing, marketing that involves *making* the right product, not hyping it.

SALINGER KNEW BETTER

Did Holden Caulfield *really* have the adventures and angst the author wrote about? Of course not. There wasn't a Holden Caulfield. *Catcher in the Rye* is a work of fiction.

So what's the difference between fiction and a lie? Is storytelling lying?

I think the distinction we make for ourselves is that novelists don't pretend that they are telling us the truth. They don't set out to deceive because they write novels, which are clearly labeled as fictional. No evil intent, no lie.

Judging from my e-mail and postings I see on blogs here and there, it seems that some people have trouble with the word "liar." "Liar" is a word that makes us angry.

When I wrote *All Marketers Are Liars*, I was trying to make a point about true lies.

Some people (mostly those that haven't bothered to read the book) think I'm telling people to lie and cheat and deceive and abandon what few ethics we've got left. Nope! I'm doing the opposite.

I start by telling you that you *are* telling a story whether you want to or not. You are a novelist, a film director, a fabulist. It's impossible to deliver the entire truth to anyone, ever, so by making choices, you're telling a story. If your blog is well designed, that's part of your story. If your blog is ugly, that's a story, too. Neither story has to do with the words. But you're still telling a story. We as marketers ought to recognize that and start acting accordingly—our competition sure is.

Then I say that telling a story that is inauthentic, inconsistent, hollow, or filled with unstated side effects isn't just wrong, it's stupid. The best lies are true! True in the sense that you don't disappoint the listener when she discovers more facts about what you do.

Any marketer who believes that they are in the business of telling the complete truth about what they do is delusional. You can't. There is not enough time, not enough attention, not enough money.

J. D. Salinger understood this when he wrote fiction. He didn't try to tell the truth. He tried to tell a story that resonated.

Be a true liar. Someone who knows he's in the storytelling business, someone who tells people about his ideas in terms they want to hear. But be someone whose stories hold up under inspection.

SATIN PILLOW, VISUALIZING THE

At the risk of boring you, I thought you might like to read the confirmation note I got from my order from CD Baby (see below) today. A far cry from Amazon's boring confirmation (do you *ever* read yours?).

A little creativity can build your brand in a big way:

Your CDs have been gently taken from our CD Baby shelves with sterilized contamination-free gloves and placed onto a satin pillow.

A team of 50 employees inspected your CDs and polished them to make sure they were in the best possible condition before mailing.

Our packing specialist from Japan lit a candle and a hush fell over the crowd as he put your CDs into the finest gold-lined box that money can buy.

We all had a wonderful celebration afterwards and the whole party marched down the street to the post office where the entire town of Portland waved 'Bon Voyage!' to your package, on its way to you, in our private CD Baby jet on this day, Tuesday, June 18th.

I hope you had a wonderful time shopping at CD Baby. We sure did. Your picture is on our wall as "Customer of the Year." We're all exhausted but can't wait for you to come back to CD-BABY.COM!

SCARCITY, THERE'S A SHORTAGE OF

What's worth more: a pile of gold or a pile of salt? Throughout history, many people have chosen the salt. Gold is pretty, but you can't live without salt, and when it was more scarce than gold, it became valuable enough to use as a currency itself. (The word "salary" is even related to the Latin for "salt.")

Today, of course, salt is close to worthless. Given the choice between a pile of salt and a pile of gold, you'd go for the gold every time, because there's less of it around.

Scarcity, it seems, has a lot to do with value.

Lord knows, we're running out of a lot of important things—clean water, free time, breathable air, the ozone layer, and honest leadership, just to name a few. At the same time, we have to worry about something that is about to affect just about every business I can think of. We're running out of scarcity.

Scarcity, after all, is the cornerstone of our economy. The only way to make a profit is by trading in something that's scarce. This is why the music and film industries are so terrified by the millions of people who download entertainment from the Internet every day. Downloading threatens to make supply virtually unlimited, and that could make the offerings of the music and film giants about as valuable as those of some kids down my street who recently tried to run a stand selling freshly made mud.

It seems as though once a category becomes successful, the headlong rush to copy it is stronger (and quicker) than it ever was before. Last week, a woman who came to a seminar at my office was desperately searching for a way to improve her mortgage brokerage business. I ruined her day when I suggested that she shut her company down and try something else. Twenty years ago, most mortgages were written by the local bank. Those banks planted the seeds of their obsolescence when they eliminated judgment from the writing of mortgages. Once they could automate a mortgage application, so could everyone else. So mortgage brokers used their low overhead and quick wits as an advantage and stole the business. Today, there are an infinite number of brokers to choose from, all offering essentially the same service. The result is that there is no scarcity, and no profit.

It's not just about product knockoffs, of course. While there are almost 500,000 lawyers practicing in the United States today, there are (gasp!) more than 125,000 in school right now. No matter what you believe about lawyers creating ever more work for ever more lawyers, there's no question that, with so many of them, they're hardly scarce.

The same thing is true for doctors, Web sites, T-shirt shops, sushi restaurants, thumbtack manufacturers, and brands of blank CD-ROM disks. There are one hundred major brands of bottled water. Someone opened a fancy ice-cream parlor in Manhattan, and then there were six.

If it's remotely digital (like music), then it's easy to mimic. And if it's easy to mimic, someone else wins if they can replicate the original—the sooner the better. When someone starts to sell exactly what you sell but for half the price, how long does your good-service, first-mover, nice-person advantage last?

Zara, the fast-growing European clothing store, can knock off a new fashion before the original designer even gets it to the upscale department stores. Suddenly, the original appears to be the copy.

So how do you deal with the shortage of scarcity?

Well, the worst strategy is whining—about copyright laws and fair trade and how hard you've worked to get to where you are. Whining is rarely a successful response to anything. Instead, start by acknowledging that most of the profit from your business is going to disappear soon. Unless you have a significant cost advantage (like Amazon or Wal-Mart), someone with nothing to lose is going to be able to offer a similar product for less money.

So what's scarce now? Respect. Honesty. Good judgment. Long-term relationships that lead to trust. None of these things guarantee loyalty in the face of cut-rate competition, though. So to that list I'll add this: an insanely low cost structure based on outsourcing everything except your company's insight into what your customers really want to buy. If the work is boring, let someone else do it faster and cheaper than you ever could. If your products are boring, kill them before your competition does.

Ultimately, what's scarce is that kind of courage—which is exactly what you can bring to the market.

SECRETS TO SUCCESS

If it's not money or brilliant programming, what will characterize the success of tomorrow's Internet?

1. *Relentless execution* This is far and away the winner. Persistence and focus and consistency. We saw how this worked for Amazon and we saw how getting distracted hurt AOL and others. It's far more important today, because markets at rest tend to stay at rest. Changing the market is hard.

2. *Resistance to compromise* Because you can do so much so fast nowadays, and because it's easy for nonexperts to chime in, the temptation is to go for the middle, to compromise, to be all things. It's that Purple Cow thing again . . .

3. *What you don't do* This is a little bit like #2. Go take a look at an Amazon page. From these you can do a Web search, search inside the book, order it new, order it used, and on and on and on. The temptation is to do everything you can do (and it might work for Amazon, but it's probably not going to work for you). The very best new Net companies understand in their heart and soul what they *won't* do.

4. *Desire to be three steps ahead* One step ahead is easy, but one step isn't enough. If you're only one step ahead, you'll get creamed before you launch. Two steps ahead is tempting. Two steps means that everyone understands what you're up to when you pitch it to them. Two steps means that you can get funding in no time. But two steps is a problem, because the really smart guys are three steps ahead. They're the groundbreakers and the pathfinders. They're the ones inventing the next generation. It's harder to sell, harder to build, and harder to get your mother-in-law to understand, but it's what's truly worth building.

5. *Doing something worth doing* Hey, nobody is going to switch to your service because you worked hard on it. Being a little better is worthless.

6. *Connecting people to people* Over and over again, connecting people with one another is what lasts online. Some folks thought it was about technology, but it's not.

7. *Monetizing from the first moment* Google without AdWords is worthless. So Adwords are built into the experience. Google isn't saying, "Hey, we have to do this because otherwise we'll go out of business," they're saying, "This actually makes the service *better.*" Given how cheap most online services are to build and run, you can't charge money if the only reason you're charging is to make a profit. Charging adds friction and selectivity. If those two elements are a drag on your service, you will fail. Hotmail's founders missed this point. Banner ads made Hotmail worse, not better, and because they didn't build useful ads into the service from the start, they never could.

8. *Not depending on a big partner* Sure it would be great if you could be on Yahoo!'s home page every day, or built into Blogger or featured on Fox every night. But it would be great if you won the lottery, too. That's a wish, not a plan.

9. *Ignoring the pundits* Including me. If I'm so smart, why don't I go build your business?

10. *Keeping promises* Even though the Net is here and it's real, that doesn't mean that the laws of business have been suspended forever. And the words "keeping promises" capture the best of what we've learned over the past four hundred years. Do what you say you're going to do and the rest is a lot easier.

SELFISH WIFI, RAZOR BLADES, AND HALLOWEEN

This one has been a long time gestating, but a scaremongering piece in the *New York Times* completely pushed me over the edge. They're trying to frighten people about WiFi connections and how unsafe they are to both the person with a network and the person using it.

As I make my travels through the Northeast, I'm stunned by how many WiFi networks my Mac encounters—and how many of them are password protected. Waiting in the doctor's office, for example, I find five networks. And every one of them is closed.

Why on Earth would someone go to the trouble to do this?

I mean, I'm sitting at an ad agency or a cosmetics firm and their network is closed. I'm standing outside of an office building and there are eighteen networks and all of them are closed. All of them!

It's like having a television on and intentionally putting up blinders so that certain people can't watch. Worse, it's like making an apple pie and putting nose plugs on people who would like to smell it!

Having the WiFi network in your lobby or your waiting room or in the street under your window open to guests will not compromise the security of your files—you need a different sort of security for that. And it won't degrade your Net performance much either (and hey, if it does, you can always turn the password protection on again, cursing me out as you do it). [Note: I'm not a computer security expert, and I'm not making a statement about the risk to your data. What I am saying is that if you're dealing in stuff that's superconfidential—like medical records or which congressman is breaking which law—then you've got no business using a WiFi network anyway.]

And yet here comes the influential *Times* with an urgent warning that all manner of pedophiles, car bombers—hey, even people who do graffiti or spit on the street—are using this major hole in our security networks to do bad deeds. Since the article focuses on the dreaded "data thieves" it's easy to assume that they're stealing data from the networks. *They're not.* They're just hiding from the FBI. But if everyone jumps up and down and starts closing their networks, these data thieves will just take one of their stolen credit cards and go to Starbucks!

There were no razor blades in apples on Halloween when we were growing up. Did you know that? Really, they made it up. Someone should tell the *Times* and its readers that if you want to be anonymous on the Net, you can go to Kinko's or go to Bryant Park or the library. It's certainly not necessary to scare the nation into closing its WiFi hot spots.

SHARP NEEDLE, BIG HAYSTACK

Last month, I posted a bunch of notices looking to hire summer interns. The ads asked people to send in a three-page PDF describing their background and their goals and encouraged applicants to really stand out and make their case.

This, of course, should be the dream opportunity for most job seekers. Instead of being treated as a piece of paper, a list of stats in a dry résumé, here was a chance to actually tell me a little about yourself.

Half the people sent in a résumé. *Just* a résumé.

"Here's my résumé" was the total content of at least 20 percent of the cover notes I got.

Part of this is the result of being beaten down. Most of the system is about following the rules, fitting in and not standing out. But a lot of it, it seems to me, is that people are laboring under a mistaken impression about what works—in life, in seeking a job, and in marketing in general.

Most people, apparently, believe that if they just get their needle sharp enough, it'll magnetically leap out of the haystack and land wherever it belongs. If they don't get a great job or make a great sale or land a terrific date, it might just be because they don't deserve it. So we spend a lot of time sharpening our needles.

Having met some successful people, I can assure you that they didn't get that way by deserving it.

What chance is there that your totally average résumé, describing a totally average academic and work career is going to get you most jobs? "Hey Bill! Check out this average guy with an average academic background and really exceptionally average work experience! Maybe he's cheap!"

Do you hire people that way? Do you choose products that way? If you're driving a Chevy Cavalier and working for the Social Security Administration, perhaps, but those days are long gone.

People ultimately judge only one thing about you: the way the engagement (hiring you, working with you, dating you, using your product or service, learning from you) makes them feel.

So how do you make people feel?

Could you make them feel better? More? Could you create the emotions that they're seeking?

As long as we focus on the commodity, on the sharper needle, we're lost. Why? Because most customers don't carry a magnet. Because the sharpest needle is rarely the one that gets out of the haystack. Instead, buyers are looking for the Free Prize, for that exceptional attribute that's worth talking about. I just polled the four interns sitting here with me. Between them, they speak twelve languages. No, that's not why I hired them. No, we don't need Tagalog in our daily work, but it's a Free Prize. It's one of the many things that made them interesting, that made me feel good about hiring them.

What's your Free Prize?

SHORTCUTS

I did an interview yesterday with a magazine that specializes in marketing. They've got hundreds of thousands of readers, most of them in the direct-mail business.

"How do you build an e-mail marketing list?" the reporter asked. She didn't like the answer. I told her that the first step was to offer something in your e-mail newsletter that people would actually *want* to read. That the second step was to promise people exactly what you intended to give them. And the third step was to create content that was so remarkable that people wanted to share it. I explained that if you take your time and keep your promises, it'll build if it deserves to build.

She wanted to know about shortcuts.

At least three times she asked me what the shortcuts were. How to do it if you were in a hurry. Most important, how to do it if your message wasn't that interesting.

It appears that American marketers still have plenty of time to do it over, but not nearly enough time to do it right.

If there were shortcuts, people smarter than you and me would have found them already. There aren't. Sorry.

SHORT WORDS AND THE KMART SHOPPERS

At the airport the other day, every announcement was preceded with (at full volume), "Attention all personnel." Sometimes, they said it twice.

The thing is, as soon as you start blasting audio, you've already got my attention. Stating that you want my attention not only doesn't get you more of my attention, it gets you *less*.

Not only is "Attention" useless, the word "all" doesn't do us much good either. After all, the entire airport is being broadcast to. And "personnel" is a fancy, bureaucratic word that doesn't mean a thing. Are they saying that they only want paid workers to listen? Paid airport workers?

I bring this up not because you're the twit who made the announcer talk in such an officious way, but because you one day may find yourself in a situation where you're writing a blog or a letter or an e-mail or whatever, and you'll be tempted to fill the space.

Don't.

Short sentences get read.

Not long ones.

While we're at it: short words are better than long ones.

SMALL IS THE BIG NEW

What do you do once you realize the power of small?

It's one thing to say, "Yep, of course, small is the new big." It's quite another to actually do anything about it.

For the last six years, I've had exactly one employee. Me. This has changed my work life in ways that I hadn't predicted. The biggest changes are:

1. The kind of project that's "interesting" is now very different. It doesn't have to be strategic or scalable or profitable enough to feed an entire division. It just has to be interesting or fun or good for my audience.

2. The idea of risk is different as well. I can write an e-book and launch it in some crazy way and just see what happens. I can build a dot-com enterprise with a questionable business model and just see what happens. Because my costs are nothing compared to those of a large organization, there are no boundaries in the way I can approach something (compared to, say, a publisher or a public company or a multinational).

Does this mean that little companies just do little things? Of course not.

What about the solo contractor I met who competes with giants by aggressively outsourcing his design and labor?

What about the architect down the street who tripled his income by leaving a huge firm and only taking on the high-leverage assignments he actually enjoys?

Or the lawyer who left a giant firm, works half as much, and actually enjoys it for the first time?

A dear friend of ours left her housewares sales firm and is now inventing things, getting them built in factories she doesn't own, and selling to retailers who are dying for innovative stuff that feels risky. She doesn't risk anything at all except her time, which is cheap now because she's on her own.

One of the implications of the Long Tail is that you don't know what's going to work. That it's easy to launch stuff, but it's hard to figure out where it's going to land. If you don't have to bet the farm on every launch, you're way more likely to launch more, and more randomly, which vastly increases your odds.

So, what do you do if you buy this idea? Quit.

Quit buying into the machine, the cog theory, the desire to fit in, the bigger-is-better mentality.

Don't grow unless it gives you joy.

Dare your employees to become freelancers instead.

Do it on a weekend until it doesn't scare you quite so much.

It's no longer about access to cash. Now it's about choosing the right model and being remarkable.

SMALL IS THE NEW BIG!

Big used to matter.

Big meant economies of scale. (You never hear about "economies of tiny" do you?)

Years ago, people, usually guys, often ex-marines, wanted to be CEO of a big company. The Fortune 500 is where people went to make a fortune, after all.

Big meant power and profit and growth.

Big meant control over supply and control over markets.

There was a good reason for this. Value was added in ways that suited big organizations. Value was added with efficient manufacturing, widespread distribution, and very large R&D staffs. Value came from hundreds of operators standing by and from nine-figure TV ad budgets. Value came from a huge sales force.

Of course, it's not just big organizations that added value. Big planes were better than small ones, because they were faster and more efficient. Big buildings were better than small ones because they facilitated communications and used downtown land quite efficiently. Bigger computers could handle more simultaneous users.

Get Big Fast was the motto for start-ups, because big companies can go public and find more access to capital and use that capital to get even bigger. Big accounting firms were the place to go to get audited if you were a big company, because a big accounting firm could be trusted. Big law firms were the place to find the right lawyer, because big law firms were a one-stop shop.

And then small happened.

Enron (big) got audited by Andersen (big) and failed (big). The World Trade Center was a terrorist target. Network (big) TV advertising is collapsing so fast you can hear it. American Airlines (big) is getting creamed by JetBlue (think small). Boing Boing (four people) has a readership growing a hundred times faster than the *New Yorker* (hundreds of people).

Big computers are silly. They use lots of power and are not nearly as efficient as properly networked Dell PCs (at least that's what they use at Yahoo! and Google). Big boom boxes are replaced by tiny Ipod Shuffles. (Yeah, I know big-screen TVs are the big thing. An exception that proves the rule.)

I'm writing this on a laptop at a skateboard park that offers free WiFi for parents to surf the Web while they wait around for their kids. They offer free WiFi because the owner wanted to. It took them a few minutes and $50. No big meetings, corporate policies, or feasibility studies. They just did it.

Today, little companies often make more money than big companies. Little churches grow faster than worldwide ones. Little jets are way faster (door to door) than big ones.

Today, Craigslist (eighteen employees) is the fourth most visited site according to some measures. They are partly owned by eBay (more than four thousand employees), which hopes to stay in the same league, traffic-wise. They're certainly not growing nearly as fast.

Small means that the founder is involved in a far greater percentage of customer interactions. Small means the founder is close to the decisions that matter and can make them quickly.

Small is the new big because small gives you the flexibility to change your business model when your competition changes theirs.

Small means you can tell the truth on your blog.

Small means that you can answer e-mail from your customers.

Small means that you will outsource the boring, low-impact stuff like manufacturing and shipping and billing and packing to others while you keep all the power because you invent something that's remarkable and tell your story to people who want to hear it.

A small law firm or accounting firm or ad agency is succeeding because they're good, not because they're big. So smart, small companies are happy to hire them.

A small restaurant has an owner who greets you by name.

A small venture fund doesn't have to fund big, bad ideas in order to put their capital to work. They can make small investments in tiny companies with good ideas.

A small church has a minister with the time to visit you in the hospital when you're sick.

Is it better to be the head of Craigslist or the head of UPS?

Small is the new big *only* when the person running the small thinks big.

Don't wait. Get small. Think big.

SOCKS

I love this Web site: LittleMissmatch.com

They sell mismatched socks for eleven-year-old girls. Hundreds of varieties, four categories so you don't clash. Only sold in odd lots. You can't buy a pair. There are 133 styles, and none of them match.

Think about how easy this was to do, and how remarkable it is. Think about how many sock marketers thought of this and then got scared and didn't go for it. Realize how turning socks into a remarkable collectible is both obvious and satisfying and likely to succeed.

I wish they came in my size.

But why should you care about socks? After all, you make something serious, you sell to big business, you have a factory, you deal in intangibles.

That's exactly why you *should* care. Socks used to be a low-margin, low-interest commodity. Littlemissmatch.com changes that by creating a fashion. Why, precisely, can't you?

SODA (THEY EVEN MAKE MASHED-POTATO FLAVOR)

"The reality is that consumers don't need our stuff," says Peter van Stolk, founder, president and CEO of Jones Soda, in a transcript of an interview with Ryan Underwood posted on *Fast Company*'s Web site. He says that's the one simple insight that made him a better marketer. As he puts it: "You're not listening to your customer when you tell them, 'You need me.' You listen to your customers when you say, 'You really don't need me.'"

SOUVENIRS—REAL COMPARED TO WHAT?

I wasn't there at the Montreux Jazz Festival in 1969. I wish I had been.

Eddie Harris and Les McCann walked onto the stage and, though they had hardly rehearsed at all, launched into an ad-libbed song that made history. Ironically enough, the song contained the line, "Real . . . compared to what?"

The vinyl souvenir of that live performance is a million-selling classic. Buy a copy if you can: *Les McCann and Eddie Harris—Swiss Movement: Montreux*. Listening to the vinyl LP isn't the same as attending the original concert, but it's convenient and sounds great.

Twenty years later, "perfect sound forever" brought us the CD version. There are no pops and crackles, but to my ears, it's just a reminder of the depth of the LP.

Then they had us move everything to MP3 format. Now I've got the CD version ripped on my iPod. There are far fewer bits of data (and quality) and it doesn't sound as good, but it reminds me of the original ("original" meaning the analog recording, not the live event, where I wasn't).

Now, I've got a Monster cable for my car that lets me broadcast the MP3 version of the CD version of the vinyl version of the live event over the FM airwaves to my car radio. It sounds like Eddie's in the Holland Tunnel. And it's not even close to music, but it reminds me of the way I felt when I heard the album.

This is not only happening to music. The cell phone conversation I have with my friend Jonathan has content, but the tone and tenor of his voice merely remind me of the way I feel when I hear him live.

And the millions of digital photos I see online don't look anything like the original high-resolution versions, which, of course, look nothing like their real-life subjects.

My dad used to tell me a joke. This guy is on a tour of the state prison with the warden. They walk into the lunchroom and see the following:

A prisoner stands up. He says, "142!"

Everyone laughs hysterically.

Another prisoner stands up. He is giggling, but manages to blurt out, "884."

The place rocks with laughter.

The tourist can't figure out what's going on. He asks the warden.

"Well, you see, these guys are all here for life sentences. They've heard every joke a million times. So, instead of retelling the jokes, they just call out the number."

"Wow," the tourist says. "Can I try that?"

The warden is dubious, but says, "Sure."

"191!" cries the tourist. The place is dead quiet. Like a tomb.

Humiliated, the tourist turns to the warden and asks what he did wrong.

"It's the way you tell it," says the warden with a wry smile.

I wonder what happens when our digital culture has nothing to do but spread pale imitations of the original experiences? I wonder what happens when the media companies that depend on our attention start losing it when all we've got is ringtones.

I think my books change a lot more minds than my blog does. But books don't spread the way digital ideas do.

It's not just traditional media, either. An e-mail doesn't communicate as much information as a meeting, and a voice mail is really hard to file. A PowerBar may have plenty of vitamins and stuff, but it's just not as good as a real meal, is it?

This phenomenon creates a big opportunity. The opportunity to provide sensory richness, to deliver experiences that don't pale in comparison to the old stuff. It's not just baby-boomer nostalgia (though that helps)—it's a human desire for texture.

At the same time, the good news from sites like JamBase.com is that they're using inherently low-resolution digital media to sell people on showing up to hear the highest-resolution live stuff.

Are you in the souvenir business?

SOY LUCK CLUB

The Soy Luck Club, my favorite place in New York, just announced the breakfast club. Pay $40 or so and you get breakfast every day for a month. "Grab and Go," it's called. If Vivian sells one hundred memberships, it's a home run. With $4000, she can certainly buy a lot of whole-wheat bagels and grapefruit, and she ends up creating a cadre of superloyal customers. Best of all, she starts *finding products for her customers instead of finding customers for her products.*

Imagine a new chain of cafés that offers a coffee club. For a flat fee, you get all the WiFi and lattes you can handle. With the markup on both, the owner does great, and people would feel terrible every time they strayed.

They say to ignore sunk costs. People are terrible at that, though.

SPECTRUM—IS IT OURS OR THEIRS?

Stop me if you've heard this before, but the Internet keeps bringing this pair of issues to our attention, and they seem to go together more and more often.

Sinclair Broadcasting tried to use the spectrum (our spectrum) to broadcast political messages through its company-owned stations. Once again, regardless of our politics, I think we need to ask the following question:

"Whose spectrum is it?"

Computers have completely reinvented what we can do with a slice of spectrum. In the bandwidth your local CBS affiliate uses, we could easily broadcast dozens of channels of digital information. We could create free Internet access around the country. But it sits there, untapped, because the FCC licensed that spectrum years ago. Just because someone has built a business around it, should it stay that way?

What if we decided to use the spectrum in ways that benefited everyone, not just media companies? For example, why not require that anyone broadcasting on the public airwaves devote one hour every night in prime time to public-interest programming and commercials? With that much inventory, the cost of running for president could be driven close to zero (all your media buys would be free).

Which brings us around again to the issue of copyright, which always manages to get me in trouble. Whose copyright is it? What's it for?

Why not have patents last a hundred years? They don't because we know that allowing a patent to go into the public domain makes it far easier for society to benefit. Other inventions can be based on that first idea.

So why not make copyrights last for five years, not one hundred? A five-year copyright would not dramatically decrease the incentive to make a movie or write a book, would it? Looking at my book sales, I can tell you that the vast majority of sales come in the first five years. Sure, Harper Lee would get hurt in the long run, but would that have kept her from writing *To Kill a Mockingbird*?

The purpose of copyright is simple: to encourage people to make stuff worth looking at and using. Not to protect the people who have already created something. And *certainly* not to protect the companies that market movies or publish books.

Both cases are the same: Our spectrum and our access to ideas are being held hostage by big companies who are dependent on the status quo. The ability of our culture to quickly evolve ideas and then to broadcast them to ever larger audiences is a fundamental building block of our success. *Why do 98 percent of us sit by idly while big companies that don't care about us legislate against our interests?*

STAGNATION

They want to make the supermarket near my house better. They plan to add free parking for all the people who want to shop in the village (where there is no free parking). They want to add more fresh produce and organic foods, as well as an enhanced deli/prepared-food section. They also want to take over an unused lot where a car dealership has stood abandoned for years, and eliminate a little-used street that messes up the traffic.

The town is up in arms!

There are petitions everywhere. People are outraged. Shocked. It'll ruin everything.

It seems as though it's easy to be against change.

There's a toxic waste dump in my town, crowned by an old, rusting, abandoned water tower. There's actually a committee to protect the water tower, claiming that it signifies an important part of our (toxic) heritage.

One more: New York State fought for years (and spent millions on legal work) to hang on to a law that is patently ridiculous—that only in-state wineries could sell online and by mail. Somehow, I guess, the in-state wineries would avoid selling to minors, but not the ones from, say, California.

The day after the U.S. Supreme Court overturned the law, our esteemed governor said that he was in favor of changing it anyway. No big deal. The world did not end.

Why is it so easy to protect the status quo, even when the status quo isn't so great?

It has to do with a discontinuity on the curve of gain and loss. Think about it this way:

How much would you pay for an extremely unlikely chance to win $100 million? Odds of a billion to one. My guess is you'd be willing to pay a token amount. Probably a dollar. They call it a lottery ticket.

Now, how much would you *sell* a long shot for (with odds in your favor—a hundred billion to one), where if a certain number came up, you'd have to give away every single item you owned?

Figure you'd lose $1 million worth of assets. Now, before you answer, remember that the amount you'd lose is just 1 percent of what you were willing to *pay* a dollar to win. The rational mathematical answer is no more than one penny. Of course, no one would sell this ticket for a penny. Most people wouldn't sell it for $1000. Take $1000 for a hundred-billion-to-one shot you'll go bankrupt? No way.

The fear of loss is far greater than the desire for gain. Unless it's carefully hidden inside a story, that's the way we feel. We're humans, not Vulcans.

If I ran the Stop & Shop supermarket near my house, I'd bluff. I'd pull bulldozers and wrecking balls into town and tell everyone I was going to demolish my no-longer-profitable store and then leave the parking lot filled with bricks so no one could park there and jog over to the wine store while using my parking lot.

The outrage would be so profound I'd have no trouble at all selling the town on a small upgrade.

All change isn't good. Not at all. But the irrational opposition to change is less good. Marketing is all about making changes. More often than not, a good way to sell change is not with the promise of gain. It's with the fear of loss. Sad but true.

START NOW—HURRY!

Sometimes it seems as though the rank and file gets nothing but the short end of whatever stick is available. Whether it's layoffs or excessive pay for senior management, the hardworking folks at the bottom end up with the shaft.

I had lunch last week with my old friend Jim. I hadn't seen him in two years, and it was a great chance to catch up. The food was great. The rest of lunch was pretty dismal.

Jim works for a big New York conglomerate. He's fifty years old, and he's got another twenty-five years of good work left in him. And he hates his job. He's stuck. He's doing exactly what he was doing the last time we had lunch. He spends most days thinking about how long it'll be before he can afford to retire—a number that, thanks to the stock market meltdown, just got a lot bigger.

Five years ago, Jim had a dream job, the sort we all envied, the kind we saw profiled in one magazine after another. Now, that very same job feels like a trap.

The big lie of the new economy is that everyone can live the life of an entrepreneur without actually becoming one.

We bought the idea that all the good stuff that people look for from an organization—job security, benefits, vacations, the safety of being able to blame your boss when things don't go well—could be accompanied by the rush of fast growth and the heady feeling we get when the bureaucracy gets out of the way and we get to discover what we can really accomplish.

We lionized the twenty-eight-year-olds who were pioneering new products or launching new divisions. We envied the lucky (but not particularly skilled or risk-taking) middle managers who made a fortune with stock options. We called ourselves "intrepreneurs," smiling because we were getting the best of both worlds.

Wrong. Very wrong. Because we missed two big ideas.

The first idea is that big companies are fundamentally broken. *Big companies are big companies because they're very good at doing yesterday's business.* They can make (and sell) their stuff faster and cheaper than the competition because they've gotten good at making and selling their existing products.

The problem is that when the world changes (and it is changing faster than ever) being good at yesterday's business isn't just useless, it's a liability. All those big companies are sweating now, because the infrastructure they built is about as useful as the Maginot Line—it's obsolete. Penguins like cold weather. When it gets warm, they're stuck. The finely tuned machinery they developed for one environment won't work so well in a new environment.

The second idea is that the stock market has been broken for just as long. The stock market is a huge mass-psychology scam, dependent on the fiction that there will always be someone more stupid than you, willing to buy those shares for more than you just paid.

A key part of this scam is investors' embracing the idea that big companies with predictable earnings are likely to continue to grow and thrive. This used to be true, of course, but in a chaotic world, it's proven wrong every single day.

The bottoming out that we're living through is a direct consequence of these two ideas becoming very clear to us at precisely the same time. Big companies can't keep growing forever at 20 percent a year perfecting yesterday's business, but the stock market didn't want to hear about that. So the big companies, with the direct encouragement of the accounting firms, lied about their results (yeah, "lied" is a strong word, but that's what it's called when you don't tell the truth).

All along, while we were giddy at the huge expansion we all enjoyed, we were missing the real point. And now we're paying for it.

The other day, I took my son to see Steve Jobs give his annual keynote at the MacWorld Expo in New York. He sat transfixed for hours, amazed at the energy and insight and enthusiasm Steve brought to the podium. I mean, Steve was acting like he owned the place.

Of course, he *does* own the place. And that's the most important lesson I think we can take away from the tumult of the last few years.

Apple introduces great products on a regular schedule. Contrast the magic of the iPod or dot Mac or Final Cut Pro with the sheer banality of most of what passes for innovation in big business. Other technology companies introduce services they expect to become profitable monopolies. Apple introduces things they're proud of.

Steve isn't trying to make the stock price go up. He's not trying to keep his current infrastructure busy or please his dealers. He's making stuff he believes in. He's continuing the legend. It's the happy coincidence of his ego and our wants.

Of course, that's only true when it's true. The rest of the time, Apple makes products that fail, that don't excite, that don't make a profit. For almost thirty years, though, there have been just enough wins to pay for the losses. He's a hero. A model for millions.

What if everyone had guts like that? What if everyone reading this chapter realized that the point of our careers (two thousand hours a year, fifty years in a row—that's a hundred thousand hours of work) isn't to crank out yet another widget? *What if, just maybe, we quit making stuff and started making a difference?*

The giant secret of the new economy was this: Entrepreneurs momentarily got a free (and fast) ride to wealth via the stock market. That connection is temporarily over, but the basic idea behind entrepreneurship is stronger than ever. In a time of rapid change, the best organizations are small and fast, and the people who run them have a chance to make an impact that will last.

It's not a coincidence that one of the by-products of the technological revolution is the death of the factory. With all the publicly available infrastructure (from cell phones to e-mail to Kinko's to outsourcing in Thailand) there's really no reason at all to build a big company anymore. And since big companies are no more profitable than little ones, it's the little ones that are most likely to spring up, make a difference, and then (without tears) disappear, only to reappear at some other time, in some other place.

This is hard to swallow for a lot of people. We grew up with parents who read *Time* or *Forbes*, not *Inc.* Our role models weren't crazed entrepreneurs, on a mission from god to accomplish something or go bust trying. We don't see ourselves wearing those shoes. Why can't the world just settle down and let us get some rest?

Alas, the world isn't going to settle down. The desire for safety is understandable, but it's being overwhelmed by Moore's law, by globalization, by competitive desire. I'm sorry if you've made it two-thirds of the way to retirement but, alas, the world got crazy on us.

The dot-coms that failed in a big way all had one thing in common—they tried to use money to insulate themselves from external change. They tried to buy success, to buy bigness, to buy stability. You can't do this, no matter how big you are.

As long as you work for someone, you have no job security. As long as your company is public, your future is in the hands of others—people who are likely not as smart as you are. And as long as you follow the instructions of others, you won't be fulfilling your destiny of really and truly making a difference in the way people live and work.

How much time do you spend every day worrying about how fulfilled and happy the CEO is? How much do you invest to be sure she's got a secure job? Big news: Your CEO spends precisely the same amount of time worrying about you.

I want you to do something for yourself. I'm begging you. It'll only take a few minutes, but I think you might enjoy it.

Imagine for a second that you just lost your job. Further, imagine that the industry in which you've been trained and are working has just disappeared.

What are you going to do? Are you going to go out and look for another job? A job at an Enron or a WorldCom? Or at a big bureaucracy with one hundred people working in accounts payable and a budget of several million dollars a year for strategy consultants?

What if there were no choice? What if you had to start something? Anything. What would it be?

You don't need a good idea to start a business—you can steal one. Find someone in another town, another state, another industry—and do what they're doing. Once you get started, your original idea is going to be replaced anyway. Smart entrepreneurs don't stick to the original business plan. You'll realize that every day is another day closer to success, and changing the plan is part of the plan.

The best part of this exercise comes when you realize that you are smart enough, motivated enough, and focused enough to actually do this. Once you decide that you could actually run the place, you'll realize that no other option is as satisfying.

Quit your job. Right now.* Stop doing something that's crazy, risky, and ill considered (your current job is all three). Stop working for the factory and start building something that people will remember.

---

*Actually, you don't have to quit right now. You could just *decide* to quit right now. One of the best parts of the infrastructure-free economy is that you can start in your spare time. Hey, it worked for eBay.

Here's the crux of the matter: Organizations where the people doing the work are the very same people who are making the decisions are more likely to succeed in the long run. Just about all the sins of American business (from environmental despoliation to accounting fraud) can be pinned on the anonymous bureaucracy. Entrepreneurs can't be anonymous—it's your decision, your policy, your work, your business—and so you're fast and honest, or you're out. There's nowhere else to pass the buck.

Is it scary? Well, just for a second, consider the alternative. You could work for Motorola or Adelphia or even AT&T, always wondering when the company is going to downsize at the same time that you are busy doing whatever the boss asked just to be sure you'll be the last to get fired.

Sounds to me like running a tiny business is totally safe in comparison.

SUBSCRIPTIONS

It's hard to imagine standing at a cocktail party and answering the question, "So, what do you do for a living?" with, "Well, I trick people into giving me money."

I just switched some domain names from register.com to another domain registry service. The guys at Register have raised subtle duplicity to a high art. After you notify them that you want to change companies, they send you a note to confirm the switch. This, of course, is a fine security move.

The note begins with several paragraphs about how great their services are, and then has a link. It appears that this might be the link to authorize the change, but it's not. In fact, it's the link to *deny* the change! Read a few more paragraphs down, and there's the authorization link. Click it within a few days or it becomes invalid.

Once you click on the link, it appears that you're done. But if you stop now, the change won't get authorized. You must now check a box on the new screen. And *then* you must click "confirm." It's easy to imagine that you're done now, and you'll close the window. But if you do, they will still deny the change.

You must go to yet another screen and once again confirm the change (that's four clicks and three screens when one click would have been sufficient).

As subscriptions, ship-till-I-tell-you-to-stop, and other business models enter the online arena (where the profit margin can be 100 percent), we're going to see a lot more of this, I'm afraid. Almost fifteen years ago, when I first did an online project for Prodigy, I was told that Prodigy's best customer was someone who paid the $10 monthly fee but never used the service. If someone *forgot* that they had signed up for Prodigy with their credit card, it might take years before they noticed the billing. While that may have seemed like the right strategy at the time, it's pretty clear that it wasn't much of a long-term strategy.

I'm the biggest fan in the world of the milkman's return. The idea of subscriptions that save time and money for both parties is a no-brainer way to run a business. People love home delivery. But if you have to trick people into doing business with you, it's not much of a strategy, is it?

TALKING RABBIT . . . SO, A RABBI, A PRIEST, AND A

Do you feel a joke coming on?

We've been taught where to look for jokes. Certain places and times feel joke-friendly, and we're alert and aware of what's coming.

The Web is changing the vernacular daily, and I discovered this firsthand with my vacation e-mail memo from last week.

Here's an excerpt:

If you need to find me, I'll be at the UN for a few days, working on the oil for food scandal. You can reach me at the UN at 212 355 4165. Then I'll be in Beijing, consulting with the government on how they can more effectively do the messaging for the upcoming Olympics. I believe that their mascot is sending exactly the wrong message, and hope to persuade them to start using a cow.

I'll be ending the week at the Beverly Hills Hilton in California (a bungalow, just ask for me at the desk). It turns out that Steven has a bit of writer's block on a project and he asked me to stop by and help out.

I thought it was a pretty funny spoof of the self-important (okay, egomaniacal) vacation posts some people have been using. No, I didn't go to China, I went to Costa Rica (more on this soon). I was surprised, though, to discover that a whole bunch of people thought I was serious.

Now, that could be because some of my correspondents have such high regard for me that they figured I really was working with Kofi Annan at the UN, but more likely it's because we just assume that e-mail vacation notices are true. Same thing happens with phishing when hackers use e-mail to steal passwords.

What else are we assuming is true, and when it might be a joke, or an opinion, or a fraud?

TECHNORATI

Do you care what other people think? If you could place hidden microphones in the dressing room of your store or the lobby of your restaurant, would you want to know what people are saying?

Head on over to Technorati and type in the name of your brand or your book or even your name. Instantly, you'll see what millions of blogs are saying. Organized eavesdropping.

Are you doing this for your products? Your issues?

No, the blogosphere isn't always right (it's only right when it agrees with you, of course). But there's so much feedback, and much of it is in great detail. Technorati announced today that they just added blog number 30,000,000 to the pile. You can filter out the junk and you'll still be left with relevant insights that you can take action on.

A friend who is a senior business development person at one of the big TV networks was delighted when I told her about the ability to turn the megaphone backward. It's worth a look.

TELEVISION IS THE NEW NORMAL

Early one morning, I'm doing my workout at the awful Marriott outside of the Minneapolis airport. Since the room is blissfully empty, I turn off the two TV sets (different channels, both blaring) and start my workout.

Fifteen minutes into it, a silver-haired executive-looking (how you do that in a T-shirt is anybody's guess) guy walks in, walks right by me, reaches up, and turns on CNN before he gets on the treadmill.

Try to imagine the opposite. You walk in while someone is watching CNN and turn it off without asking. Never happen.

It's clear to me that the media onslaught is the default. We're so used to having the white noise of TV and the Web that not only can't we live without it, we assume no one else can either. What's also clear is nobody really *watches* it anymore (especially the commercials). It's just there.

I remember how special a TV show (any TV show) was in 1966 when I first started watching TV seriously. How everyone remembered every commercial and we all watched the same shows. I still remember some *Batman* episodes like I saw them yesterday. But I have no idea what CNN broadcast yesterday in the gym.

Last thought on this topic: In one study, more than 80 percent of the people with a TiVo digital video recorder admitted that they skip every single commercial.

THEY DON'T CARE, THEY DON'T HAVE TO

I don't like traveling.

That said, my trip the other day set a new record. I chalk it up to the new "we don't care, we don't have to" economy. In many segments, so much profit has been squeezed out that there's no room to hire and train great people. And there's not enough competition to harm the uncaring industry leaders.

I get to JFK with plenty of time. Good thing, too, because the parking lot next to the terminal is closed. The signs are optimistic, though, and point you to the relocated short-term parking. Same crazy pricing, of course.

Well, it turns out that it takes half an hour on the bus to get from the parking lot to the terminal. They have half as many buses as they need, and at $24 a day, it's not because they can't afford it. It's because they don't have to care.

Finally I get to American, an airline that gave up a long, long time ago. The line for security is thirty people long. But wait! There's a sign that says, BUSINESS CLASS, GOLD, PLATINUM, ETC. I walk over to the sign. The harried woman checking boarding passes says, "Go to the end of the line."

"But there's a sign."

"I know there's a sign. We ignore that."

As I stand in line for ten minutes, I watch this act repeated with no less than ten people. It never occurs to the TSA or to American to take down the sign. They don't care. They don't have to.

I get on the plane. It hasn't been refurbished in a decade or more. The seats are creaky. The flight costs more than ten times as much as JetBlue, but nothing about it is remarkable in any way. The amazing thing is that I recognize the staff from past flights. Good people.

People capable of trying. But they don't care anymore, because management gave up a long time ago.

I get to the Avis counter at SFO. The two women behind the counter have no other customers. I am not making this up—they literally are cackling with glee when my paperwork is messed up. The best thing that happened to them all day. And then when I present my credit (not debit) card, they cackle that they don't take debit cards, and engage me in a spirited debate about whether or not it is a debit card after all. *They don't care, they don't have to.*

THINKING BIG

I just finished giving a talk to a group of four hundred high-powered (high-leverage, high-paid) credit card execs. As I left the hotel, I passed a much smaller room, where a seminar for local CPAs was going on.

The snacks didn't seem as good. The booklets weren't that interesting either. But what occurred to me is that the folks in the second room were just as smart and just as talented as the execs in the first room.

The first group was enjoying the benefits of aiming high. They didn't get these jobs because they were smarter or had better connections or had gone to Harvard. No, they were starting with the same raw materials as the group in the second room. The difference, I think, was that a long time ago, the people in the second room had made a decision about what they deserved, or what they were capable of, or what they were going to stick with. And it was a bad decision.

No, not everyone should be a bank executive. But no one who aspires to be a bank executive should sell themselves short because of a decision they made a long time ago. In a world where the past matters a lot less than it ever did before, where it's easier than it ever was to hit the reset button, it's sad to see someone choosing to be stuck. So if you want to, switch.

Hey, the snacks are better.

TORCHBEARERS

I've never been a big fan of the Olympics. To me, most of the pageantry is hackneyed and off-putting—and I've never forgiven them for not including Ultimate Frisbee as a sport. Most of all, what's the deal with curling?

But one part of the Olympics that fascinates me is the torch relay that kicks off the event. Apparently a riff on some legend from ancient Rome (or ancient Greece, I can never remember), the torch relay involves carrying a single flame from one spot to another—preferably a spot that's pretty far away.

Unlike every other moment of the Olympics, this one focuses all of our attention on a single person, a single detail. No multiple-event, three-ring circus here. It's one runner, one flame. If the torch-bearer falls, it's a big deal. If she doesn't make it to the next runner, she lets down everyone ahead of her in line, as well as all of the runners who carried the torch before her.

When people in the workplace confront change and all of the other challenges that make up business life, there is one thread that runs through all of the choices that they make: Either they're torch-bearers, or they're not.

Over the past few months, I've spent some time working with friends at one of the biggest Internet venture firms on the East Coast. Entrepreneurs think that the selection process used by venture capitalists is a big mystery. They're dying to know how venture capital firms decide who gets the big bucks and who gets nothing. The answer is surprisingly simple.

When venture capital firms look for entrepreneurs on whom to risk their money, they aren't searching for a great idea, or even great credentials. No, what they're searching for is this: the certainty that the person who brings them a business idea is going to carry the torch for that idea as long as it takes, that the idea will get passed on, and that the business will make it across the finish line.

The really great start-up companies in Silicon Valley, the ones that overcome every obstacle and manage to press on, even when it looks as if they're going to fail, are run by torchbearers. If there is one thing that separates Silicon Valley from almost any other place I've been, it's not the technology, the traffic jams, or the lack of a decent Italian restaurant—it's the culture. The place is teeming with torchbearers, with folks who are willing to take responsibility for carrying a flame.

As more and more of us emigrate to Free Agent Nation, a place where people are their own chief executives, the trend toward rewarding torchbearers will only increase. The biggest chasm in our society has become the gap between people who embrace the torchbearer's responsibility to customers, investors, and companies, and those who are just there for the job.

A lot of folks I talk to speak wistfully about what they would do if they were "in charge." I've got news for them: If they're *willing* to be in charge, people will put them in charge! In my view, the huge rewards that we're seeing for people who are brave enough, crazy enough, and talented enough to carry the torch for a new business are entirely justified. Why? Because there aren't nearly enough torchbearers around.

During the last decade, more money was spent to fund new business ventures than in any other century in the history of the world. Yet a huge amount of money sat uninvested, because there was no place to invest it. Are we really out of good ideas? No way. I've got a file cabinet filled with them, and you probably know of a few as well. Is there a shortage of engineers who are capable of implementing those ideas? Nope. There are plenty of engineers, too.

So, if it's not a lack of money, ideas, or engineers that is slowing down our shift to the new economy, what is it? Exactly the same thing that's holding up your company's transition to a new way of doing business—the absence of someone who is willing to stand up, look everyone in the eye, and say, "I'll make it happen."

Here's how I know that I'm talking to a torchbearer:

First, torchbearers don't make excuses. Our current economic good times won't last forever. At some point, the venture capital funds will dry up. And when those tough times come, they will present a perfect opportunity for the phonies to fold their tents. Filled with vitriol and busy looking for a lawyer so that they can sue someone, these entrepreneurial also-rans will find a way to blame their troubles on other people. Real torchbearers run uphill with the same grace and style that they bring to gliding downhill.

Second, torchbearers often attract a crowd. People are fascinated by individuals who are willing to carry responsibility. All too often, people add their own burdens to those that their leader must already carry—but, in any case, they're usually delighted to follow along. And sometimes these folks are loyal and hardworking enough to follow a torchbearer uphill as well as downhill.

Third, most torchbearers don't realize how unique they are, how powerful their role is, or how difficult their task is. Even though they could make outrageous demands and insist on all kinds of special treatment, most of them are happy just to handle their task.

Fourth, torchbearers often care more about forward motion than they do about which route to take. You won't find them tied up in endless strategy meetings, looking for the perfect solutions. Instead, you'll find them out on the road, picking their way through boulders and weeds—moving, moving, moving, because they realize that moving is often the best way to get where they're going.

Fifth, and most important, real torchbearers don't stop until they finish. In the life of any torchbearer, there's a balance between devotion to duty and the pursuit of joy. A torchbearer never forgets about or shortchanges a duty, even when that means postponing joy.

Are you a torchbearer? Probably. The challenge is to find the right project, the right challenge, the right moment—and then to do it. Once you've shown that you can do that, the world will beat a path to your door.

TRADITION!

Last week, the family went to see a Broadway musical.

As occasionally happens, the star didn't show up. An understudy took his place, and there was a slip of paper in the Playbill informing the audience that a second-string actor would be appearing.

The lights went down, the orchestra started, the curtain went up. A few extras wandered onto the stage. Then the main character appeared.

The audience applauded.

Why?

Why was the audience applauding for the understudy? Virtually everyone in the audience knew that the big star wasn't there.

I'm sure that in the old days, when Gene Kelly or Audrey Hepburn appeared onstage, there was the gasp of recognition and the gratitude the audience felt that a big star had chosen to spend valuable time with us, the audience. So the applause is a natural by-product of that emotion.

Here, though, was an actor we hadn't paid to see, an actor who was sure to do his best, but he hadn't done a thing for us.

So why applaud?

Tradition!

There are too many choices in our lives. Too many brands of soft drink, too many kinds of cell phone, too many ways to fly from New York to LA. There are too many social choices as well—when to clap, how to say hello, what sort of greeting to leave on your cell phone.

As a result, more often than not, we resort to tradition. We do what we've always done because it's safer and easier.

You should care about this.

You should care if you're marketing an idea or a product that requires people to upset an existing tradition. Changing the way we do things (whether it's the design of a bicycle or the structure of the electoral college) is hard indeed. Realizing that being better is not *nearly* enough helps you understand the magnitude of your marketing challenge. In fact, traditions rarely change quickly just because the alternatives are better. True story: Walking down Newbury Street in Boston on Friday, less than a block from about twenty great and cheap restaurants, I heard one tourist say to another tourist, "Well, we could have lunch at Burger King." Why? Tradition!

Should you care that every single voice mail greeting says, "Hi, you've reached Karen's voice mail. Please leave a message at the tone"? I think by now you know what to do, but still you get instructions every time.

You should also care if you're trying to build something big and important. Because big and important things often come from changing the tradition. And if you can invent a new tradition, a new tradition around your innovation, that's when you win big.

L'chaim.

TRUST AND RESPECT, COURAGE AND LEADERSHIP

What would happen if your friends and colleagues treated you the way marketers do?

What if your spouse sold your personal information to anyone who would pay for it? If your boss promised you miraculous changes and then failed to deliver? If your co-workers refused to talk to you unless you spent half an hour on hold first?

What if the people you liked and trusted made promises to you in order to get your attention and cooperation, and then broke those promises whenever they could get away with it?

Most of us wouldn't choose to work with people who disrespect us as much as marketers do. Most of us wouldn't choose a career where everything we interact with is prettied up and dumbed down.

Why do we hate marketers so much?

We don't just hate them. We ignore them. We distrust them. In fact, when a marketer actually keeps his promise to us, we're so surprised we go and tell everyone we know.

I got a call yesterday from a company that wanted to "confirm my order." When I returned the call, I discovered that there was no confirming . . . it was just a come-on from a company I had never heard of to sell me something new.

Somewhere along the way, marketers stopped acting like real people. We substituted a new set of ethics, one built around "buyer beware" and the letter of the law. Marketers, in order to succeed in a competitive marketplace, decided to see what they could get away with instead of what they could deliver.

As businesses have become commodities, many of them have decided that respect is the first thing they can no longer afford. If you've ever been herded onto a cattle car airline, or put on interminable hold by a cell phone company, you know the feeling. One telecom executive confided in me last week, "After we sell you an account, we never ever want to hear from you again. If we hear from you, it's bad news." Hey, it's just business.

The few successful marketers we hear about again and again (we hear about them so often that they seem trite) are all on our short list because they still show their customers respect. Fidelity, the Ritz-Carlton, Linux—none of them talk down to their audience.

The magic kicks in when marketers are smart enough and brave enough to combine trust with respect. When a marketer doesn't frisk you on the way out of a retail establishment, or trusts you to make intelligent decisions, you remember it. The number of companies that keep their promises and respect their customers' intelligence, alas, is quite tiny.

Of course, this means that a huge opportunity exists. It means that if you seek the very best slice of the market (the individuals and companies that can spend money—wisely—on new things) you'll likely do best if you eschew trickery and misdirection and pandering and instead focus on customers that will embrace a realistic and honest approach to doing business. The most profitable customers are often the most difficult to defraud. Rule one: Smart marketers treat their customers like respected colleagues and admired family members.

The ironic thing is this: At the same time that marketers have coarsened commercial relationships, they've spread their ethical mantra (or lack of one) to everyday folks as well. At the start of this riff I asked, "What would happen if your friends and colleagues treated you the way marketers do?" Well, in many cases, it turns out that they do.

Now, apparently, it's okay if a company reneges on a pension commitment. Now, if the contract doesn't specifically spell out how one company will treat another, it's okay to rip the other off as long as there's a loophole. Now, apparently, it's quite alright to treat your friends and colleagues the same way a marketer treats his prospects.

If an organization makes a promise, then keeps it, we're delighted. If a manager or an employee or a co-worker takes an extra minute or jumps through an extra hoop to honor a commitment to you, it's something you'll remember for a long time—precisely because it's such a rare occurrence.

Therein lies the real opportunity—to follow in the footsteps of the great marketers by reclaiming the interactions that used to be commonplace. Have the courage to make promises and keep them. Do more than you promised, not just what the contract says. Assume your colleagues are smart, and show leadership by respecting their work as if it were your own. Rule two: Treat your colleagues the way a smart marketer would—with respect. And keep your promises.

THE TWO OBVIOUS SECRETS OF EVERY SERVICE BUSINESS

1. Take responsibility

2. Pay attention to detail

The thing that's so surprising is how little attention is paid to these two and how often we run into people (business to business or b2c) who are totally clueless about them.

You'd be stunned to see a hotel clerk stealing money from the till or a bartender smashing bottles or a management consultant drawing on the client's wall with a magic marker. But every single day, I encounter "that's not my job" or "our Internet service is outsourced; it's their fault." More subtle but more important are all the little details left untended.

All the magazine ads in the world can't undo one lousy desk clerk.

All businesses are service businesses, and experience is the product.

UBIQUITY

Want soup? The very best soup in the entire world is served by Al Yaganeh, owner of Soup Kitchen International on West Fifty-fifth Street in New York. Slandered in a notorious *Seinfeld* parody, Al's restaurant is busier than ever. Some of the folks in the thirty-minute-long line (waiting to buy a $6 bowl of soup!) are insensitive clods who saw the TV show and want to experience a real celebrity moment. Others are longtime customers who are willing to brave the cold to get the real thing.

At the same time that hundreds of hungry people are waiting to get a unique bowl of soup from Al, millions are eating lunch at the most ubiquitous restaurant in the world: McDonald's. In fact, every single day, McDonald's serves a meal to one out of fourteen Americans.

Take a drive through Illinois—home to McDonald's head-quarters—and you might discover that many of the towns you pass don't have one "real" restaurant. No diner, no place for a fancy night out. Just a Hardee's, a Pizza Hut, and, of course, a McDonald's. This is not a phenomenon limited to tiny towns near Springfield. There are thousands of McDonald's franchises across the country, along with chains like Arby's, Subway, T.G.I. Friday's, and countless others churning out anonymous, forgettable meals to people in a hurry. Hey, it's what we asked for.

So what's wrong with selling out? Paradoxically, it seems that once you become popular, you also become very unpopular. Suddenly, those in the know aren't as awed by Wolfgang Puck—not when his name is displayed in major airports across the country. They look down their noses at Yo-Yo Ma. They disdain Andy Warhol.

What is it about ubiquity that breeds contempt?

Every day, successful entrepreneurs have to make important choices about whether to expand, to open another branch, to fran-chise, to license. Once you've figured out a winning strategy, it seems only rational to cash out by letting the market have what it wants: more of you!

As long as you're giving the market what it wants, what's the problem? If *some* is good, isn't *more* better?

Here's the problem: The moment you take your special, authentic, limited-edition product and leverage it, make it widely available and common, the very people who loved it inevitably rebel. "Starbucks isn't what it used to be," they tell you. The tastemakers who made you successful in the first place turn on their heels when they smell that you're not authentic anymore.

When a product is everywhere, when it's hyped in the media and advertised on the sides of buses, sometimes it seems as if the product exists and succeeds precisely *because* it is everywhere. Before ubiquity, when it seemed as if the product (or its creator) wasn't in it just for the money, somehow that felt more real, more special, more authentic.

Marketing has always been one of the most despised aspects of business. Brands, logos, salesmanship, positioning, and focus groups have gained a reputation for insincerity and corporate greed. Most of this comes from people's desire to have something real—and to get it from someone who isn't trying quite so hard to sell it.

Are we ever authentic? Is fresh goat cheese that is made in tiny batches on a farm in France any different from huge vats of goat cheese produced by Kraft somewhere in Wisconsin and delivered weekly to your local supermarket? What if you couldn't tell them apart in a taste test?

Sure, the vistas, the smell of the sheep, and the excitement of a true discovery make the first kind of cheese seem to taste far better than the second. But isn't that just another form of marketing? Why does the intention of the creator have so much influence on our perception of the product?

If you're lucky enough to create something authentic, you have real choices. You need to decide how important it is to be real, how much of yourself you have tied up in the authentic experience that you've created. Most of all, you need to decide what you'd like to do all day. Some of us can be happy taking today's flavor and selling it like crazy. Others need to have a deeper relationship with their craft, something that establishes a connection between themselves and their product. If you ever get a cup of soup from Al, look into his eyes. You'll see what I mean.

People who create something authentic but then sell out almost always end up unhappy. Why? Because once you sell out, any new success you have doesn't come from your authenticity. You're in a new business now. Ken Burns is just as authentic as he ever was. But he's not rewarded for that. He's rewarded for ubiquity. Could you be happy with that?

Before you pull the trigger and sell out and scale up, consider a few questions: Is it better to be big than to be (perceived as) real? Is spreading the word more important than being admired by a tiny coterie of truly devoted fans? Should financial rewards come to those who make good stuff for the masses?

Could you be happy practicing your authentic task for the rest of your life?

If you do get big, you won't be practicing authenticity for the rest of your life. When you sell out, you're making a trade. The big market wants reliability and conformity. The big market won't reward you for being authentic.

Authenticity. If you can fake that, the rest will take care of itself.

UGLY, THE WEB IS

Maybe I'm just in a visual mood, but I was struck as I surfed around today at how ugly many Web pages are (eBay's, for example). Typefaces that fight one another instead of work together. Things that flash for no reason. Hierarchies of size and color that are irrational.

Milton Glaser talks about why the supermarket is the way the supermarket is. Why is Tide in that multicolored box? It turns out that the original boxes evolved when you still had to ask for what you wanted from the guy behind the counter. The boxes needed to be bright in order to attract your attention from a ways away. Once the vernacular was set for the early winners, everyone else followed.

I wonder if we're about to get stuck here as well. As we enter the broadband world, with better browsers and all sorts of tools to improve the Web experience, is everyone going to be stuck emulating what succeeded in 1999?

USPS'S YELLOW JERSEY

For years, the United States Postal Service has been gladly sponsoring Lance Armstrong. It started as a small endeavor, but as he went on to dominate the sport of cycling, the USPS spent more and more and crowed about all the free advertising they were getting.

The Postal Service didn't get much "free advertising" out of sponsoring Armstrong. They mostly got some graft and free tickets and trinkets and stuff. I mean, do you really think someone sees Lance Armstrong and says, "Oh yeah, I gotta go out and mail some stuff!"?

Unmeasurable, amorphous, feel-good branding can go too far, and this is a fine example of that. The sponsorship of Armstrong is almost without value because it does nothing whatsoever to increase public awareness or consumption of the USPS, nor does it even give them much of a halo effect. Think about it: Are many companies going to consider switching from FedEx to USPS for overnight shipping (the only place they don't have a mandated monopoly) because of seeing a postal service logo in *Sports Illustrated*?

VERBS (GERUNDS, ACTUALLY)

I had two great seminars in my office this week. Not only do cool people show up to my seminars, but they push me to think hard about new ways to talk about things that work.

Today, we talked about nouns and verbs.

"Investments" is a noun. "Investing" is a verb.

"Paint" is a noun. "Painting" is a verb.

"Gift" is a noun. "Shopping" or "giving" is a verb.

People care much more about verbs than nouns. They care about things that move, that happen, that change. They care about experiences and events and the way things make us feel.

Nouns just sit there, inanimate lumps. Verbs are about wants and desires and wishes.

Is your Web site a noun or a verb?

What about your management style or the services you offer?

A few years ago, the rage was to turn products into services. Then it was to turn services into products.

I think the next big thing is to turn nouns into verbs.

P.S. Actually they're not verbs. They're gerunds. The kind of person who would tell you to use a gerund instead of a verb is the sort of person you don't want to sit next to on an airplane.

VIDEO? DO YOU ACT DIFFERENTLY WHEN YOU'RE ON

It's been twelve years since the videotaped beating of Rodney King started a riot in LA.

In that time, the percentage of people with a video camera at home has increased dramatically. And the number of streetcorners and businesses that capture everything on tape has gone way up as well.

Odd segue: Today, in anticipation of a dinner party, I stopped at a lobster seller in Chelsea Market in Manhattan. I asked for a six-pound lobster. The pricing at the store is $9.95 a pound for small lobsters and $8.95 a pound for lobsters six pounds and up.

The lobster weighed (I'm not making this up) 5.97 lbs. For reference, that's just less than a pound by the weight of a penny. Feed the lobster a plankton and it would be six pounds.

The man behind the counter started to ring me up at $9.95 a pound. I pointed out the price breakdown and the guy shrugged and said, "It doesn't weigh six pounds."

Two co-workers came over and, with precisely the same uncomprehending grin, repeated his point. I added a couple of pennies to the scale to push it over six pounds, but they weren't swayed.

So the two questions are, "Do you think the owner wanted them to act this way?" and "Would they have acted differently if they were on camera?"

I believe that the best motivation is self-motivation. That teaching people the right thing to do is far more effective than intimidating them into acting out of fear.

But I also know that people act differently when they think no one is watching.

I've been receiving more and more mail from enraged customers (thanks, but I have enough!). These are people who are outraged when they are deliberately mistreated by someone who should know better.

As the number of "owners" goes down (because the big chain outlets, telecom oligopolies, and centrally controlled media keep increasing in number), it's harder to find people who act the way we might like.

I wonder what happens once it's on tape?

VIRAL?, WHAT MAKES AN IDEA

For an idea to spread, it needs to be sent and received.

No one sends an idea unless:

1. they understand it

2. they want it to spread

3. they believe that spreading it will enhance their power (reputation, income, friendships) or their peace of mind

4. the effort necessary to send the idea is less than the benefits

No one "gets" an idea unless:

1. the first impression demands further investigation

2. they already understand the foundation ideas necessary to get the new idea

3. they trust or respect the sender enough to invest the time

This explains why online ideas spread so fast and why they're often shallow. Nietzsche is hard to understand and risky to spread (risky because you don't want to sound dumb or make your friends feel dumb), so it moves slowly among people willing to invest the time. Numa Numa, on the other hand, spread like a toxic-waste spill because it was so transparent, reasonably funny, and easy to share.

Notice that ideas never spread because they are important to the originator.

Notice, too, that a key element in the spreading of the idea is the capsule that contains it. If it's easy to swallow, tempting, and complete, it's a lot more likely to get a good start.

But that doesn't mean that there's no role for mystery or for ideas that unfold over time. In fact, the unmeasurable variable here is style. Howard Dean's ideas spread at the beginning—not because of the economic ramifications of his immigration policy, but because of the factors above. The way they were presented fit into the worldview of those who spread them.

Another key in the spreading of ideas is the visual element. Visually engaging concepts, like the iPod, spread faster in the real world than ephemeral concepts. Pictures and short jokes spread faster online because the investment necessary to figure out if they're worth spreading is so tiny.

And of course, plenty of bad ideas spread. Panic, for instance, is a superbad idea at all times, but it spreads faster than most ideas do. That's because spreading an idea is rarely a thoughtful, voluntary act. Instead, it often relates emotionally to the core of who we are, and we often do it without thinking much about the implications.

WAFFLES ARE ALWAYS ON THE MENU

There was an astonishing (but not that surprising) string of news this week.

The record industry sued a "little old lady" named Sarah Ward. She's not that old, but she's little and she's not a pirate. She's never even downloaded the software you need to download music. The RIAA has dropped the suit, but Amy Weiss, their spokesperson, says, "We have chosen to give her the benefit of the doubt and are continuing to look into the facts. . . . This is the only case of its kind."

Now, regardless of how you feel about litigation as a business strategy, refusing to apologize is just a bad idea. This is clearly *not* the only case of its kind. Instead of stonewalling, why doesn't the RIAA say, "This is terrific! She's an honest citizen and we're proud of her. We made a mistake and we apologize. We're sending Ms. Ward a hundred CDs to apologize for bothering her. If there are any other cases like this one, we'll drop them immediately."

Moving on, the *Wall Street Journal* ran a tiny article about Clorox. It seems that Clorox ran an ad featuring slimy water mains and pipes, encouraging New Yorkers to use a Brita water filter. New York complained, calling it "a blatant mischaracterization of the world's safest, purest water supply."

Mary O'Connell, our next waffling spokesperson, speaking on behalf of Clorox, said, "The ad was never intending [sic] to be critical of the [sic] New York City's water system. It was more about the pipes that carry the water in apartment buildings."

Sometimes it's hard to tell if these folks are intending to be caricatures, or if it just turns out that way. *Of course* the ad was criticizing the water system. If it wasn't, why would I need a Brita water filter? Why don't they just tell the truth?

Moving on to one of my favorite organizations, the Motion Picture Association of America has a two-pronged approach to fighting the future piracy of movies. The first is a low-budget ad campaign saying, "Movies, they're worth it." According to the *New York Times*, the campaign profiles, "among others, a set painter, stuntman and make up artist."

The second prong? A lesson plan (including crossword puzzles featuring phrases like "digital theft" and "Movielink") created in conjunction with Junior Achievement. The plan is designed to indoctrinate teenagers with the Downloading Is Bad mantra.

Well, forgetting the huge success rate that advertising campaigns have had in reducing things like tobacco use (intentional use of sarcasm), does anyone really think that this is the answer? And when did Junior Achievement start acting as a spokesperson for maintaining entrenched industries? (Movielink is a business run by the studios.)

The reason that the ads feature the relatively low-paid craftspeople is that, of course, people don't really care if Julia Roberts or Wesley Snipes make another few bucks. The problem, of course, is that ads like this never work, and even if they did, the idea that you should pay $30 to go out to the movies to support a makeup artist you've never met is an awfully hard sell.

No, I don't think downloading movies is right or legal or even convenient. I do believe, however, that it's going to happen more and more, and people in the industry ought to tell the truth—to one another and to us. The only thing that will save the existing infrastructure is an out-of-house experience that really and truly *is* worth paying for. That, and an in-house experience that is supereasy and very cheap. The music industry could have killed Napster with a $10 a month all-you-can-hear plan (which would have easily tripled their profits) and Hollywood could do the same. But they won't.

WAKE-UP CALLS, A WAKE-UP CALL ABOUT

Staying at the Westin hotel in Florida to give a speech today. The staff here is very by-the-book, doing things because they're told to, not because it comes naturally. My favorite example: When you ask for a wake-up call in the morning, they automatically respond, "Would you like a follow-up call fifteen minutes later?" I said no. They asked me the same question when I called an hour later to change the time. Same answer from me.

So this morning, as is usual when I travel, I woke up an hour earlier than I wanted to. Before going to work out, I called to cancel my wake-up so the ringing phone wouldn't bother the neighbors. The receptionist then asked, "Would you like me to cancel the follow-up call as well?"

Obviously, there's no reason on Earth that someone who is already awake and is canceling their wake-up call would still want to be reminded of the call fifteen minutes later. Especially if they didn't ask for the reminder call in the first place. But there it is in the script, so it's an error that's repeated over and over.

I know it's more difficult, but hiring people who can think for themselves is usually a better long-run strategy than scripting every conversation. If that's the plan, it's probably better to get an automated system. And not just at a hotel in Florida . . .

WALLS, CLIFFS, AND BRICKS

Whenever you try to take a prospect or a customer or a student or an employee through a process, you run the risk of losing them. You lose a few at every step. Sometimes just a few out of a hundred drop out along the way. Sometimes, though, it's a much bigger number.

Too often, we forget to measure, to discover the wall, the one step in the process that loses a huge portion of the population. Maybe if we left that step out, we'd get a little bit less from the few, but we'd get more from a whole bunch of people.

I was asked to register an Apple product while the software was installing. I made it to step five, and they wanted to know not just the kind of product, but the "Marketing part number."

I bailed.

The benefits of being registered (dubious at best) were overwhelmed by the hassle of finding out this number. Bye.

Now the marketing gurus at Apple get *no* customer data instead of *most* of the data. My bet is that this is a wall, a place where a huge percentage of people abandon the process.

The same thing happens when people learn trigonometry or apply to your firm for a job or decide whether or not to read about your new products. If each step increases the chance for benefits and isn't too difficult, the user will clear the hurdle. But the moment you have a step that's too hard, too time-consuming, or offers too little, people stop.

WEB DESIGNERS

I ran into an old colleague ("old" as in we worked together on Prodigy's online game Guts in 1990, so don't tell me you've been online a long time, okay?). Susan is a very talented Web designer, and like most Web designers, her customers are sort of in between the "Oh boy, we need a Web site, let's hire someone!" stage of panic and the "Oh no, the economy is in the tank, let's cut costs!" stage. Good work is hard to find.

I promised to drop her a note about the burgeoning niche I see for Web designers, and here it is—circa 2003:

Susan,

Within two years, companies are going to spend about $5 billion a year on search engine advertising, adwords, keywords, and other smart ways to get strangers to click on over to their sites. (Note: I was right!)

Further proof that the Web is now officially a direct-marketing business.

Yet at the same time all these companies are aggressively spending to build the *right* kind of traffic (not the "Hey, I tricked you with a pop-up ad or seduced you with a bikini ad") they're dropping the ball because they're wasting the traffic they get.

Less than 10 percent of these advertisers regularly measure results. Which means that traffic shows up at Web sites and then leaves. The visitors leave because the offer on that page is no good, or because it doesn't match the ad they clicked on.

Few advertisers are changing their offer pages hourly—which is what they ought to do.

What a waste.

People like Andrew Goodman (his site is Traffick.com) understand this. They realize that testing, measuring, and evolving is the secret to direct marketing. There are no once-and-for-all secrets. It's a process, not an event.

So who's going to do this work?

I think it's going to be the next generation of Web designer.

I think it goes like this:

You say to the prospect: "I will work with you to build a four-page engine of revenue. The idea: You (the client) load it up with targeted traffic that you buy by regularly trying and testing adwords and other relevant, measurable media.

"Then, I will regularly, constantly tweak (or redesign) the four-page site to turn those strangers into friends (and maybe, if your product is great and your follow-up is appropriate, you can turn those friends into customers)."

The thing is, it's probably cheaper to constantly measure and evolve and redesign a four-page offer site than it is to do the annual four-hundred-page Web site overhaul. And there's no question it's more effective.

It takes patience. It takes a lack of ego. It takes a willingness to be creative and to try new stuff, to measure what works, and to do it again and again.

The great news about direct marketing is that when it works, you know it worked. That makes it easy to get new clients.

The future belongs to disciplined designers, talented copywriters, and patient, honest, and respectful clients/marketers.

Have fun with it!

WHAT DID YOU DO DURING THE 2000s?

Hindsight is 20/20. People are already looking back on the 1990s and wishing that they had had more courage. When you look back on this decade, now half over, what will you have to say for yourself?

Here's a question that you should clip out and tape to your bathroom mirror. It might save you some angst fifteen years from now.

The question is, "What did you do back when interest rates were at their lowest in fifty years, the crime rate was close to zero, great employees were looking for good jobs, computers made product development and marketing easier than ever, and there was almost no competition for good news about great ideas?"

Many people will have to answer that question by saying, "I spent my time waiting, whining, worrying, and wishing." Because that's what seems to be going around these days. Fortunately, though, not everyone will have to confess to having made such a bad choice.

While your company has been waiting for the economy to rebound, Reebok has launched Travel Trainers, a very cool-looking, lightweight sneaker for travelers. They are selling out in Japan—from vending machines in airports!

While Detroit's car companies have been whining about gas prices and bad publicity for SUVs (SUVs are among their most profitable products), Honda has been busy building cars that look like SUVs but get twice the gas mileage. The Honda Pilot is so popular, it has a waiting list. And Toyota, of course, is mopping up the industry with the Prius.

While Africa's economic plight gets a fair amount of worry, a little start-up called KickStart is actually doing something about it. The new income that its products generate accounts for 0.5 percent of the entire GDP of Kenya. How? KickStart manufactures a $75 device that looks a lot like a StairMaster. But it's not for exercise. Instead, KickStart sells the machine to subsistence farmers, who use its stair-stepping feature to irrigate their land. People who buy it can move from subsistence farming to selling the additional produce that their land yields—and triple their annual income in the first year of using the product.

While you've been wishing for the inspiration to start something great, thousands of entrepreneurs have used the prevailing sense of uncertainty to start truly remarkable companies. Lucrative Web businesses, successful tool catalogs, fast-growing PR firms—all have started on a shoestring, and all have been profitable ahead of schedule. The Web is dead, right? Well, try telling that to Meetup, a Web site that helps organize meetings anywhere and on any topic. It has 200,000 registered users—and counting.

Maybe you already have a clipping on your mirror that asks you what you did during the 1990s. What's your biggest regret about *that* decade? Do you wish that you had started, joined, invested in, or built something? Are you left wishing that you'd at least had the courage to try? In hindsight, the 1990s were the good old days. Yet so many people missed out. Why? Because it's always possible to find a reason to stay put, to skip an opportunity, or to decline an offer. And yet, in retrospect, it's hard to remember why we said no and easy to wish that we had said yes.

The thing is, we still live in a world that's filled with opportunity. In fact, we have more than an opportunity—we have an obligation. An obligation to spend our time doing great things. To find ideas that matter and to share them. To push ourselves and the people around us to demonstrate gratitude, insight, and inspiration. To take risks and to make the world better by being amazing.

Are these crazy times? You bet they are. But so were the days when we were doing duck-and-cover air raid drills in school, or going through the scares of Three Mile Island and Love Canal. There will always be crazy times.

So stop thinking about how crazy the times are, and start thinking about what the crazy times demand. There has never been a worse time for business as usual. Business as usual is sure to fail, sure to disappoint, sure to numb our dreams. That's why there has never been a better time for the new. Your competitors are too afraid to spend money on new productivity tools. Your bankers have no idea where they can invest safely. Your potential employees are desperately looking for something exciting, something they feel passionate about, something they can genuinely engage in and engage with.

You get to make a choice. You can remake that choice every day, in fact. It's never too late to choose optimism, to choose action, to choose excellence. It only takes a moment—just one second—to decide.

Before you finish this paragraph, you have the power to change everything that's to come. And you can do that by asking yourself (and your colleagues) the one question that every organization and every individual needs to ask today: Why not be great?

WHAT THEN?

Assume that:

Hard drive space is free

WiFi-like connections are everywhere

Connection speeds are ten to one hundred times faster

Everyone has a digital camera

Everyone carries a device that is sort of like a laptop, but cheap and tiny

The number of new products introduced every day is five times greater than it is now

Wal-Mart's sales are three times as big

Any manufactured product that's more than five years old in design sells at commodity pricing

The retirement age is five years higher than it is now

Your current profession is either obsolete or totally different

What then?

WHO'S WHO?

All the cues we use to figure out who's real and who's not appear to be fading away.

Years ago, there were "real" books and self-published books. The real books were worth buying and reading, while the self-published books were from vanity presses. Today, of course, some of the best stuff is self-published, whether as a book or a blog.

Multilevel marketing used to feel just a little creepy. Vitamins or cosmetics got sold by MLM. Today, of course, it's not surprising to hear about car companies or even doctors rewarding people with cash or services for referrals.

The Republican Party just announced that it's paying a 30% commission to anyone with a Web site who collects money on their behalf. That sort of tactic used to be reserved for fledgling start-ups or small grassroots organizations.

Wearing a fine suit that fit you right was a great cue to others that you were successful and powerful and about to make something happen. Today, it's just as likely that your potential partner is going to show up in a turtleneck and jeans.

Hotmail accounts used to indicate anonymity and they gave a fly-by-night aura to the people using them. You wanted the e-mail addresses of people you interacted with to have permanence—stuff like ford.com. Today, of course, Gmail (which is nothing but Hotmail 2.0) is the flavor du jour for movers and shakers. Famous people and executives have Gmail addresses.

Having your headquarters in Manhattan used to be a sign of real success. People even made a business out of selling post office boxes at the Empire State Building. Today, you're more likely to find aggressive, responsible companies sprouting up in Colorado, Dubai, and Singapore.

The best Web sites (belonging to the best organizations) used to be designed by Razorfish or Organic or Scient. They were big and fancy and expensive and complex. Today, it's not surprising to find a successful business with a one-page site that cost $300 to build.

Advertising used to be about expensive spreads in the *New York Times* magazine. Today, text-only AdWords ads on Google are the most likely to be paying for themselves.

It used to be true that being public and traded on the NYSE was a sign of permanence and ethics. Today, after Enron and United and Xerox, it's the previously unknown (and private) companies that just might be the best to do business with.

So, how do we tell the good from the bad? In a connected world where people don't have letterhead, don't wear suits (maybe don't even own suits), work out of tiny rented office suites (or the living room), have a simple Web site and buy only AdWords, have an answering machine instead of a PBX, don't have a receptionist or a sculpture out front—in that world, how do we tell?

As we've stripped away a lot of the extraneous expenses and signaling mechanisms, are we in a race to the bottom (if "bottom" means raw, not bad)? I can no longer count on the best books coming from a major publisher, on the best articles being in the biggest magazines (in fact, I can usually assume that if it's the cover story of a major magazine, it's insipid). I can no longer assume that someone with a sketchy résumé or a simple Web site isn't serious about what they're up to.

Ten years ago, there was a neat and orderly process for companies that wanted to go public and cash out. It started with some time spent as a student at Stanford and then proceeded to lunch with the right venture capital guys. There were people to see and tickets to punch. There was also a standard process for authors and salespeople and nonprofit administrators and teachers and just about everyone else. But today, cutting the line appears to be the best way to get what you want.

At this point in my riff, I'm supposed to insert a breathtaking insight, something that will turn your head around and make it all make sense. I'm not sure I can. I think maybe the insight here is just that puzzling times lie ahead.

Welcome to the blended times. The moment when big meets small. We're seeing the juxtaposition of the impermanent and the permanent, the accepted and the false. For a while, it's going to be awfully confusing. We'll get ripped off, waste time, become even more skeptical than ever before.

But soon, I think, we'll walk out to the other side.

I have no certainty as to what the other side looks like, but I'm pretty sure the winners are those that treated their customers and their constituents with respect and did it with honesty. Trust and respect are the two things we haven't figured out a shortcut for.

WHO YOU KNOW DOESN'T MATTER

I once wrote, "What you know is more important than what you do," and I labeled this one of the top ten lies told to maintain the status quo. A day later, I got an e-mail saying, "I am starting a business from the ground up right now. It seems that I cannot get in *any* door unless I know somebody. Please let me know your thoughts."

Here's why I wrote what I wrote:

When your idea is gaining traction, the easy and obvious and natural thing to do is to fear that you won't succeed because you don't know the right people. After all, we see Donald Trump's getting in NBC's door, and we see some famous author on a talk show or some rock star with a video on MTV twenty years after he hit his prime. *It just doesn't seem fair or right that all too often access is determined based on relationships or past glories, not some other measure of quality.*

I'm all for the momentum that builds for a creator once she establishes a brand or a hit. But the facts belie the excuse that who you know matters. You can hate the fact that you don't know anyone, but you can't blame your failure on that.

Microsoft, for example, almost always fails when they introduce something new. Most successes (in books, music, movies, politics, nonprofits, etc.) don't come from where the established wisdom tells us they're going to come from. No one bet on Phish or Boing Boing or Google or Dan Brown.

Yes, it looks like the big guys (McKinsey Consulting, Stephen King, General Foods) always manage to win, but what's really happening is that the big guys slowly fade away and the real growth comes from where no one expected it.

In a world where things are viral, you're more likely to succeed with passive networking (strangers recommending you) than the old-school, active kind. In other words, make great stuff, do your homework, build your audience, and when you've got something worth talking about, people will talk about it.

WHY (ASK WHY?)

The woman next to me on the flight had thin, sharpened spikes, two of them, eight inches long. They're called knitting needles, and they're allowed on the plane. The guy on the other side was bemoaning the fact that they took away his nail clippers.

The little kid in row 8 had to walk thirty-five rows to the back of the plane to use the bathroom because it's a grave breach of security for him to use the empty bathroom seven rows in front.

They x-ray sneakers at LaGuardia.

The hotel sent me down the street to a health club because the hotel's workout room was under construction. The health club wouldn't let me use the facilities until I filled out a form with my name and full address and contact information. Why? Insurance regulations. Apparently this is also the reason you can't watch a mechanic repair your car or visit the kitchen of a restaurant.

My doctor's office doesn't have a fax machine.

The stellar Maison de Chocolate café in New York doesn't serve herbal tea.

The government of New York made it illegal to buy wine on the Internet.

If your frontline people are unable to answer a "why" question, what do you tell them to do?

Most bureaucracies don't want these questions working their way up the chain. Most bureaucracies encourage their people to be the first and only line of defense. "That's our policy." "I'm sorry, but there's nothing I can do about that." "Insurance regulations, sir." The goal is to get the customer (questioner) to go away.

To go away.

They want you to go away.

Does that make any sense at all? The single most efficient (and lowest-cost) technique for improving your operations is answering the why questions! You should embrace these people, not send them away.

"You know, sir, I have no idea why you have to do that. But I can tell you that I'll find out before the end of the day."

WOOT.COM AND THE EDGE

Woot.com goes all the way to the edge in that *they sell just one product a day.* This is an extreme way to deal with product selection (about a millionth the size of Amazon) and very effective in attracting interesting customers and having them spread the word. What could be good enough or cheap enough to be the only product of the day?

The second thing they do that's neat is that they support RSS. Which means you don't have to remember to go to their site every day. You can subscribe. I love subscription-based businesses.

WORDS

In 2004, efforts to change social security revolved around two words.

"Privatization" it seems, has bad test numbers. So those who would privatize it don't call it that anymore.

"Reform," on the other hand, is on the march. "Reform" is a great word in terms of establishing a frame for a debate, because re-form assumes something is broken and how can anyone be against fixing something that's broken?

Don't minimize the impact of the right word.

WORKING CLASS

A recent conference in New York computed that approximately 90 million Americans are working-class. About one in three adults.

They define "working-class" as having a job where the worker has little control over her actions—her goals, her time, the outputs created.

In that category, I'd guess, you'll find cashiers, punch press oper-ators, janitors, and keypunchers. People who work on the clock (and against the clock) and do what they're told to do.

It's worth noting that they didn't use the term "blue-collar." An enormous number of white-collar jobs are now working-class. This is due to a combination of factors: computerization, faster mea-surement, more competition, consolidation into ever bigger corpo-rations.

Here's the fascinating uptake from my point of view:

We (you, me, everyone) is complicit in this intellectual down-sizing.

We asked for it.

The American worker, long a responsible iconoclast, an individualist in search of greater productivity and new opportunities, now just wants to be told what to do.

I think working-class is a state of mind, not a socioeconomic description.

WRAPPERS

For the past twenty years or so, I've had a bad habit. I buy compact discs. Only one or two a week—but one or two a week adds up. So last week, I threw out what had become my collection of more than a thousand CDs.

Well, I didn't really throw out the CDs themselves. I threw out the jewel boxes that the CDs came in. With the new CD changers that hold three hundred CDs each (for only $250!), it's just easier to store CDs in the changer than it is to keep them in their jewel boxes.

I gathered up stacks and stacks of jewel boxes (which weighed a ton) and left them on the curb for the garbage collectors. And in the twenty-four hours that followed, at least a dozen people in cars pulled over, got out, and started to paw through the boxes.

It took them only a few seconds to determine that the jewel boxes were empty. But that didn't stop them: Each and every person kept pawing through the pile. They couldn't bring themselves to believe that so many CD cases, usually coveted, were now worthless. One guy even took a few of the empties with him—for what reason I can't begin to imagine.

Of course, the jewel boxes are worse than useless without the music. They take up space, and they're not particularly attractive. Few home decorators rush out to buy jewel boxes in bulk to distribute in key locations around a house to give it that finishing touch before the photographers from *Architectural Digest* arrive.

Here's the question that the whole episode suggested to me:

What is it about packaging—about a wrapper—that is so important?

Here's my answer: People are quick to attach emotional memories to packaging, all the more so when what is held within that packaging is something ethereal. Anyone who has paid to put her wedding dress in storage knows what I mean. You're never going to wear it again, your kids are unlikely to want it, but you keep it because it's an important wrapper. It was the packaging around a romantic, once-in-a-lifetime—and hard-to-recapture—personal experience. Long after the cake has been cut and the rice has been thrown, it's the one tangible thing that you can take with you. That wedding dress is the wrapper on your wedding day, the physical manifestation of a warm and fuzzy concept.

In the old days, virtually everything had to come with some sort of wrapper. The packaging was as much a part of the product as it was a part of the brand.

As our economy continues to become more digital, the role of the wrapper becomes a vitally important concept. Some pundits riff about all products becoming services and all services becoming products. I don't think that's what it's about. I think it's about our starting to separate goods and services from their wrappers.

The music business, of course, has this very problem coming out of its ears. If first you throw out the jewel boxes, and then you throw out the polycarbonate disks, can you really charge $14 for the music? Napster is a huge threat precisely because it makes clear just how many layers of wrapping come with the music—and just how little value such wrapping actually holds.

But it's not only in the land of the CD that we find this problem. There's been quite a kerfuffle in the book business as well. When authors can throw away the paper and the cover, charge $4 or $1—or nothing at all—for a book and still profit from the exercise, it gives book publishers an excellent reason to quake. After all, publishers have organized themselves to be in the wrapper business. But if the wrapper now is nothing but a lot of prelandfill material, everyone in the book-wrapping business will have a lot of trouble making sense of what they do every day.

And those are the easy examples. How about your cell phone? Is it an irreplaceable, useful object, or just a wrapper for really valuable things such as conversations and data exchange? Tellme Networks Inc., a start-up in Silicon Valley, is betting on the latter. Dial 800-555-TELL, and you can have a really fascinating phone conversation with a computer. It will look up stock information or weather, and will even dial an airline for you—all for free. And Tellme doesn't care at all which phone you use. Phones will get cheaper and cheaper, but if Tellme does its job right, its service will become more and more valuable. In a few years, cell phones are going to be very close to free—wrappers without value. What we do with them, on the other hand, will be where a ton of money stands to be made.

At the same time that we're abandoning some traditional wrappers, some businesses are becoming ever *more* obsessed with the wrapper. They understand that their businesses are really all about wrappers, and so they offer their T-shirts, their soaps, their teas— even their computer workstations—in wrappers and packages that satisfy our inner need for beauty. The pleasure that we get by pulling out a Palm V when everyone around us has a IIIe is irrational. It's based on the kinesthetic joy that we get from holding the latest and greatest. That's worth something, and Palm understands its worth. Go to a conference, and all the "irrelevant" wrapper stuff—the uniforms, the look and feel of the place—makes the rest of the conference that much more important and enjoyable.

In the age of e-mail and faxes, do we really need to use FedEx envelopes to send most documents? Unless a document is an original that must be signed, probably not. Yet businesses continue to use them. Why? Because the envelope (FedEx's version of the jewel box) makes it more likely that the letter will get read.

So who's in danger? How will the increasing chasm between wrappers and contents make life difficult for some companies? I think it will happen to companies in the middle, the ones that hesitate to go for the edges. Here are a couple of quick ideas to get you thinking about your choices.

If your company makes contents, get out of the wrapper business as fast as you possibly can. Giving away your e-book will dramatically increase the number of people who read it. More than 2 million people have read *Unleashing the Ideavirus* so far—all because I got rid of the physical stuff that makes a book expensive. If you're in the wine business, and your wine is well reviewed and has a huge following, maybe it's time to sell a special vintage directly to your customers, bypassing liquor stores and foregoing fancy bottles. Sell the wine—not the bottle!

If you're in the wrapper business, get better at it! Beer should come in truly beautiful bottles, and those bottles should make a great noise when they are opened. Emulate the cosmetics industry in your packaging, Nordstrom in your customer service, and Apple in your sheer sexiness. Too many companies are afraid to admit that they're in the packaging business. They're happy to invest big money in a new plant, but they view spending similar money on user experience as some sort of soft expense.

Here are a couple of tests: Take a page from the *New York Times*, cut out a two-inch square from it, and give that piece of paper to a friend. Odds are, she knows exactly what newspaper she's reading. Have another friend shut his eyes, get into a Mercedes-Benz, and close the door. Odds are, he'll know exactly what kind of car he is sitting in. At first glance, neither of those experiments has anything to do with the actual products. Yet they have everything to do with them. The way that the *Times* looks and feels affects how I interpret the news that I read within its pages. The way that the door on a Mercedes shuts is at least as important to most drivers as the car's acceleration.

I walked into a supermarket in Saranac Lake, New York, last week. It was part of a big chain, one that has some pretty upscale markets around the country. Not here, though. The lighting was poor. The shelves weren't very well arranged. I knew within five seconds that I wasn't going to make any silly, spur-of-the-moment (read: "profitable") purchases.

Of course, this supermarket, like all supermarkets, is nothing but a wrapper itself. It's a giant jewel box for food, a wrapper designed to convey packaged goods from companies that make them to consumers who buy them. A supermarket is a wrapper filled with more wrappers. And because the store's manager had stopped trying to make all that wrapping attractive, that store was leaving huge profits on the table.

I know that this idea of our being packaging obsessed seems, at first, to be superfluous and wasteful. But if you've chosen to thrive in the packaged world, then that is the path you've chosen. To go halfway down that road, to go to all the trouble of having a product, a sales force, and even real estate, and then not to finish it off by creating joy in the process for the user—what a waste!

The Web has really ripped a hole through the wrapping that has been sheltering the wrapper folks. On the Web, you can't hear the crinkling, see the lighting, smell the leather, or enjoy the sultry sound of a handsome salesperson's voice. The Web, the engineer's revenge, is all about content and commodities, not sexiness and wrappers. What do you do? I would do three things:

1. *Make your Web site crisp, simple, and elegant—but don't try to replicate the joy or the wonder of your wrapper.* Instead, first do no harm. Go to most consulting firms' Web sites, and you'll see that it is too easy to do too much online. Get what you need from your prospect's attention—and then stop.

2. *Get permission from people to follow up with tools that support your packaging.* Send them a certificate for a free test-drive of your latest BMW on a nearby racetrack, or get them to call your ace customer service people by phone.

3. *Create unique intermediate products that are either cheap or free in order to get people started with your experience.* Burt's Bees worked with drugstore.com to give away a free ten-pack of its lip balms

and skin creams to anyone who made a purchase on the site. If the product experience is strong enough, your effort will have been money well spent. Why? Because once I use some of Burt's stuff, I may fall in love with the experience and buy from Burt's again and again, paying handsomely for the package each time.

There's one other thing that you can do if such approaches fail: Get out of the wrapper business entirely. Rededicate your company to making things that do something better. Wrappers may be fun, sexy, and media-worthy, but you'll never go hungry in the long run if you can offer people something that is really and truly better. After all, as Freud once observed, a cigar may be just a cigar. But no one thinks twice about the cellophane wrapper.

YAK SHAVING

Apparently turned into a computer term by the MIT media lab five years ago, "yak shaving" was recently referenced by my pal Joi Ito. It's the single best term I've learned this year.

I want to give you the nontechnical definition, and as is my wont, broaden it a bit.

Yak shaving is the last step in a series of steps that occurs when you find something you need to do.

"I want to wax the car today."

"Oops, the hose is still broken from the winter. I'll need to buy a new one at Home Depot."

"But Home Depot is on the other side of the Tappan Zee Bridge and getting there without my E-ZPass is miserable because of the tolls."

"But wait! I could borrow my neighbor's E-ZPass."

"Bob won't lend me his E-ZPass until I return the moshi pillow my son borrowed, though."

"And we haven't returned it because some of the stuffing fell out and we need to get some yak hair to restuff it."

And the next thing you know, you're at the zoo, shaving a yak, all so you can wax your car.

This yak-shaving phenomenon tends to hit some people more than others, but what makes it particularly perverse is when groups of people get involved. It's bad enough when one person gets all up in arms yak shaving, but when you try to get a group of people together, you're just as likely to end up giving the yak a manicure.

Which is why solo entrepreneurs and small organizations are so much more likely to get stuff done. They have fewer yaks to shave.

So, what to do?

Don't go to Home Depot for the hose.

Take a chance. Start now. Create something that gets feedback. Listen. Repeat.

YOU ARE YOUR REFERENCES

References don't matter now that everybody's life is on public record.

My sister (who's a brilliant manager and team leader) is looking for a new job. She showed me her résumé a few days ago, and there, in small print at the very bottom, were four words that appear on almost every résumé—and that are now irrelevant: "References available upon request."

Like millions of other job seekers, she was willing to share selected opinions about herself once a company expressed interest. The thing is, it doesn't matter anymore. The reason? Your references are everywhere, all the time, whether you want to share them or not.

Wherever we go, we leave electronic footprints. When you post a complaint on Epinions.com, a review on Amazon, or a comment in a newsgroup, your opinions are shared, with everyone, forever. Buy a house, default on a credit card, switch jobs a few times—it's all there, online, for everyone to see.

The cost of a background check is a fraction of what it used to be. Private detectives don't do legwork anymore. They check their e-mail, type in a few numbers, and—wham!—the data (more than you can imagine) is right there.

Of course, it's not just employees who are leaving a trail. Organizations face an even bigger challenge. Consider the case of a company that hired me to give a few speeches around the country. Instead of paying me as we contracted (with the money's going to charity), they bounced three checks. After trying to call them, write them, and work with them, I finally had to hire a lawyer. They never paid. In the old days, that would be that. But today, there's a record online. A quick Google search of the company name would lead you to my blog, which would make you think twice about doing any sort of business with them.

If you run a restaurant, every patron is keeping score for Zagat. If you're a politician, every potential voter is a potential online pundit as well. It's pretty easy to get paranoid about this. Pretty easy to imagine that every customer is a potential brand destroyer. But every customer is also a potential brand builder. Dozens of people have posted positive reviews on PlanetFeedback (now known as Intelliseek) and Epinions.com for brands you wouldn't expect, like Chili's restaurants. Here are excerpts from one posting: "Do you like service that is exceptional? Do you like having a fair price for what you get? You can get all of this at Chili's, because it has all that you want in a restaurant. . . . I had a chicken fried steak with corn on the cob and mashed potatoes. The chicken fried steak was as big as the plate, and it is made with Black Angus beef."

Wow!

One thing is becoming crystal clear: You are your references. If a friend tells me a play is no good, I don't go. A friend's recommendation will also determine my choice of lawn care service or an island to vacation on. My publisher just sent me an e-mail asking about a potential author—and if I don't back up the author's version of our relationship, he won't get the contract.

No person or company can escape their past. You can no longer change your prices with impunity, because the old price lists may be cached at the Internet Archive's Wayback Machine, which regularly takes snapshots of Web sites and stores them forever. With a little care, you won't hire a manager with a history of abusing his employees, because the lawsuits are all on record.

So what should we do? Should we fret and live in fear of our past actions and words' coming back to haunt us? I don't think so. There's a bright new opportunity just sitting here, waiting for organizations and individuals to take advantage of it: Spend your future creating your past, starting right now. Live your life out loud, well aware that everything you say can (and will) be used against you (or for you). Treat every customer as though he could turn into a testimonial. Treat every vendor as if she could give you a recommendation. And then, when the time comes, the seeds you've sown will pay off.

Blogs, newsgroups, professional organizations, and all the rest are perfect for someone who wants to leave a vivid, positive trail. You can choose to use the new tools or to become a victim of them.

My sister? She's no longer offering to supply her amazing references upon request. Now she's sending them instead of her résumé.

YOUR VERY OWN PRINTING PRESS

Thirty years ago, everyone in the TV business believed in the three-channel universe. Cable was a myth. That's why the big networks did such a bad job of starting cable networks. They couldn't believe that it was even remotely likely to succeed.

Of course, the first twenty channels did succeed. In a very big way. Billions of dollars' worth of success.

It took about a decade, but the TV business recalibrated. The industry now believes that they have reached the natural number of networks and that's it.

What happens, I asked, when TiVo has Java and TCP/IP and there are a million channels?

The people in the TV business can't imagine this. They can't imagine a world where there might be twenty A&E networks, or where there might be a channel just for shows on how to build a model airplane.

XM and Sirius radio and the Net just increased the number of radio stations by a factor of one hundred.

And the *New York Times* reports that 175,000 books are published every year. And rising.

And we just hit 30,000,000 blogs, up from 100 five years ago.

The number of channels for just about anything keeps going up. The number of *good* channels, where "good" means a built-in, high-traffic, nondiscerning audience, keeps going down. The number of good newspaper PR outlets is down to a handful. The number of retailers with shelf space that really matters is tiny. Yes, you can get your thing out there. No, you can't expect that distribution (or carriage, as they say in TV) is going to make you successful.

In other words, owning a printing press is not such a big deal. Knowing the buyer at Bed Bath & Beyond isn't much better.

ZEBRA CAKE, FAMOUS

In the old days, of course, McDonald's was Purple. They were remarkable. They were unique.

Why?

They offered food that was consistent nationwide, and no one else did. They offered national advertising, and no one else did. They offered a limited menu of popular food with a satisfying mouthfeel aimed at the masses, and no one else did. They offered a quick, low-investment eating experience, and no one else did.

The point is that the rules keep changing. *Today's Purple Cow is tomorrow's mad cow.*

It's hard to stay remarkable. It won't just happen for you. Learn to evolve or watch it go away.

I thought about this when I was making a zebra cake from Famous (the brand) chocolate wafer crackers and cream. Sure, it's a cool retro-Proustian dessert. But no way I'd want to be *that* brand manager. Growing that brand is impossible. The glory days for this product are long, long gone, and no amount of wishing will bring them back. Famous? Not anymore.

BONUS #1: KNOCK KNOCK:
A BOOK ABOUT WEB SITE DESIGN

Just about everything you think you know about Web sites is wrong. What the establishment has taught you about Web design and strategy is largely self-serving, expensive, time-consuming, and completely ineffective.

This riff is designed to change all that.

How's that for a promise?

If you don't have a Web site problem or you're not interested in solving it, reading this section will be a complete waste of time. On the other hand, if you're trying to figure out how to use Google AdWords or other advertising techniques to connect with your prospects, customers, donors, students, or users, then I'm betting you'll find some useful information inside.

This manifesto tries to identify just a few important (and overlooked) ideas and sell you hard on putting them to work for you. I believe that your problem (if you have a problem) isn't that you don't have enough data. You have too much data! You don't need a longer book or more time with a talented consultant. What you need is the certainty of knowing that you ought to do something (one thing); then you need the will to do it.

No wasted words. Let's go.

BIG PICTURE: WHAT A WEB SITE DOES

Big Picture #1:

A Web site must do at least one of two things, but probably both:

- Turn a stranger into a friend, and a friend into a customer.
- Talk in a tone of voice that persuades people to believe the story you're telling.

Big Picture #2:

A Web site can cause only four things to happen in the moments after someone sees it:

- She clicks and goes somewhere else you want her to go.
- She clicks and gives you permission to follow up by e-mail or phone.
- She clicks and buys something.
- She tells a friend, either by clicking or by blogging or phoning or talking.

That's it.

If your site is attempting to do more than this, you're wasting time and money and, more important, focus.

In this guide, we'll start with Big Picture #1, because it's first.

WHY BOTHER?

A guy goes on a sales call. After a while, the purchasing agent says, "Are you trying to sell me something?"

The salesman hesitates, then stammers, "Well, no, of course not. . . . I'm just trying to talk with you."

Understandably, the purchasing agent is incensed. "If you're not here to sell me something, get out and stop wasting my time."

Sometimes it's hard to embrace the fact that, yes, you are trying to sell something. It might be a product or a service or just an idea. You might be trying to raise money for your university or help a battered woman find the nearest shelter. But you are trying to do something with your Web site. If you're not, get out.

So what are you trying to do? Have you got real clarity among the people on your team?

A Web page isn't a place the way Starbucks is a place. A Web page is a step in a process. The steps on the stoop in front of your house understand (if steps understand anything) that they exist in order to get you up or down. If you asked the architect what any particular step is for, she wouldn't hesitate. The answer is obvious. The purpose of this step is to get you to the next step. That's it.

So what's *that* Web page for? What about *this* one?

It seems really simple, doesn't it? It's not. It's not simple because many Web pages are compromises, designed to do three or six or a hundred different things. HTML is a powerful tool that is constantly misused by people who believe that just because they can do something, they should.

So bear with me for a moment, and pretend you have a Web page that does just one thing.

And that it leads to another page that does just one thing.

And soon (as soon as possible), your Web pages lead people to do the thing you wanted them to do all along, the reason you built your Web site in the first place.

BUY TRAFFIC

Even two-year-olds know how knock-knock jokes work. You always start with the same line. You always get a response. You respond in a structured, predictable way. Then you get another response. And then there's a punch line.

It's a step-by-step progression that makes it quite easy to build new knock-knock jokes. Some of the same step-by-step thinking goes into building a process that gets you what you want. (Notice that I didn't say "building a Web site." That's because the process takes place *outside* of your Web site at times.)

Creating a knock-knock joke is very straightforward. First, you announce the joke. The jokee then chooses to ignore you or to engage. The exchange that follows is simple. And sometimes the jokee gets the joke and smiles.

For this part of the guide, I want to assume that you're buying the traffic that comes to your site. I'm starting here because any fool with money can buy traffic. And if you like the results you get from that traffic, you can buy more traffic. If the boss wants you to double traffic, you can double traffic. Buying traffic is predictable and scalable and makes you look smart. If you're getting traffic for free as a result of a head start or good search engine placement, then it's a natural resource. And like the oil in Texas, it's going to run out soon. So I want to pitch you on building a renewable traffic resource—buying traffic.

So, you buy traffic. Let's get into a little detail about the smart way to do that.

Everyone's heard of Google, but a surprisingly small number of people understand how Google makes billions of dollars a year. They do it with those little boxes that show up next to the search results.

Google calls this their AdWords program. Other sites offer similar programs, but since AdWords is the biggest, we'll use it as an example. The deal is pretty elegant:

- Pick a word or a phrase that describes your product. (You can even select words that you don't want used as keywords.)
- Write a short headline followed by a sentence that makes a promise.

■ Figure out how much you're willing to pay to get one person to click on that ad one time (and visit whatever page you'd like them to visit).

■ Figure out how many people you want at that price.

That's it. Go to http://adwords.google.com and put in your info. So, for example, you can buy "Florida retirement home" and bid $1.20 per click. Tell Google you're willing to take up to one thousand people a day. You might get fewer (see below), but you won't get more.

Here's why you might get fewer people than you asked for:

■ There isn't enough Google traffic. (The only people who see your ad are people who typed in the phrase you're looking for, and as big as Google is, some stuff is still obscure.)

■ You're not bidding high enough to be listed up top (where more people click).

■ People hate your ad and don't click on it. If your ad is really bad, Google will send you a note and fire you. Imagine that—a media company firing an advertiser for running ineffective ads.

There's an art to writing an effective AdWords ad, but that isn't nearly as important as the math behind it. Okay, it's easier than math. It's arithmetic.

Let's say you tell Google you're willing to pay $1 per click.

Of the people who get to the page you send them to, figure that 20 percent read what you have to say and decide to click on to the next step in the process. And 20 percent against $1 equals $5. (If that bit didn't make sense, make a picture and you'll see what I'm getting at. If one out of five people gets to the second page, you had to buy five clicks to get one live one, which means that she cost you $5.)

You just spent $5 to get someone to that next step.

In that next step, you ask for some information, maybe even a credit card number. Only 5 percent of the people who are confronted with this step actually go ahead and do what you need them to, so now your cost is 5 percent against $5, which equals (gasp) $100.

You ended up paying $100 for each desired outcome. $100 per sale.

The good news is that some of those people will tell their friends, and so you get additional customers for no additional cost, because that traffic is free. Say that the average word-of-mouth value is two (each customer brings two friends, which means that when you buy a new customer, you're really buying three). Your cost per outcome is now $33.33.

So, our arithmetic makes it clear what your online marketing and Web strategy is accomplishing—new customers for about $33 each.

What if you could make that first page more efficient?

What if, instead of catching 20 percent of the people who saw it, **that first page got 50 percent?**

And what if, instead of converting 5 percent of the people who saw the second step, **you got 10 percent?**

And finally, what if your tell-a-friend tools got people to convert **three friends instead of two?**

Now the arithmetic looks like this:

Fifty percent against $1 equals $2 for each person to the first step.

Ten percent against $2 equals $20 to make one sale.

A word-of-mouth value of three means you get four customers for the price of one, which means a total cost of $5 each.

Wow.

You've just turned a project that lost money (at $33 a customer, you're *losing*—I'm making this up—$3 a sale) into one that mints money (at $5 a customer, you're *making* $25 in profit).

If you're losing $3 on each new customer, then marketing is an *expense* and you won't grow. If you're making $25 on each new customer, you have an infinite amount of money to spend "buying" customers at that price—and marketing is now an *investment*.

Congratulations, you're a hero.

Once you've got the process down, you can start sharpening your pencil when it comes to acquisition. You can buy pay-per-click ads on sites like Yahoo! You can use the various ad networks to run your ads on other sites. You can buy ads on blogs or even on the sides of buses. As long as you can measure the cost per click, and as long as the clicks cost less than they deliver in profit, you win.

Here's an important note for anyone who isn't "selling" something. Just because this analysis uses dollars doesn't mean it doesn't apply to you. Let's say you design the Web site for a college, and you determine that the site's function is to enable students to read the course catalog online instead of having to use a printed version. The same math applies.

No, the students aren't giving you cash, but yes, the idea of increasing the percentage of people who follow each step is still clear. If you put up some interesting but irrelevant links, and people follow those and lose their way, that's costing you. It costs you in terms of the efficiency of what you set out to do. A good Web site gets the largest percentage of people to do what you set out to have them do in the first place.

Here's our first big rule:

View your site as a series of steps, steps that go from a stranger's clicking on an ad all the way to a satisfied customer's telling ten friends about you. Figure out which step is least efficient and focus all your energy on making it more efficient. Measure everything!

There's plenty more to talk about on this topic, but let's get the lay of the land. On to Step #2, Persuasion.

TELL A STORY

The examples in this section can be found at http://sethgodin.type pad.com/photos/knockknock/index.html. I'm enclosing black-and-white facsimiles here for your reference.

All Web sites are not the same. Compare figure 1 with figure 2:

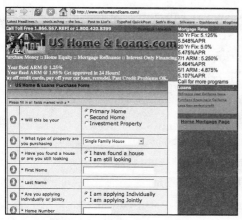

Figure 1

Figure 2

Obviously, they're selling different things. One site wants you to refinance your most valuable possession (your house) and go hundreds of thousands of dollars into debt. The other site wants to sell you a $90 sweater.

Once you realize that the purpose of a Web page is to start a conversation, it helps to anthropomorphize a little bit. If the first page were a person, how would it dress? Would you talk to him if he met you in a bar? In a bank?

What about the second page? Does it have a personality?

All Web pages are created equal: Seventy-two pixels per inch, a fixed choice of colors, the same size. It costs just as much to put up the pixels on the first page as it does on the second. Yet they tell very different stories.

All of the cues people rely on to make decisions are muted online. There's no smell or touch or location. There's very little sound. So we obsess about subtle cues of typeface or color or photography. It's hard to overestimate just how much these things matter.

So, for all those years when the guys in the tech department were trying to shame you into adding all sorts of cool Web features, I have to admit that they were right. A little. They were a little right because those features send a signal to some people. If I'm looking for a cool firm, a firm that understands technology, a firm that wants to signal to me how much they care about technology, then a Flash intro is a fine way to tell that story.

But it's only a tiny part of what I'm trying to sell you on. The same story doesn't work for everyone. There's no way you'd want to find a mortgage at Ibex. They tell an effective story—for a clothing company. That's very different from the story you ought to be telling, isn't it?

So, here's another general principle:

Like it or not, every page on your site has a tone of voice. That tone must match the expectations of the visitors or they will misunderstand who you are (or worse, flee). Choose a tone that matches or exceeds the tone of your successful competitors.

Here's another example: This is the (now obsolete) Web site for an open-source RSS reader. The goal is to attract techies and early adopters and media folks. The problem is that it looks like a different kind of site. It looks like a small business-to-business company that's struggling to find its voice.

Compare that site to this one: Same number of pixels, totally different tone.

The challenging thing here, of course, is that one person's appropriate vernacular is another person's design excess. There's no way to predict what the visitor's worldview is going to be, no way to know that a given person is going to get it.

Which leads to another general principle:

You have to choose.

You are never going to please everyone, so you shouldn't try. If you do, you'll fail at pleasing anyone. Instead, imagine who your very best audience is and go straight for the heart of that group. Ignore everyone else.

Your best audience? Your best audience has three components:

1. It's large.

2. It's likely to click on your AdWords or find you in some other way.

3. It's likely to respond to your message.

If it's not #3, the other two don't matter. If it's not #2 and #3, then #1 doesn't matter. But if all three work—if you can find a large enough audience that's interested enough to click and focused enough to respond to the story in the vernacular you use to tell it—then that's the audience you want.

TREAT DIFFERENT PEOPLE DIFFERENTLY

A first-time visitor to your site is a completely different challenge from a repeat visitor. Someone who is returning to your site already knows who you are and what you offer. She trusts you, and she's back to look for something specific.

A new visitor, on the other hand, is busy getting a first impression. So why would you show both of them the same information?

Why make them the same offers? Why use the same vernacular?

The good news is this: It's technically trivial to set a cookie and show repeat visitors something different.

Armed with that knowledge, you're now free to talk differently to different people.

Don't let technical myths change your marketing. Yes, you can easily show different pages to returning visitors. And yes, you should do just that.

THOUGHT: NO SUCH THING AS A WEB SITE

As a marketer, you've got a bunch of Web pages. You can call this collection your "Web site" if you want to, but it's really a bunch of connected Web pages.

This is a critical distinction if you want your Web site (okay, sorry, couldn't help it) to deliver more profit and be more efficient.

When you send someone to your Web site, *don't* send them to your home page. Hey, don't even have a home page!

You can have as many entrances to your site as you want. I call these pages "landing pages."

A landing page is the place you link your ads to. If you've got a music store and your ad says, "The Complete Carole King Catalog on Sale," you shouldn't link to your home page. Instead, you ought to link to a special page you built that matches your ad.

Of course!

Once you look at it this way, it makes perfect sense. You wouldn't tell a knock-knock joke that started one way but ended with a different punch line. That wouldn't work. Same thing is true of the connection between your ads, your marketing, and your landing pages.

We've been trained by engineers to see a Web site as a pyramid, with a home page at the top and an ever increasing range of choices as the user digs deeper.

Instead, I'd like you to see a Web site as a series of processes, as different from each other as each customer is different.

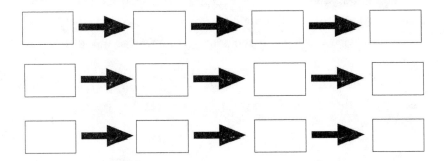

A returning customer ought to see one page, preferably one based on her past behavior.

A customer who clicked on an AdWords ad for "Garage Door Openers" ought to see an offer for a garage door, not your standard home page that requires her to restate why she came in the first place.

What do you want me to do?

If *you* don't know the answer, how can you expect the prospect to know?

At every step along the way, you need to stake out a position. It must say (without saying it), "The smart thing to do is click here. The best way to solve your problem is to click here." The American Bowling Congress (ABC) will invalidate a score of 300 in bowling if they find that the alley has been waxed to encourage the ball to go down the center. A waxed lane isn't fair to other bowlers.

But a waxed Web site is fair to you and to your users. You want to create a grooved path, a simple, easy-to-follow series of steps that get people from here to there. Will every person follow it? Of course not. But more people will follow the waxed lane if you create that path for them.

ASIDE: WHAT ABOUT SEARCH ENGINE OPTIMIZATION?

There are dozens (okay, thousands) of companies that will happily work with you and your team to do search engine optimization (SEO). SEO is the art of making your site attractive to the automated spiders that Google and other search engines send around the Web. By changing your site (and helping you get the right inbound and outbound links), a talented SEO firm can change your ranking—sometimes quite a bit.

Why does this matter?

We know that about 15 percent of the people doing a Google search look over at the AdWords ads. We also know that more than 70 percent ignore the ads and rarely bother to look at the second or third page of search results. This means that someone types in, say, "Florida retirement home" and chooses from one of the top five or six returned entries; then they're gone.

If you're number 8 out of the 1,590,000 matches, you lose.

In the past, I've been hard on SEO, mostly because of the way clients misuse it. They build static, boring, selfish Web sites and then try to make them work by ranking high in Google. What a waste! It's like waving your hand to get called on in second grade—but not knowing the answer when you do.

If you've done the right kind of optimization—the optimization of first click to sale, the optimization of first click to satisfied customer—then (and only then) will your SEO investment pay off.

TEST AND MEASURE

People hate to hear this. Sorry.

You need to change your pages all the time. Daily, even.

You need to change the offers you make and the way you make them. Then you need to see what happens. Sometimes your results will get better. That's good; keep doing whatever you just did. Sometimes, though, your results will get worse. That's good; you just discovered what doesn't work.

If you change your site all the time, you'll demolish any competitor who assumes she got it right the first time and is stuck now.

Why do people hate this step? Because it feels like a lot of work. Actually, failing is a lot of work. Updating your site all the time is sort of fun.

Whenever you can set up an evolutionary system, you win.

Evolution is a simple idea: lots of semirandom mixing followed by an abrupt battle for supremacy. The fit ones win and replicate; the ones that lose disappear.

Web pages can work the same way. Challenge your staff or your freelancers to create a page that can beat your current standard. Put up completely different landing pages, and see which offers and which stories and which typefaces and which colors and which prices win.

THREE OTHER THINGS I'D LIKE TO SAY

Choice is a bad thing. Time and again, studies have demonstrated that when faced with too many choices, people flee. They get unhappy. They regret their decision.

Nothing is easier than giving people too many choices on your Web site. In a broadband world, the cost of a click to the user is much smaller than it used to be. Break down your choices and play it like twenty questions. Instead of saying, "Here are the twenty-five things we offer," offer me three or four broad categories. Then, when I click, focus on the four or five narrower categories that are totally relevant to my last choice. This is the way it works in retail ("Are you looking for men's or women's clothing?").

Contact is a good thing. If you have a Web site, it's probably because you want to interact with your customers. So give me a phone number and an e-mail address. A real one, one that goes to a person, and quickly! Put it on every page.

Eliminate dead ends and error pages. If you have a search box on your site, it better give me a result even if it doesn't find a match.

Instead of saying "sorry" and giving me nothing in exchange for my hard work, give me a discount, or a secret item, or at least a joke.

You can't make me do something, but you can make it easy for me. No, I won't recommend your site to all my friends. But if I did want to do that, is there an easy way for me to do so? Too often, marketers build totally selfish recommendation tools into their sites. People skip them because, after all, why would they want to do that? Every once in a while, though, there is something worth recommending. If you can make it easy, it's more likely to happen.

I can't state this strongly enough: The number one complaint that businesses with Web sites bring to me is that they can't make their Web site pay off. They're desperate. They've bought AdWords and SEO and banners and even a hot-air balloon but while they can buy a spike in traffic, they can't convert that traffic into anything worthwhile.

They can't convert it because they have a Web site that was designed by an engineer or a true believer, not a marketer.

Good marketers understand that a Web page isn't some special window on the truth. It's not literature. It's just another marketing device.

As a device, your page is there to get the viewer from one place to another. From stranger to friend. One or two clicks, in, then out. Knock knock.

Here are the three questions you must answer about every single page you build:

1. Who's here?

2. What do you want them to do?

3. How can you instantly tell a persuasive story to get them to do #2?

If you can't pull off #3, then don't bother building a page. Take small steps. Make promises, and keep them. Test and measure.

BONUS #2: WHO'S THERE? A BOOKLET ABOUT BLOGS

Just about everything that the Web was built on is disappearing. Fast.

If you're confused, join the club. The rules are different and everything is new.

Every few years, it seems, some pundit announces that this time it's different, that all the rules have changed and the big guys should watch out.

Let's see, the last time that happened was seven years ago. And we saw the music industry tank, politics change forever, JetBlue mop the floor with Delta and American, Amazon continue to give agita to retailers in the real world and, oh, yes, the TV networks destroyed.

Well, it's happening again. This time you're ready. I wrote this booklet to help you understand a few simple rules that will make crystal clear what's at stake and how it works.

How's that for a promise?

This is not a FAQ, it's not the blogging bible, it's incomplete, and you may very well already realize everything that's in here. But my guess is that you and your team haven't focused all your energy and all your efforts on maximizing along some of these principles. That's why I wrote them down.

We start with three basic assumptions and then follow up with a handful of rules that seem to apply to most of what's going on online.

Here's are the goals you should hope to accomplish:

- Understand how and why the mainstream media is dying.
- Figure out why your organization needs to take a fundamentally different approach to the Web.
- Embrace the fact that you can't just change your tactics. The truth of what you do and who you are has to change as well.

■ Realize that all of this is very inexpensive and very quick. The hardest part is finding the will do it right.

No more wasted words. Let's get started.

FIRST TRUTH: CLUTTER

There are 80,000 new blogs every day.

There are 19,000 different beverages at Starbucks.

There are nineteen flavors of Oreo.

There are 172 professional sports teams in the United States.

On September 28, 2004, a search on "podcast" in Google turned up 24 matches. As I write this, the number is 17,000,000.

The amount of noise we're living with is exploding. There's an exponential increase, but we're not noticing it because it's happening a little bit at a time. If it were suddenly turned off and we were transported back to a three-network universe, a world with three car companies, six radio stations, two kinds of laundry detergent, and two newspapers, you'd go crazy looking for something to distract you. Just because you're used to the noise, though, doesn't mean it's not there.

And it is changing everything.

When you apply for a job, so do a thousand other people.

When you see a for-sale listing, so do a thousand other people.

When you bid on a grilled-cheese sandwich on eBay, so do a thousand other people.

And when you want people to come to your blog or your Web site, so do a million (ten million, a billion!) other people.

You've just read that, but you don't really believe it. You are almost certainly living in a different world, a world where you expect that some people actually care about you. Your boss nods her head when she hears about clutter, but turns right around and continues to build and market stuff as if it were 1969.

No one cares about you. Almost no one even knows you exist.

SECOND TRUTH: QUALITY

It's easy to wring your hands and whine about the decline of Western civilization.

Every time I pass a sign on a business that says QUALITY AT ITS BEST, I cringe.

Every time I have to check my voice mail with the horrid interface, or throw out another Misto olive oil sprayer because it's hopelessly clogged, I shake my head in sorrow.

But the fact is that more stuff is better (and cheaper) than it ever was before. You can buy far better food, access more free content of value, call further and more often. You name it, most everything is better (or if not better, then much cheaper) than it used to be.

The relentless march of quality improvement means that mistakes—from your bank to your shoes—are a lot less common. When I was a kid, a pair of sneakers that were just good enough cost about ten times (in today's dollars) what the same pair would cost today.

And nowhere is this more obvious than in the content you find online. Twenty years ago—no, even ten or five years ago—it just wasn't there. You couldn't find it at the library for free or at the bookstore for money.

As a result, we've become astonishingly picky. Picky about what we buy, and what we watch, and what we read. In a world where there's a lot of clutter and where everything is good enough, most of the time we just pick the stuff that's close or cheap or familiar. But when it's something we care about, we go to enormous lengths to find the very best.

THE BEST WAY TO FIND BLOGS

Visit Technorati. When you get there, search on your name, or your organization's name, or your brand or your town or your religion. I think you'll be surprised at what you find. People are talking about you. Listen.

THIRD TRUTH: SELFISHNESS

The idealists who started the blogging trend built a few components into the idea of blogging that made it thrive. The first was the idea that blogs selflessly link to one another. If someone writes something that you want to respond to, you include a link to it on your blog.

They also invented the idea of a blogroll, which is a listing of a blogger's favorite bloggers. This seemingly small gesture ended up having huge importance for blogs, because Google used all the cross-linking to reward these blogs with a higher ranking. In other words, generosity paid off.

The more you linked, the more you were linked to. The more you were linked to, the higher your Google rank. Which meant more traffic. And on and on.

But, even though bloggers are selfless, blog readers are selfish. They (we) really have very little choice when you think about it. We are selfish because we only have a little bit of time and there's too much to read. So, as a result, we are very strict about what's on our short list. We are merciless in deleting a blog from our reader if the blogger posts too often about stuff that's not relevant to us. We are always hovering over the mouse button, ready to flee a site at a moment's notice.

Boing Boing is one of the most popular blogs online, and for good reason. It's funny and interesting and everyone else reads it, so I do, too. But when I get to my blog reader and there are 125 new posts, well, I have to pause for a moment and decide whether it's worth keeping up. One day, it might not be.

TIME OUT FOR A FEW DEFINITIONS

A *blog* is just a Web page with some clever formatting software behind it so that anyone (including you) can build it and update it with no technical know-how.

The key elements that make a Web page a blog (other than the blogging software) seem to be:

1. time-stamped snippets

2. postings in reverse chronological order

A blog unfolds over time, with the most recent posts first.

Blogs often, but don't always, include comments from readers, a blogroll listing other blogs, a way to search the archives and past posts, and a bio of the blogger. Until recently, it was unusual for a blog to be written by anyone other than a single individual. Today, though, it's not unusual to find team blogs (like www.huffingtonpost .com) and blogs written by organizations.

Want to see a classic blog? Visit buzzmachine.com to hear Jeff Jarvis talk about media—and everything else.

RSS is a system that allows a blog (or any Web site) to alert an *RSS reader* that it has been updated. That's a mouthful, and while I don't care particularly about the technology, I care a lot about the implications.

RSS means that a user can subscribe to any Web site that supports RSS. It means that once the user has an RSS reader (and there's one inside of My Yahoo! and Firefox and Safari and soon just about every browser) she can pick a dozen or a hundred blogs and have them home delivered.

This is huge. It's huge because it completely undoes the clutter issue.

Once your *feed* (that's what they call the RSS broadcast) is in my RSS reader, it's going to stay there until I take it out. It means that you get the benefit of the doubt. It means you've earned attention.

If there are 20,000,000 blogs in the world and only 32 blogs in my RSS reader, guess which ones get read first?

Podcasting may not be what you think it is. It has nothing in particular to do with iPods, for example. A podcast is a sound file with an RSS feed.

Why is the feed part important?

There have been sound files on the Web forever. (The first example, I think, was on the Ben & Jerry's Web site a million years ago. They had a cow that mooed. But I digress.)

The sound files just sat there, because they're impossible to browse. It's too hard to find the file you want. It takes too long.

When Dave Winer came up with the idea of adding RSS to sound files, he did something brilliant. He allowed any Web surfer with an RSS reader to subscribe to audio!

This changed sound publishing the way home delivery changed the newspaper business.

Now, instead of having to run out and find listeners for every recorded dialogue or radio-type show you put together, your podcast automatically notifies every one of your subscribers. And if any of those subscribers are using iTunes, they can have your podcast show up in their iPod the next time they charge their batteries and sync it up.

Now, it's easy to set up your RSS stream in iTunes so that every single morning on the way to work, you can hear what you want to instead of what Imus wants you to hear.

Radio is officially dead, especially when wireless Internet access makes it to your car.

Imagine how powerful a podcaster becomes when she has three million people listening to her every single day on their computers at work or on their Rio MP3 players at the gym.

A Few More Bonus Definitions A *ping* is a technical term that doesn't concern us, but the term has evolved to also signify reminding someone or asking someone about an idea. "I'll ping John and see what he says," or "Thanks for the ping on this, I'll blog it."

A *trackback* is an automatic link to any blog that comments on your blog. This is the cement that links one blog to another. Once you turn on trackbacks, your readers (and you) can see who else is saying what about you.

IRC is a wide-open sort of chat room. You can easily set one up and make it easy for your blog readers to talk among themselves, and talk to you.

THREE KINDS OF BLOGS

Yes, I know there are two kinds of people in the world—those who believe that there are two kinds of people and those who don't. But there really and truly are three kinds of blogs.

Cat blogs are blogs for, by, and about the person blogging. A cat blog is about your cat and your dating travails and your boss and whatever else you feel like sharing in your public diary. The vast majority of people with a cat blog don't need or want strangers to read it.

If you've got a cat blog, you should embrace that fact and stop wondering where all your traffic is. Alas, this riff is almost completely useless to you. You already have what you want!

Boss blogs are blogs used to communicate to a defined circle of people. A boss blog is a fantastic communication tool. I used one when I produced the fourth-grade musical. It made it easy for me to keep the parents who cared about our project up to date, and it gave them an easy-to-follow archive of what was going on.

If you don't have a boss blog for most of your projects and activities, you should think about giving it a try. Boss bloggers don't need this riff either, because you already know who should be reading your blog and you have the means to contact and motivate this audience to join you.

The third kind of blog is the kind most people imagine when they talk about blogs. These are blogs like InstaPundit and Scobleizer and Joi Ito's. Some of these blogs are by individuals (call them citizen journalists or op-ed pages) and others are by organizations trying to share their ideas and agendas. These are the blogs that are changing the face of marketing, journalism, and the spread of ideas. I want to call these *viral blogs*.

They're viral blogs because the goal of the blog is to spread ideas.

The blogger is investing time and energy in order to get her ideas out there. Why? Lots of reasons—to get consulting work, to change the outcome of an election, to find new customers for a business, or to make it easier for existing customers to feel good about staying.

The math behind viral blogs is astonishing. One person, $20 a month in overhead, and an audience of several hundred thousand people! Even better, a viral blog stuffed with good ideas is going to influence millions of people who never even read the original. For example, Chris Anderson posted his "Long Tail" idea on a blog. There are now 1,040,000 Google matches for the expression he invented.

This is a riff for viral bloggers. It's about how to make your ideas spread far and wide and have more impact.

If you're writing for strangers, that means you're building a viral blog. The first principle is to make your entries shorter.

Use images and tone and design and interface to make your point. Teach people gradually.

On the other hand, if you're writing for colleagues, you've got a boss blog. That means you can make your entries more robust.

Be specific. Be clear. Be intellectually rigorous and leave no wiggle room.

The stuff you're putting on your marketing site or in your blog or even in your brochures or in your business letters is too long. Too much inside baseball. Too many unasked questions getting answered too soon.

The stuff you're sending out in your e-mail and your memos is too vague.

Figure out who you're writing to before you put finger to keyboard!

FIRST LAW: IT'S NOT WHO YOU ARE, IT'S WHAT YOU SAY

Remember Dan Rather? Tom Brokaw? Remember the *Los Angeles Times* and even Procter & Gamble?

It used to matter a lot where an idea came from. When an idea came from a mainstream media company (MSM) or from a Fortune 500 company, it was a lot more likely to spread. That's because media companies had free airwaves or paid-for newsprint, while big corporations had the money to buy interruptions.

Big companies and MSMs were able to sell us stuff like SUVs and wars overseas. They created panic about Alar on apples and got us excited about MP3 players. There was a word for someone outside the mainstream with a big idea: "crackpot."

Today, all printing presses are created equal. And everyone owns one. Which means that a good idea on a little blog has a very good chance of spreading. In fact, nowadays an idea from outside the mainstream might have an even better chance of spreading.

Few people today treat ideas from outside the mainstream as immediately suspect. In fact, there are many people who give these ideas *more* credence, not less. Bloggers are no longer outsiders.

A hundred years ago, the FCC created the broadcast-media monopolies of TV and radio. When there were only a few channels, the people with a channel had a lot of influence.

But there are *millions* of blogs. Which means that having a blog does not automatically mean you are powerful.

Nobody, it seems, reads a lousy blog for very long. Even lousy posts don't get read. Take a look at the comment counters on some very popular blogs. They can vary by 300 percent to 10,000 percent. That's because the good ideas spread and the not-so-good ideas just sit there.

An aside: "Good" doesn't have anything to do with quality or ethics or even profitability. In this case, I just mean attractiveness. Good ideas, by my definition, are the ones that spread. At least in this section.

SECOND LAW: ACTUALLY, IT DOESN'T MATTER WHAT YOU SAY, IT MATTERS WHO YOU ARE

Remember what I just said in the first law? That's not really true. It used to be, of course, but not anymore. At the beginning, it didn't matter who you were, because blogs didn't have subscribers or people who believed in them or trusted them or were committed to them. Now, though, things are different.

So bear with me for a moment, while I revisit and retract.

When Doc Searls or Cory Doctorow or Joshua Micah Marshall says something, of course it matters who said it. They are the Dan Rathers of our age. For a while.

The bloggers with a following get both the benefit of the doubt and a far bigger megaphone. Because they reach more people, they're likely to have their words echoed more quickly. And one thing we've learned from the blogosphere (yes, it's really called that) is that ideas that echo are echoed again. In other words, a meme (that's a new term for an idea that spreads) will get picked up merely because everyone else is talking about it.

And so the bloggers who have earned a following are more likely to spread spreadable ideas, which of course further reinforces their position at the top of the pyramid.

For a while.

Because if those bloggers get lazy or stupid or selfish, their audience will flee.

They will flee far faster than they fled CBS. It won't take years. Sometimes it only takes a month or two. A blogger may discover that members of her audience have taken her off their RSS readers because she posts too often and it is too hard to keep up with her, or because she's getting too selfish and self-promotional. Boom. They're gone and they don't come back.

The traditional MSM powers are watching their audiences shrink daily. But these are lifelong audiences with deeply entrenched viewing habits, so the shrinkage is slow. Losing your blog audience happens much faster.

So, yes, it matters who says it. Powerful bloggers are louder.

And yes, the first two laws conflict. But no, they don't really. Because ideas that stick and people who have power are different than they used to be.

People come to me all the time believing that if I would just link to them, just highlight them, they'd be unstoppable. Alas, this isn't true. What's true is that if you write something great, and do it over and over and over again, then you'll be unstoppable. Whether or not someone helps you.

Hugh MacLeod is a great example of this. His gapingvoid.com blog gets far more traffic than my blog, but he started from scratch just over a year ago. No magazine column, no books, no help from the MSM. He just wrote and wrote and agitated enough that people noticed what he had to say.

THIRD LAW: "WITH" AND "FOR," NOT "AT" OR "TO"

Social media, blogging especially, is social. Not antiseptic or anonymous or corporate.

This means that the writing skills you and your organization have honed aren't going to help you very much. When you write *at* your audience, or even *to* your audience, you've made it really clear that you think that they are unlike you, and that you think they are yours.

It is not *your* audience, of course. The audience belongs to itself. And if you talk as if they are not like you, then it's awfully difficult to keep up your position of power. The subterfuge of omniscience is way easier to perpetrate on television, where you have makeup and the editing room. It's easy on radio, because you have an FCC license and they don't. But it's hard to do on a blog, because your audience has one too!

So we're talking about dramatically changing the relationship between writer and reader. This isn't a chat room. It's not a dialogue between two people of equal authority. Instead, the blogger is at the center of the hub. He has the power to set the agenda of the blog and to have the last word if he chooses (on *his* blog anyway). That means that a blogger is still the author/publisher/journalist. What's different is that his power to control the conversation is dramatically decreased by the ability of the audience to talk back on their own blogs, and by their ability to ignore him.

The best blogs walk a very fine line between civility and anarchy, between passion and privacy. We've all visited blogs where the writer lets her hair down just a little too much. Okay, a lot too much. I don't want or need to know about your cat's operation, thank you.

The best blogs start conversations, they don't control them.

Nobody gets to be Dan Rather, ever again. But the audience desperately wants you to be a leader, to stand for something, to speak up, to bring new ideas and challenging thoughts into their lives.

This isn't for everyone. Not everyone wants to engage in emotional discourse about your topic. But the days of media for the masses are long gone. We miss you, Walter Cronkite.

Remember the most important point of all: I'm busy, so if you weird me out or confuse me or disrespect me, I'm out of here.

FOURTH LAW: ON THE INTERNET, EVERYBODY KNOWS YOU'RE A DOG

In the famous *New Yorker* cartoon, nobody knows you're a dog on the Internet. While the cues online are far more subtle than they are in almost any other medium, because we're so attuned to distinguish the good from the bad and the real from the fake, every little hint matters.

You may believe that all blogs are the same, and you may believe that as a blogger you are anonymous. I'm not buying it.

Surfers notice which service your blog is hosted on. We notice your Skype handle and the font you use on your blog or your home page. We notice everything when we need to.

The newspaper was sitting on the floor of my living room, at least thirty feet away. Not only could I tell it was the *New York Times*, I could even tell that it was the bottom half of the Wednesday restaurant review section, just from the layout.

How many times have you left a Web page before you even bothered to read a sentence? You wouldn't let a doctor with a pierced tongue do heart surgery on you, and you're not going to believe what you read on a blog that looks like a cat threw up on it.

In the IM world, teens are extraordinarily good at figuring out who's authentic and who's not. They can't even tell you how they know—maybe it's the speed the person is typing, or the word choices, but whatever the clues, they know. So do you.

This means that faking it online is actually more difficult than doing it in the real world.

Hire a great interior decorator and your store looks great for years. But if your online presence isn't consistent and authentic and honest over time, people are going to notice. And they'll flee.

WHAT ABOUT COMMENTS?

It's an act of faith that blogs ought to have comments. After all, as the Cluetrain guys said, markets are conversations.

Exactly. Markets, not marketing.

Marketing is not a conversation. Marketing is an act that starts a conversation, but it doesn't have to include one, at least not from the beginning. Marketing, like publishing, is ultimately about one person or one entity sharing a point of view. If they get it right, that idea spreads.

Hosting a conversation on your blog is a totally valid strategy. It makes it easier for you to see what people are saying, and to then modify your ideas to give those ideas more power going forward. It also is a service to your readers, because it locates the conversation right next to the idea itself.

My blog doesn't have comments, though. There are two reasons for this. The first, which is childish, is that I hate reading angry rants about my ideas, and having comments on my blog made it harder and harder for me to post because I lived in fear of trolls (the angry little men living under the bridge). The other reason, more practical, is that we now live in a world where many people have blogs. So if you've got something you want to say about one of my ideas, go ahead and track-back it and put it on *your* blog. Your nonanonymous blog. Your blog that puts your comment in context with all your other comments.

Comments are thus more thoughtful. Trackbacks lead to greater credibility for the person commenting (and a higher page rank) and also introduce my blog to readers of your blog.

There are some who will read this and worry that I'm telling you to ignore the conversation. I'm not. Go to Google and do a search on *Jeff Jarvis Dell*. You'll see how Dell totally blew it. In public.

An influential blogger was calmly but loudly pointing out where Dell went wrong on one order. Using easy and cheap technology, Dell ought to be tracking each and every blogger that has something to say about them. And then they ought to reach out to the unhappy and mollify them, while reaching out to the happy and amplifying their emotions. Dell ought to learn from those who are willing to take the time to post, and use that learning to make their products (and their ideas) better.

Imagine customer support that works like that. Instead of calling a number and waiting forever, you just post your problem on your blog, as specifically as you possibly can. Then the company uses a blogreader/RSS tracker to search all 20 bazillion blogs. They do this all the time. Within minutes, they see your post and then contact you directly—or post their answer right there in the comments section of your blog.

If the comment/fix they posted worked, and it was quick, you would likely post your satisfaction right there on your blog. The interaction is performed in public, and the satisfaction is evident. This process helps the company get new customers.

By bringing the interaction from the company side to your side, the game changes, doesn't it?

BLOGS ARE LIKE MOVIES

Blogs work best when people read them over time. One frame of a movie isn't enough to win an Academy Award, and one post on a blog isn't enough to make a huge difference.

My friend Jerry calls this drip marketing. It works like an ancient water torture, one drop at a time, building until it has an impact. A blog is a chance to talk to people who want to listen, to aggregate an audience that wants to listen to you, spread your ideas, and talk back to you.

Because of RSS, a blog allows you to be patient and kind and to not worry so much about first impressions. You're already in a relationship with your readers. Just be mindful of the fact that the minute you break your promise, the relationship is over.

What sort of promise? Well, there's a popular blog in which the blogger decided to cook every single recipe in the *Joy of Cooking*. She has thousands of readers. The moment, though, she decides to use the blog to start relentlessly selling a brand of coffee, they'll leave. Because that's not the deal.

It's quite possible to have a blog that's all about you. About your company or your cat or your boyfriends. Who knows what people will read (they certainly watch who knows what on TV). The thing is, the expectations have to be clear from the beginning.

SO WHAT?

So every post on a viral blog should be designed to get you another RSS subscription.

Every blog post should be designed to be important enough that another blog will eagerly post a link or quote you or reprint the whole thing.

Every blog post will be read because I want to read it, not because you want me to.

A BOSS BLOG

A friend sent me over to Adobe's new blog. It's one software developer after another writing about the stuff they're working on, minutiae about new products. I lasted about a minute. There should be a warning that says, "Not for everyone!"

That's okay as long as the expectations are set properly. I can't imagine that Adobe's blog is going to get them one new customer. There won't be one person who sees this insider dope and decides to buy Illustrator. I can't even imagine that someone will choose to surf over and check this blog out instead of, say, Amihotornot.com. But that's okay. As long as Adobe doesn't overinvest, as long as they understand that this is going to be a slow, low-return process on building communication and ultimately loyalty, it's a great idea.

The Adobe blog is a boss blog. It's a blog for a company that wants to have more direct communication with its most important customers.

A blog is a terrific platform for this, and it's hard to imagine why any company in a similar situation would hesitate to have one. Quark lost millions of dollars in sales over a decade in which they did everything they could to *not* communicate with passionate customers. Verizon bends over backward, it seems, to alienate their most profitable customers.

A boss blog—where you end up telling the truth—is a terrific way to reinforce good feelings among a core constituency. But don't confuse it with a viral blog. A boss blog filled with inside information isn't going to get you new customers tomorrow.

P.S. It's pretty clear to me that once RSS and the blogosphere break the world into tiny interconnected pieces, there's not a lot of benefit to being big or overstaffed or deep in resources—not when it comes to your blog. The best blog efforts are genuine and interesting and swift and worth reading. And that has nothing at all to do with being big, or being the CEO, or getting approval from your boss's boss.

TALKING AND LISTENING
This is where it all leads.

It turns out that marketing is really about two things. Talking and listening.

For a long time, though, marketing was about just one thing—talking.

Talking *at* people through radio ads or TV ads or posters on the street. Talking *at* people through product design or features or pricing.

For someone who wants to be in show business, marketing was seductive. You got to put on a show every day.

Then, a few decades ago, the *listening* became important. Focus groups started running the show, with high-paid marketers paying special attention to small, self-selected groups in darkened rooms in shopping malls.

Companies *said* they were listening, but they were really using the focus groups to justify the things they wanted to do in the first place. A few decades ago, for example, the automobile market told Detroit that they wanted high-quality, fuel-efficient cars. Detroit wanted to ignore the message, so they stacked their focus groups so that they could hear what they wanted to hear.

That's not going to fly anymore. The feedback loops are too fast, and while you can ignore the market, you can't do it for long. The Net is busy changing things all over. Here's a recap of how talking and listening have changed.

Talking Old, one-way talking is being killed by clutter.

TV is down.

Radio is down.

Newspapers and magazines are down and almost out.

Customers are ignoring you all the time.

But, it turns out that enabling your best customers to tell their friends about you is up, way up. Making remarkable stuff that is worth talking about is up.

The most important kind of talking is storytelling. Not top-down dictation, but stories that resonate, stories that are authentic, stories that spread.

Listening Skewed focus groups are down.

Unfiltered, nonanonymous blog feedback is up.

Listening at your call center is up.

Rapid product cycles that involve users in product design are up.

So is open source, in which the users *are* the designers.

Talking directly to your publicly unhappy customers is up, too.

Platforms are the next big thing because they enable you to build tools that make it easy for your clients or customers to talk and listen to one another. So, eBay is different from Brooks Brothers, because eBay enables users to listen, and to talk. MySpace.com is different from MTV because MySpace.com allows users to listen, and to talk.

Blogging, then, is a platform that enables your organization to talk to the people who want to hear you. RSS makes the publication of your ideas crisp and focused. And the blogs of your clients and your users and your customers are the way they talk back to you. The question is whether you're willing to listen and to take action.

AND WHAT NOW?

If your organization isn't watching what's being said about you in the blogosphere, you're in big trouble. Instead of learning, you're clueless.

Instead of trying to fix problems before they snowball, you're waiting for the avalanche. And instead of amplifying the good feedback, you're allowing it to fade away.

If you care about your personal brand and career and impact, you need a blog. And you should start the cycle of getting better at blogging.

Being better has nothing to do with following conventions. It's not about how standardized your blogroll is, how frequently you post, or how well you maintain comments and trackbacks. These are all distractions on the way to building what you actually need.

What you need is a committed group of subscribers, a substantial and influential RSS audience that will stick with you as you tell your story. Measure yourself on what gets linked to and commented on and spread. Measure yourself on what leads to more (and better) subscribers.

Then, over time, take your readers on a journey. Teach them what you'd like them to know, and the rest will take care of itself.

ACKNOWLEDGMENTS

This book is the result of six years of almost daily writing. And I need to thank every single person who read my blog, or read a *Fast Company* column, or wrote a letter to the editor, or posted about my blog on their blog. I need to thank every copy editor, line editor, agent, and bzzagent as well. I need to thank the people who built the software that allows me to do this for a living, and the folks who take the time to hear me speak. But, of course, I can't, because this book is too long already. You know who you are.

There are two kinds of people I need to mention in the meager space allotted to me here. The first are the people who said no. That's where creativity comes from, at least my creativity. When people say it's never going to work or that they can't or won't help, it just makes it more challenging and more interesting. And I'm forced to find another way to get the ideas out there. I've been told "no" by family members, agents, editors, business partners, venture capitalists, big-time advertisers, employees, bosses, publishers, landlords, hotel clerks, speakers' bureaus, and the guy at security at LaGuardia. Before you spend a lot of time cursing the people who won't embrace your next big idea, thank them first. Without them, you'd be ordinary.

"Ordinary" is no way to describe Alan Webber and Bill Taylor, though. The cofounders of *Fast Company* magazine are my heroes. Not only did they found and chronicle a movement that changed the world, they also changed *my* world. Bill did it with a single article, and Alan did it by editing every one of my columns while he was at the magazine. When they left, they left all of us a huge void. Thanks, guys, for my big break. I miss working with you more than you know.

This book is dedicated to Alex and Mo.

The original content and date of each article, color pictures, comments, and other annotations can be found at www.sethgodin.com/smallisthenewbig.

INDEX

W Hotels, 114
WiFi, 140, 217
  coffee clubs, 222
  free connections, need for, 210–211
Willie Wonka, 112
Wilson, Fred, 106
Winer, Dave, 297
woot.com, 176, 264
Word of Mouth Marketing
    Association (WOMMA), 97
work
  blogs about, 76–77
  choosing to be stuck at, 235
  commission-based vs. hourly, 43–44
  competence as antithetical to success
    at, 44–50
  employment Web sites, 119–120
  fear of criticism at, 52–53
  freelance, pleasure of, 215–217
  giving feedback at, 81–83
  hard, new meaning of, 18–20
  initiative vs. tasks at, 32
  intellectual downsizing of, 265–266
  job titles, new meaning of, 35–37
  lack of job security at, 121,
    228–229

  new rules for success at, 42–43
  paradox of finding, 121–122
  Purple Cow approach for job
    seekers, 180–181
  reputation as references, 272–274
  stress from bosses at, 107–108
  success at, via "Local and Big Max"
    route, 124–127
World Trade Center, 217

Xerox, 134

Yaganeh, Al, 243
Yahoo!, 24–25, 106, 147, 162, 171,
    190, 203, 210, 217
Yale University, 202
Yang, Jerry, 24–25
Yoyodyne Entertainment, 131
Yo-Yo Ma, 244

Zara clothing, 207
Ziglar, Zig, 74
"zooming," 48–49
  companies' inability at, 198
  instead of change, 25–28
  ways companies stop, 136